**AA**

# Pocket Guide
## to
# LONDON

**Editor:** Robert Baker

**Maps:** prepared by the
Cartographic Department of the
Automobile Association.
Tube Map © London Transport

**Filmsetting by:**
Turnergraphic Limited,
Basingstoke, Hampshire

**Printed and bound by:** Purnell
Book Production Ltd, Paulton, Avon

**ISBN 0 86145 528 2**
**AA Ref: 59239**

Published by the Automobile
Association, Fanum House,
Basingstoke, Hampshire
RG21 2EA

# Contents

# About this Book

**London in your pocket —**
This new pocket size guidebook is set out in easy-to-use sections, designed to help you make the most of your visit to London.

**Useful Information**

In planning your trip you may want to obtain as much general information as possible. Here we have researched everything you should want to know, including general tourist information, how to get around the city, sightseeing tours, entertainment, even such detail as the times of Changing the Guard at Buckingham Palace.

**Gazetteer**

All the famous places to visit, listed in alphabetical order throughout. Here we give all the necessary information:- name, address, telephone enquiry number and map location grid reference.

After a brief description of the place of interest we list opening times, admission charge (or free!) and any facilities (such as lectures, guided tours, special exhibitions, etc) available.

**Around the streets of London**

London's history has been preserved in the many fine buildings, churches, squares, monuments, statues, plaques and much else of interest that can be found throughout the capital. Here we give you an insight into London's past and the origins of what makes up the streets of London today.

**London map and Street Index**

The twelve page central London map and the street index are designed to help you find your way around. Shown on the map are places of interest, car parks, buildings, underground stations etc.

**Opening dates**

The dates quoted in the gazetteer are inclusive, so that Apr-Oct indicates that the establishment is open from the beginning of April to the end of October.

**Donation and Charity Boxes**

Some of the places of interest listed in the book are administered by Charities, Trusts and Associations. They are responsible for carrying out much of the restoration work in order to promote Britain's heritage and rely on public generosity to continue their work. They do not charge for admission, but donations are appreciated.

**Ancient Monuments**

**AM** Ancient Monuments in England are in the care of the Historic Buildings and Monuments Commission for England (popularly known as English Heritage), with the exception of seven properties in and around London which are administered by the Department of the Environment. The address of English Heritage is PO Box 43, Ruislip, Middlesex, HA4 0XW.

**The National Trust**

**NT** Indicates properties which are administered by the National Trust for Places of Historic Interest or Natural Beauty, 42 Queen Anne's Gate, London SW1H 9AS.

# AA

## *Pocket Guide to*

## LONDON

# USEFUL
# INFORMATION

tourist information, accommodation,
entertainment, transport, shops, sport,
ceremonies, etc

# Tourist Information

The London Visitor and Convention Bureau (LVCB) is the official Tourist Board for London. Full facilities, help and advice from multi-lingual staff on all aspects of tourism, accommodation, theatre and cinema ticket bookings is available.

**Written enquiries to:**
**Central Information Unit**
**London Visitor and Convention Bureau**
26 Grosvenor Gardens, London SW1W 0DU

**Personal callers to:**
**London Visitor and Convention Bureau Tourist Information Centre**
Victoria Station Forecourt SW1
Open: daily 9-8.30 (July & August : extended hours)

**Telephone Information Service (LVCB)**
01-730 3488
Open: Mon-Fri 9-5.30 (automatic queueing system)

**Harrods Tourist Information Centre (LVCB)**
Harrods, Knightsbridge SW1
Open during store hours

**Selfridges Tourist Information Centre (LVCB)**
Selfridges, Oxford Street W1
Open during store hours

**H M Tower of London Tourist Information Centre (LVCB)**
West Gate, H M Tower of London EC3
Open: daily April-October, 10-6

**Heathrow Tourist Information Centre (LVCB)**
Heathrow Central Station, Heathrow Airport, Middlesex
Open: daily 9-6

**Local Information Centres at:**

**City of London Information Centre**
St Paul's Churchyard EC4
Tel: 01-606 3030

**Clerkenwell Heritage Centre**
33 St John's Square EC1
Tel: 01-250 1039

**Croydon Tourist Information Centre**
Katherine Street, Croydon, Surrey
Tel: 01-688 3627 Ext 45146

**Greenwich Tourist Information Centre**
Cutty Sark Gardens SE10
Tel: 01-858 6376

**Hillingdon Tourist Information Centre**
22 High Street, Uxbridge, Middlesex
Tel: Uxbridge (0895) 50706

**Kingston-upon-Thames Tourist Information Centre**
Heritage Centre, Fairfield West, Kingston-upon-Thames, Surrey
Tel: 01-546 5386

**Lewisham Tourist Information Centre**
Borough Mall, Lewisham Centre SE13
Tel: 01-318 542112

**Richmond Tourist Information Centre**
Central Library, Little Green, Richmond, Surrey
Tel: 01-940 9125

**Tower Hamlets Tourist Information Centre**
88 Roman Road E2
Tel: 01-980 3749

**Twickenham Tourist Information Centre**
District Library, Garfield Road, Twickenham, Middlesex
Tel: 01-892 0032

**The British Travel Centre.** Operated by the British Tourist Authority, British Rail and American Express, offers a comprehensive tourist service for Great Britain. Services include British Rail ticket bookings, bureau de change, accommodation, theatre, air, coach, sightseeing tours bookings, etc.

**British Travel Centre (BTA)**
4-12 Lower Regent Street
London SW1
Open: all year Mon-Sat, 9-6.30, Sun 10-4
Telephone Information Service 01-730 3400 (Mon-Sat 9-6.30)

## Telephones

There are hundreds of public payphones throughout the capital, most still found in the distinctive and easily recognisable red phone boxes. Additionally, many pubs, restaurants, hotels, post offices, and other places open to the public have payphones which you may use. There are four types of payphones:

**Pay-on-answer** phones are the older type. They take 10p coins only, and are more suitable for inland calls.

**Coin-operated payphones:** dial direct to anywhere in the UK and to all countries to which International Direct Dialling is available. They take 2p, 5p, 10p, 20p, 50p and £1 coins.

**Phonecard phones** are quickly becoming more widely available. To use these phones you must first buy one of the special cards which are available from post offices and shops displaying the 'Phonecard' sign. You may then make any number of calls up to the value of the card, whenever you wish, without the need for cash but only from the special Phonecard phones.

In all cases, instruction on how to use the phones will be clearly displayed by the set.

**Creditcall Payphones:** phones that accept Visa, Mastercard, Diners Club, and American Express credit cards are now being installed in the London area and at airports.

Instructions for use are given on notices next to these phones.

The dialling code for London is 01. This should be omitted when dialling a telephone number from within the London area.

The following telephone numbers can be dialled free of charge for telephone assistance:

**Operator**          100 (104 for international calls)
for difficulties in obtaining a dialled number.

### Directory Enquiries

To find out a London number                    142
To find a number outside London                192
(You will need to give the full name and address)

## Useful Tourist Telephone Information Numbers

**Breakdown Assistance**
Automobile Association                          01-954 7373
                                                (24hr service)

British Telecom provides certain recorded information services which are of help to visitors:-

**Tourist Information**
Leisureline
(Recorded information of the day's main events in London)

English 01-246 8041
German 01-246 8045
French 01-246 8043

**Children's Information**

| | |
|---|---|
| Children's London — events and competitions | 01-246 8007 |
| Kid's Line — individual enquiries Mon-Sat 4-6 | 01-222 8070 |

| | |
|---|---|
| Arts Line — Information service for disabled people on the Arts and Leisure activities in London | 01-388 2227/8 |
| Cricketline — During Test and other major matches | 154 |
| International telegrams (also Telemessage — United States only) | 193 |
| London Weather Centre — individual enquiries | 01-836 4311 |
| Motoring travel delays within 70 miles around London | 01-246 8021 |
| Motorsport Information | 01-246 8066 |
| Newsline — news bulletin updated every hour | 01-246 8080 |
| Raceline — horse racing information and results | 168 |
| Restaurant Switchboard — information on eating out in London 9am-10pm | 01-444 0044 |
| Sports Line — General sports summary | 01-246 8020 |
| Timeline — speaking clock | 123 |
| Travel Information — National summaries | Rail 01-246 8030 |
| | Road 01-246 8031 |
| | Sea 01-246 8032 |
| | Air 01-246 8033 |
| Weather — recorded forecast for London area | 01-246 8091 |

**Emergency Services**

If you are involved in any serious accident, or if you need the police in an emergency, you should always dial 999 in any telephone box (these calls are free), and ask for Fire, Police, or Ambulance.

London Transport Police (for reporting thefts and other crimes which take place on London Transport); telephone 222 5600.

If you are injured and require medical attention in Central London, University College Hospital (Gower Street, WC1), the Middlesex Hospital (Mortimer Street, W1), St Thomas's Hospital (Lambeth Palace Road, SE1), and the Westminster Hospital (Horseferry Road, SW1), all have 24-hour casualty departments. Several chemists have extended opening hours; these include Boots, Piccadilly Circus, W1 (Monday-Friday 8.30am-8pm, Saturday 9am-8pm), H D Bliss, 5 Marble Arch, W1 (9am-midnight daily), Underwoods, 75 Queensway, W2 (9am-10pm daily), and the Churchill Pharmacy, 268 Oxford Street, W1 (8.30am-midnight daily). All foreign visitors to Britain can take advantage of the accident and emergency services of the National Health Service without charge.

Emergency dental treatment can be obtained, at a charge, from the Emergency Dental Service: telephone 677 6363.

**Lost property**

If you lose anything while travelling on buses or the underground, you should write or go to the London Transport Lost Property Office at 200 Baker Street, NW1, adjoining Baker Street underground station. This office is open Monday to Friday, 9.30am-2pm (closed Saturdays and Sundays). (For Lost Property information ring (01)-486 2496).

For property lost in London taxis or in the street, report any loss to the nearest police station.

Taxis only: write to the Metropolitan Police Lost Property Office, 15 Penton Street, N1. It would be helpful to quote the plate number of the taxi in which you travelled. If you lose anything in a store, hotel, airport, etc., contact the premises in question. Should property be lost on a train or at a railway station, contact the arrival/departure station of your journey.

**Post Offices**

In the UK, the only place you can buy stamps, post parcels, and send telegrams is at a Post Office. (Letters, cards, and small packages can also be posted in the hundreds of distinctive red pillar boxes dotted around the capital.) Each district in London has its own chief Post Office, and there are also many smaller sub offices. The London Chief Office is in King Edward Street, EC1; it is open for all kinds of postal business on Monday to Friday from 8am to 7pm, except on public holidays, and on Saturdays from 9am to 12.30pm. The Trafalgar Square Post Office, 22-28 William IV Street, WC2 (tel: 930 9580) is open for all kinds of business, Monday-Saturday 8am-8pm, and 10am-5pm on Sundays and public holidays (except Christmas Day). The smaller offices in which to transact your business are often combined with a general shop or newsagent, and are normally open from 9am to 5.30pm, Monday to Friday, and on Saturday mornings.

**Banks**

All banks are open between 9.30am and 3.30pm Monday to Friday (3pm in the City), and some now open on Saturday mornings. They are closed on Sundays and Public Holidays. There are 24-hour banks at Heathrow and Gatwick airports. Most banks now operate a queueing system. When changing foreign currency, banks usually give the best rates at the lowest commission charges. Bureaux de Change are located throughout the capital and are usually open longer hours than banks, in the evenings and at weekends, but check the rates of commission they charge — they can be very high. Wherever you change money or cash cheques, exchange rates and charges should be clearly displayed.

**Public conveniences**

London has a large range of well-signposted public loos, but their opening times are sometimes erratic. New individual coin-in-the-slot, French-style conveniences are being erected in Central London; these cost 10p. There are conveniences in hotels, large stores, pubs, and at stations — but be sure you have plenty of change in advance; charges vary.

**Tipping**

It is customary to tip for the following services: taxi-drivers; porters, doormen, bell-boys, and room-service waiters; tour guides; barbers and hairdressers; cloakroom attendants; and in restaurants, except where the menu specifically says that service is included.

## Foreign Embassies, Consulates and High Commissions

**Australian High Commission**
Australia House, Strand WC2
Tel: 01-438 8000

**Austrian Embassy and Consular Section**
18 Belgrave Mews West SW1
Tel: 01-235 3731

**Belgian Embassy**
103 Eaton Square SW1
Tel: 01-235 5422

**Canadian High Commission**
Canada House, Trafalgar Square SW1
Tel: 01-629 9492

**Danish Embassy**
55 Sloane Street SW1
Tel: 01-235 1255

**Finnish Embassy**
38 Chesham Place SW1
Tel: 01-235 9531

**French Embassy**
58 Knightsbridge SW1
Tel: 01-235 8080

**German Embassy of the Federal Republic of Germany**
23 Belgrave Square SW1
Tel: 01-235 5033

**Greek Consulate General**
1a Holland Park W11
Tel: 01-727 8040

**India High Commissioner**
India House, Aldwych WC2
Tel: 01-836 8484

**Irish Embassy**
17 Grosvenor Place SW1
Tel: 01-235 2171

**Italian Consulate General**
38 Eaton Place SW1
Tel: 01-235 9371

**Japanese Embassy**
46 Grosvenor Street W1
Tel: 01-493 6030

**Luxembourg Embassy**
27 Wilton Crescent SW1
Tel: 01-235 6961

**Malta High Commission**
16 Kensington Square W8
Tel: 01-938 1712

**Netherlands Embassy**
38 Hyde Park Gate SW7
Tel: 01-584 5040

**New Zealand High Commission**
New Zealand House, Haymarket SW1
Tel: 01-930 8422

**Norwegian Embassy**
25 Belgrave Square SW1
Tel: 01-235 7151

**Portuguese Embassy**
11 Belgrave Square SW1
Tel: 01-235 5331

**Spanish Consulate General**
20 Draycott Place SW3
Tel: 01-581 5921

**Swedish Embassy**
11 Montagu Place W1
Tel: 01-724 2101

**Swiss Embassy**
16 Montagu Place W1
Tel: 01-723 0701

**United States of America Embassy**
24 Grosvenor Square W1
Tel: 01-499 9000

# Accommodation in London

London offers a wide choice of accommodation, ranging from the luxury hotels of Mayfair to the more modest accommodation around Victoria and Paddington.

## Hotel Booking Service

A provisional bed booking service for the same or next night is available, to personal callers only at one of the London Visitor and Convention Bureau's five central Information Centres — at Victoria and Heathrow Stations, Harrods, Selfridges, and the Tower, or at the British Travel Centre in Regent Street (see page 6 for addresses and opening hours); you will find all the help you need at these centres. A returnable deposit must be paid when making a reservation there, and this is deducted from your final bill; in addition a small non-returnable booking fee is charged.

The London Visitor and Convention Bureau can help with advance hotel booking, by giving at least 4 weeks written notice to:-

Hotel Accommodation Service
London Visitor and Convention Bureau,
26 Grosvenor Gardens SW1

Telephone 01-730 3488 (automatic queueing system — please hold until receptionist answers).

Listed opposite are brief details of AA Appointed hotels, by Postal District numbers.

*KEY*    * Star classification of AA Appointed hotel
R Hotel classified with red stars
(considered to be outstanding within its
star rating)
Listed Approved hotel

Details of Appointed hotels are in the annual AA
guide *Hotels and Restaurants in Britain.* Details of
Listed hotels are in the AA guide *Guesthouses,
Farmhouses and Inns in Britain.*

---

**E1 — Stepney**
****    Tower Thistle     01-481 2575

**E18 — South Woodford**
Listed    Grove Hill     01-989 3344

**N8 — Hornsey**
Listed    Aber     01-340 2847

**NW1 — Regents Park, Baker Street, Euston & King's Cross Stations**
***    Harewood     01-262 2707
***    Kennedy     01-387 4400

**NW2 — Cricklewood, Willesden**
Listed    Clearview House     01-452 9773
Listed    Garth     01-455 4742

**NW3 — Hampstead and Swiss Cottage**
****    Holiday Inn, Swiss Cottage     01-722 7711
***    Charles Bernard     01-794 0101
***    Post House     01-794 8121
***    Swiss Cottage     01-722 2281
Listed    Frognal Lodge     01-435 8238

**NW4 — Hendon**
***    Hendon Hall     01-203 3341

**NW7 — Mill Hill**
**    TraveLodge, M1 Scratchwood Service Area
(Access from Motorway only)     01-906 0611

**NW8 — St John's Wood**
****    Ladbroke Westmoreland     01-722 7722

**NW11 — Golders Green**
Listed    Central     01-458 5636
Listed    Croft Court     01-458 3331

**SE3 — Blackheath**
Listed    Bardon Lodge     01-853 4051

**SE9 — Eltham**
Listed    Yardley Court     01-850 1850

**SE11 — Kennington**
**    London Park     01-735 9191

**SE19 — Norwood**
Listed    Crystal Palace Tower     01-653 0176

**SE23 — Forest Hill**
Listed    Rutz     01-699 3071

**SE25 — South Norwood**
Listed    Toscana     01-653 3962

**SW1 — West End, Westminster, St James's Park, Victoria Station,
Knightsbridge, Lower Regent Street**
*****R Berkeley     01-235 6000
*****    Hyatt Carlton Tower     01-235 5411

| | | |
|---|---|---|
| ***** | Hyde Park | 01-235 2000 |
| ***** | Sheraton Park Tower | 01-235 8050 |
| **** | Cavendish | 01-930 2111 |
| **** | Duke's | 01-491 4840 |
| ****R | Goring | 01-834 8211 |
| **** | Holiday Inn Chelsea | 01-235 4377 |
| **** | Stafford | 01-493 0111 |
| *** | Lowndes Thistle | 01-235 6020 |
| *** | Royal Horseguards Thistle | 01-839 3400 |
| *** | Royal Westminster Thistle | 01-834 1821 |
| *** | Rubens | 01-834 6600 |
| *R | Ebury Court | 01-730 8147 |
| Listed | Arden House | 01-834 2988 |
| Listed | Chesham House | 01-730 8513 |
| Listed | Easton | 01-834 5938 |
| Listed | Elizabeth | 01-828 6812 |
| Listed | Hanover | 01-834 0134 |
| Listed | Willet | 01-730 0634 |
| Listed | Windermere | 01-834 5163 |

**SW3 — Chelsea, Brompton**

| | | |
|---|---|---|
| ****R | The Capital | 01-589 5171 |
| *** | Basil Street | 01-581 3311 |
| Listed | Eden House | 01-352 3403 |
| Listed | Garden House | 01-584 2990 |
| Listed | Knightsbridge | 01-589 9271 |

**SW5 — Earl's Court**

| | | |
|---|---|---|
| *** | London International | 01-370 4200 |
| ** | Hogarth | 01-370 6831 |

**SW7 — South Kensington**

| | | |
|---|---|---|
| **** | Gloucester | 01-373 6030 |
| *** | Rembrandt | 01-589 8100 |

**SW19 — Wimbledon**

| | | |
|---|---|---|
| Listed | Trochee | 01-946 1579 |
| Listed | Wimbledon | 01-946 9265 |
| Listed | Worcester House | 01-946 1300 |

**W1 — West End — Piccadilly Circus, Soho, St Marylebone, Mayfair**

| | | |
|---|---|---|
| *****R | Claridge's | 01-629 8860 |
| *****R | The Connaught | 01-499 7070 |
| *****R | The Dorchester | 01-629 8888 |
| ***** | Churchill | 01-486 5800 |
| ***** | Grosvenor House | 01-499 6363 |
| ***** | London Hilton | 01-493 8000 |
| ***** | Inn on the Park | 01-499 0888 |
| ***** | Inter-Continental | 01-409 3131 |
| ***** | May Fair | 01-629 7777 |
| ***** | Ritz | 01-493 8181 |
| ****R | The Athenaeum | 01-499 3464 |
| **** | Britannia | 01-629 9400 |
| ****R | Brown's | 01-493 6020 |
| **** | Cumberland | 01-262 1234 |
| **** | Holiday Inn — Marble Arch | 01-723 1277 |
| **** | London Marriot | 01-493 1232 |
| **** | Montcalm | 01-402 4288 |
| **** | Park Lane | 01-499 6321 |
| **** | Portman Inter-Continental | 01-486 5844 |
| **** | St George's | 01-580 0111 |
| **** | Selfridge | 01-408 2080 |
| **** | Westbury | 01-629 7755 |

| | | |
|---|---|---|
| *** | Berners | 01-636 1629 |
| *** | Chesterfield | 01-491 2622 |
| *** | Clifton-Ford | 01-486 6600 |
| *** | Mandeville | 01-935 5599 |
| *** | Mount Royal | 01-629 8040 |
| *** | Stratford Court | 01-629 7474 |
| ** | Bryanston Court | 01-262 3141 |
| ** | Regent Palace | 01-734 7000 |
| Listed | Hotel Concorde | 01-402 6169 |
| Listed | Georgian House | 01-935 2211 |
| Listed | Hart House | 01-935 2288 |
| Listed | Montagu House | 01-935 4632 |

**W2 — Bayswater, Paddington**

| | | |
|---|---|---|
| **** | Royal Lancaster | 01-262 6737 |
| *** | Central Park | 01-229 2424 |
| *** | Hospitality Inn | 01-262 4461 |
| *** | London Embassy | 01-229 1212 |
| *** | Park Court | 01-402 4272 |
| *** | White's | 01-262 2711 |
| ** | Coburg | 01-229 3654 |
| Listed | Ashley | 01-723 3280 |
| Listed | Camelot | 01-723 9118 |
| Listed | Dylan | 01-723 3280 |
| Listed | Garden Court | 01-727 8304 |
| Listed | Nayland | 01-723 3380 |
| Listed | Pembridge Court | 01-229 9977 |
| Listed | Slavia Hotel | 01-727 1316 |

**W4 — Chiswick**

| | | |
|---|---|---|
| Listed | Chiswick | 01-994 1712 |

**W5 — Ealing**

| | | |
|---|---|---|
| *** | Carnarvon | 01-992 5399 |

**W6 — Hammersmith**

| | | |
|---|---|---|
| *** | Novotel London | 01-741 1555 |

**W8 — Kensington**

| | | |
|---|---|---|
| ***** | Royal Garden | 01-937 8000 |
| **** | Kensington Palace Thistle | 01-927 8121 |
| **** | London Tara | 01-937 1115 |
| *** | Kensington Close | 01-937 8170 |
| ** | Hotel Lexham | 01-373 6471 |
| Listed | Apollo | 01-373 3236 |
| Listed | Atlas | 01-373 7873 |

**W11 — Holland Park, Notting Hill**

| | | |
|---|---|---|
| *** | Hilton International Kensington | 01-603 3355 |

**W14 — West Kensington**

| | | |
|---|---|---|
| Listed | Avonmore | 01-603 4296 |

**London WC1 — Bloomsbury, Holborn**

| | | |
|---|---|---|
| **** | Hotel Russell | 01-837 6470 |
| *** | Bloomsbury Crest | 01-837 1200 |
| *** | London Ryan | 01-278 2480 |
| ** | Bedford Corner | 01-580 7766 |
| Listed | Mentone | 01-387 3927 |

**WC2 — Covent Garden, Leicester Square, Strand, Kingsway**

| | | |
|---|---|---|
| *****R | Savoy | 01-836 4343 |
| **** | Waldorf | 01-836 2400 |
| *** | Drury Lane Moat House | 01-836 6666 |
| *** | Royal Trafalgar Thistle | 01-930 4477 |
| *** | Strand Palace | 01-836 8080 |

# Entertainment

**What's on in London (Newspapers and Magazines)**

For detailed information on concerts, theatres, films, exhibitions and special events in London, see the entertainment section of the following newspapers:- the evening newspaper *The Standard*, *The Independent*, *The Guardian*, the Friday edition of *The Times* or the *Sunday Times*. The London Visitor and Convention Bureau also produces regular free leaflets on events and entertainment. Alternatively, the weekly magazines *What's On & Where To Go*, *Time Out* or *City Limits* — on sale at bookstalls and newsagents.

**Booking**

Tickets can be booked, of course, at the box offices of the individual theatres and concert halls. Many now accept credit card booking, which means you can telephone the box office to reserve your seats, quote your credit card number, and then collect the tickets half-an-hour before the performance begins. Some places have special phone numbers for credit card bookings, and these are pre-fixed *cc* in the listings which follow. Or you can use the services of ticket agencies such as Keith Prowse (tel: 01-741 9999); or try First Call (tel: 01-240 7200), a new telephone booking service mainly for credit card holders wanting theatre and concert tickets. It is open 24 hours a day, seven days a week.

**Late Theatre Booking**

The Half-Price Ticket Booth in Leicester Square, a chalet-type building opposite the Swiss Centre, is open to personal callers only and sells tickets from 12-2pm for matinee performances and from 2.30pm-6.30pm for evening shows. Tickets are for that day only; a booking fee is charged.

## Theatres

**Adelphi**
Strand WC2
(tel: 01-836 7611)

**Albery**
St Martin's Lane WC2
(tel: 01-836 3878;
*cc* 01-379 6565)

**Aldwych**
Aldwych WC2
(tel: 01-836 6464)

**Ambassadors**
West Street WC2
(tel: 01-836 1171;
*cc* 01-741 9999)

**Apollo**
Shaftesbury Avenue W1
(tel: 01-437 2663)

**Apollo**
Victoria, 17 Wilton Road SW1
(tel: 01-828 8665;
*cc* 01-630 6262)

**Astoria**
Charing Cross Road WC2
(tel: 01-734 4287)

**Barbican**
Barbican EC2
(tel: 01-628 8795;
*cc* 01-638 8891)

**Comedy**
Panton Street SW1
(tel: 01-930 2578;
*cc* 01-839 1438)

**Criterion**
Piccadilly W1
(tel: 01-930 3216;
*cc* 01-379 6565)

**Donmar Warehouse**
Earlham Street WC2
(tel: 01-836 3028;
*cc* 01-379 6565)

**Duchess**
Catherine Street WC2
(tel: 01-836 8243;
*cc* 01-741 9999)

**Duke of York's**
St Martin's Lane WC2
(tel: 01-836 5122;
*cc* 01-836 9837)

**Fortune**
Russell Street WC2
(tel: 01-836 2238;
*cc* 01-741 9999)

**Garrick**
Charing Cross Road WC2
(tel: 01-836 4601;
*cc* 01-379 6433)

**Globe**
Shaftesbury Avenue W1
(tel: 01-437 1592)

**Her Majesty's**
Haymarket SW1
(tel: 01-930 6606;
*cc* 01-930 4025)

**ICA Theatre**
Carlton House Terrace
SW1
(tel: 01-930 0493)

**Jeanetta Cochrane**
Theobalds Road WC1
(tel: 01-242 7040)

**King's Head**
Upper Street N1
(tel: 01-226 1916)

**Lyric Hammersmith**
King Street W6
(tel: 01-741 2311)

**Lyric**
Shaftesbury Avenue W1
(tel: 01-437 3686;
*cc* 01-434 1050)

**Mayfair**
Stratton Street W1
(tel: 01-629 3036)

**Mermaid**
Puddle Dock EC4
(tel: 01-236 5568)

**The National Theatre**
South Bank SE1
(tel: 01-928 2252;
*cc* 01-928 5933)

**New London**
Drury Lane WC2
(tel: 01-405 0072;
*cc* 01-404 4079)

**The Old Vic**
Waterloo Road SE1
(tel: 01-928 7616;
*cc* 01-261 1821)

**Open Air Theatre**
Regent's Park NW1
(tel: 01-486 2431;
*cc* 01-379 6433)

**Palace**
Shaftesbury Avenue W1
(tel: 01-437 6834;
*cc* 01-379 6131)

**Palladium**
8 Argyll Street W1
(tel: 01-437 7373)

**Phoenix**
Charing Cross Road WC2
(tel: 01-836 2294;
*cc* 01-741 9999)

**Piccadilly**
Denman Street W1
(tel: 01-437 4506;
*cc* 01-379 6565)

**Prince Edward**
Old Compton Street W1
(tel: 01-437 6877;
*cc* 01-439 8499)

**Prince of Wales**
Coventry Street W1
(tel: 01-930 8681;
*cc* 01-930 0844)

**Queen's**
Shaftesbury Avenue W1
(tel: 01-734 1166)

**Royal Court**
Sloane Square SW1
(tel: 01-730 1745)

**St Martin's**
West Street WC2
(tel: 01-836 1443)

**Savoy**
Strand WC2
(tel: 01-836 8888;
*cc* 01-379 6219)

**Shaftesbury**
Shaftesbury Avenue WC2
(tel: 01-379 5399;
*cc* 01-741 9999)

**Strand**
Aldwych WC2
(tel: 01-836 4143)

**Theatre Royal, Drury Lane**
Catherine Street WC2
(tel: 01-836 8108)

**Theatre Royal**
Haymarket SW1
(tel: 01-930 9832)

**Vaudeville**
Strand WC2
(tel: 01-836 9987)

**Victoria Palace**
Victoria Street SW1
(tel: 01-834 1317;
*cc* 01-828 4735)

**Westminster**
Palace Street SW1
(tel: 01-834 0283)

**Wyndhams**
Charing Cross Road WC2
(tel: 01-836 3028;
*cc* 01-379 6565)

**Young Vic**
66 The Cut SE1
(tel: 01-928 6363)

---

## Cinemas

**ABC 1 & 2**
Shaftesbury Avenue WC2
(tel: 01-836 8861)

**Academy 1, 2 & 3**
Oxford Street W1
(tel: 01-437 2981)

**Cannon (Baker Street)**
Marylebone Road NW1
(tel: 01-935 9772)

**Cannon**
Charing Cross Road WC2
(tel: 01-437 4815)

**Cannon**
Haymarket SW1
(tel: 01-839 1527)

**Cannon Moulin**
Great Windmill Street
W1
(tel: 01-437 1653)

**Cannon**
Oxford Street W1
(tel: 01-636 0310)

**Cannon**
Panton Street SW1
(tel: 01-930 0631)

**Cannon (Piccadilly Circus)**
Piccadilly W1
(tel: 01-437 3561)

**Cannon Premier**
Swiss Centre, Leicester
Square WC2
(tel: 01-437 2096)

**Cannon**
Tottenham Court Road
W1
(tel: 01-636 6148)

**Cannon Royal**
Charing Cross Road WC2
(tel: 01-930 6915)

**Cinema 1**
Barbican EC2
(tel: 01-628 8795)

## Curzon (Mayfair)
Curzon Street W1
(tel: 01-499 3737)

## Curzon (West End)
Shaftesbury Avenue WC2
(tel: 01-439 4805)

## Dominion
Tottenham Court Road
W1
(tel: 01-580 9562)

## Empire
Leicester Square WC2
(tel: 01-437 1234)

## Leicester Square Theatre
Leicester Square WC2
(tel: 01-930 5252)

## Lumiere
St Martin's Lane WC2
(tel: 01-836 0691)

## Metro
Rupert Street W1
(tel: 01-437 0757)

## Minema
145 Knightsbridge SW1
(tel: 01-235 4225)

## National Film Theatre
South Bank SE1
(tel: 01-928 3232)

## Odeon
Haymarket SW1
(tel: 01-930 2738)

## Odeon
Leicester Square WC2
(tel: 01-930 6111)

## Odeon
Marble Arch W2
(tel: 01-723 2011)

## Plaza 1, 2, 3 & 4
Regent Street W1
(tel: 01-437 1234)

## Prince Charles
Leicester Place WC2
(tel: 01-437 8181)

## Renoir
Brunswick Square WC1
(tel: 01-837 8402)

## Screen on Baker Street
Baker Street W1
(tel: 01-935 2772)

## Warner West End
1, 2, 3 & 4
Cranbourn Street WC2
(tel: 01-439 0791)

## Concert Halls

### Barbican Centre
Barbican EC2
(tel: box office 01-628
8795; recorded
information on events
01-628 9760;
cc 01-638 8891)

### Royal Albert Hall
Kensington Gore SW7
(tel: 01-589 8212;
cc 01-589 9465)

### The South Bank Arts Complex
SE1
(tel: 01-928 3191;
cc 01-928 8800)
This includes three
concert halls,
The Royal Festival Hall,
Queen Elizabeth Hall
and the Purcell Room

### Wigmore Hall
36 Wigmore Street W1
(tel: 01-935 2141)

## Opera and Ballet

### The London Coliseum
St Martin's Lane WC2
(tel: 01-836 3161;
cc 01-240 5258)

### Royal Opera House
Covent Garden WC2
(tel: 01-240 1066;
recorded information
01-240 1911)

### Sadler's Wells
Rosebery Avenue EC1
(tel: 01-278 8916;
recorded information
01-278 5450)

Royal Albert Hall

## Church Concerts

There are many churches in London which hold lunchtime recitals or concerts. For full details and programme tel: 01-606 3030. A few of the popular churches are:

**All Hallows-by-the-Tower**
Byward Street EC3
1pm Mondays;
12.15pm and 1.15pm
Thursdays

**Holy Sepulchre**
Holborn Viaduct EC1
1.15pm Tuesdays,
Wednesdays, Fridays;
1.20pm Thursdays

**St Bride**
Fleet Street EC4
1.15pm Wednesdays

**St John's**
Smith Square SW1
1pm Mondays; and

1.15pm alternate
Thursdays

**St Lawrence Jewry**
Gresham Street EC2
1pm Mondays and
Tuesdays

**St Martin-in-the-Fields**
Trafalgar Square WC2
1.05pm Mondays and
Tuesdays

**St Mary-le-Bow**
Cheapside EC2
1.05pm Thursdays

**St Mary Woolnoth**
Lombard Street EC3
1.05pm Fridays

**St Michael-upon-Cornhill**
Cornhill EC3
1pm Mondays

**St Olave**
Hart Street EC3
1.05pm Wednesdays
and Thursdays

**St Paul's Cathedral**
EC4
12.30pm Fridays

**Southwark Cathedral**
Borough High Street SE1
1.10pm Mondays

## Open-Air Music

During the summer, military bands offer free lunchtime entertainment in the Royal Parks, and in certain City Parks and squares.

**Royal Parks:**
military and brass
bands play free most
lunchtimes in Hyde
Park, St James's Park,
and Regent's Park.
Phone 01-211 3000 for
information.

**City sites**
(phone the City
Information Centre on
01-606 3030 for
details)

**Finsbury Circus
Gardens**
Moorgate EC2:
lunchtime band
concerts, usually
Wednesdays.

**Lincoln's Inn Fields**
WC2: military bands,
usually Tuesday and
Thursday lunchtimes.

**Paternoster Square**
EC4: military bands,
daily, lunchtimes.

**St Paul's Steps**
EC4: sit in full view of
St Paul's and listen to a
full military band
concert; usually
Thursdays.

**Tower Place**
EC3: military bands,
usually Fridays.

**Victoria Embankment
Gardens:**
SW1: riverside setting
for military bands,
massed bands, and
light orchestras, most
lunchtimes of the
week.

**Other sites:**

**Battersea Park Concert
Pavilion**
SW11 (tel: 01-633
1707). Imaginative

programme of musical
events, lunchtime and
evenings.

**Holland Park Court
Theatre**
W8 (tel: 01-633 1707).
A small open-air theatre
which stages opera and
ballet and concerts
during July.

**Kenwood**
Hampstead Lane NW3
(tel: 01-348 1286).
Leading orchestras give
symphony concerts in
this beautiful setting by
the lake on Saturday
evenings during June
and July. To be seen to
be 'in', take a picnic.

**Parliament Hill**
NW3 (tel: 01-485
4491). Massed bands
play beside the lake on
Saturday evenings
during the summer.

# London's Transport

The visitor arriving in London will need to know first of all how to get about the capital. Fortunately, though Greater London is over 610 square miles in size, twice as large as New York or Paris, it is served by one of the finest transport systems in the world.

You have a choice of three means of public transport: the familiar red London bus, the Underground railway — or 'tube' — network, and the London Taxi.

The buses and Underground are controlled by London Regional Transport whose headquarters is at 55 Broadway, Westminster SW1. This authority maintains Travel Information Centres at the following underground stations in Central London:

| | |
|---|---|
| Charing Cross Station | 8.15am-6pm |
| Euston Station | 7.15am (8.15am Sun) — 6pm (7.30pm Fri) |
| King's Cross Station | 8.15am-6pm (7.30pm Fri) |
| Oxford Circus Station | 8.15am-6pm (9.30pm Thurs) (Closed Sun) |
| Piccadilly Circus Station | 8.15am-9.30pm |
| St James's Park Station | 8.15am-5pm (Mon-Fri) except public holidays |
| Victoria-British Rail | 8.15am-9.30pm |
| Heathrow Terminals 1, 2, 3 Underground Station | 7.15am-9.30pm |

(Also Heathrow Terminal buildings, see page 22)

They answer all queries about travel in London, as well as issue tickets, book tours, and sell publications. Or you can telephone 01-222 1234 anytime, day or night. (For Lost Property information telephone 01-486 2496)

## The Underground

There is a map of the Underground at the back of this book.

As with many capital cities, the quickest and most efficient means of public transport in London is the Underground railway — known as 'the tube'. With more than 275 stations, the Underground covers a wide area reaching out from central London to the suburbs where it rises above ground as an ordinary surface railway. There is almost always a tube station close at hand throughout London, and trains run frequently between 5.30am and 0.15am (until 11.30pm on Sundays). There are no all-night services, however, and it is important to note that certain stations are closed at weekends.

There are large Underground maps posted at all stations, in the booking halls and on all platforms, and each car displays a map of that train's route. Each line has a name and is clearly indicated in a separate colour; it is usually easier to follow the colours than go by the names of the lines.

| | |
|---|---|
| Bakerloo line | — brown |
| Central line | — red |

District line        — green
Circle line          — yellow
Jubilee line         — grey
Metropolitan line    — purple
Northern line        — black
Piccadilly line      — dark blue
Victoria line        — light blue

Signs throughout the tube stations show the way to the line required, but make sure you wait on the correct platform and board the right train by checking the direction indicators both on the platform itself and on the front of the train.

A list of fares is displayed in ticket halls; you must buy a ticket before you begin your journey, either from the booking office or from automatic machines (these will save you queueing and some of them give change), and keep it safe to either show or surrender at your destination.

Under-14s travel at a reduced fare, as do 14- and 15-year-olds with a Child Rate Photocard — these are available free from Post Offices in the London area. Under-fives travel free.

**Buses**  One of the best ways of seeing London is to take a seat on the top deck of one of its famous double-decker buses. The fact that the traffic may be slow on occasions is no great handicap, but offers a wonderful opportunity for leisurely sightseeing. Buses operate from about 6am to midnight on most routes, including those connecting the main-line railway stations, and offer a comprehensive service in central London and the suburbs. A network of special All Night buses runs through central London serving Piccadilly Circus, Leicester Square, Victoria, Trafalgar Square, Hyde Park Corner, Marble Arch, and many other parts convenient for theatres, cinemas, and restaurants. However, do check times before using these buses; their stops have distinctive blue and yellow route numbers.

You should pick up a free, detailed bus map from any Travel Enquiry Office or Underground station. Each bus route is identified by a number which appears on the front, sides and back of each bus. The final destination also appears on the front and back, and a short list of major ports of call on the sides. Bus-stop signs, which generally list the numbers of the buses which stop there, are displayed on a red or white background. Red backgrounds denote 'Request Stops', where the bus will only stop if hailed in good time; the white background signs are compulsory stops.

On double-decker buses, there are usually conductors who control the number of passengers allowed on and collect fares; on single-decker buses you give your fare to the driver.

Under-14s pay a reduced flat fare until 10pm, as do 14- and 15-year-olds with a Child Rate Photocard, and up to two under-fives per person travel free. Remember to keep your ticket until you leave the bus.

**Concessionary Fares**

If you intend using public transport in London extensively, there are a number of special tickets and passes available which will save you money and waste a good deal less of your precious time. With most of them you can travel when you like, as often as you like; there's no need to queue for separate tickets in the normal way or search for change on buses. They can be bought from any London Transport or LVCB Information Centre, or any Underground station.

With the **London Explorer Pass** you get unlimited travel on all London's red buses (except the Official Sightseeing Tours) and almost all the Underground — even to and from Heathrow by Airbus or tube — for 1, 3, 4 or 7 days, with special low prices for the under-16s.

**Red Bus Rover** tickets allow unlimited travel for one day on any of London's normal bus services.

The newest faresaver — and timesaver — in London is the **Capitalcard**. The combined British Rail, Underground, and bus network in Greater London is divided into five concentric zones. You just choose which zones you most wish to travel in, and buy the appropriate Capitalcard. You can then travel on any combination of train, tube, and bus within your selected zones, any number of times, for the duration of the ticket's validity (seven days or a month). There is also a **One Day Capitalcard** which gives you unlimited off-peak travel for the day throughout the whole of Greater London, by train, tube and bus: the only restriction is you have to travel after 9.30am, Monday to Friday (no restrictions at weekends). You can also buy combined British Rail tickets and seven-day or monthly Capitalcards, and One Day Capitalcards, from most stations outside Greater London, which is a great saving if you are not actually staying in the capital.

Within London, Capitalcards can be bought from any British Rail or Underground station. Before buying one, you will need a Photocard: just take a passport-size photograph of yourself with you when you buy your first ticket and you will be issued with one free. (There are instant-photo booths at the major railway and tube stations; these are coin-operated, so be sure you have the right change with you.)

# British Rail

Britain's extensive rail network links all major cities in the country with London. British Rail offer travel facilities at **The British Travel Centre**, 4-12 Lower Regent Street SW1. (tel: 01-730 3400). Here you can buy rail tickets and make reservations, book tickets for theatres and sightseeing tours, arrange accommodation, and change foreign money. The Centre is open from 9am to 6.30pm, Monday to Saturday and on Sundays from 10am to 4pm.

British Rail also have **Travel Centres** at:
14 Kingsgate Parade, Victoria Street SW1
87 King William Street EC4
407 Oxford Street W1
170b Strand WC2

Here you can purchase rail tickets and obtain full information on British Rail services/holidays etc. They are open Monday to Friday from 9am to 5pm. There are also Travel Centres at these main London terminals:
Cannon Street, Charing Cross, Euston, King's Cross, London Bridge, Liverpool Street, Paddington, St Pancras, Victoria and Waterloo

**Railway Terminals**    The principal mainline stations linking London with various parts of Britain and timetable telephone numbers are:

| | | |
|---|---|---|
| King's Cross | 01-278 2477 | East and north east England and Scotland via the east coast. |
| Liverpool Street | 01-283 7171 | East Anglia, Essex |
| Fenchurch Street | 01-283 7171 | Essex |
| St Pancras | 01-387 7070 | East Midlands |
| Euston | 01-387 7070 | West Midlands, north west England, Scotland via the West coast and North Wales. |
| Victoria | 01-928 5100 | South and south east England |
| Waterloo | 01-928 5100 | South and south west England |
| Charing Cross | 01-928 5100 | South east England |
| Paddington | 01-262 6767 | South west England, South Wales and Oxford area. |

Full details of scheduled rail services are shown in local timetables. Free copies are available from British Rail stations and Travel Centres.

British Rail fares are calculated on the distance travelled. It is generally cheaper to travel after the morning rush hour (9.30 Monday to Friday), and at any time over the weekend. Buy a Cheap Day Return or, for longer journeys, a Saver Return ticket. You must buy a ticket before travelling, and surrender it either to the guard on the train or to the ticket-collector on the platform at your destination. Children under five travel free; under 16, half price.

**Rush Hour**    From Monday to Friday the buses and trains of London Regional Transport carry a daily average of over 6,000,000 passengers. In Central London all forms of public transport become extremely crowded between 8am-9.30am and 4pm-6.30pm when most of London is travelling to and from work. London's rush hour is really most uncomfortable, and if travel can be arranged outside these times, the visit will be considerably more enjoyable. Buses and tubes also get quite busy at lunchtime, but not as bad as during the rush hour.

**Taxis**    The London taxi is one of the friendliest sights a visitor will see. The traditional colour is still black, though in recent years red, blue and yellow vehicles have added a splash of colour to London's fleet. But the distinctive shape remains. Taxis are a salvation for those who get lost; after midnight they are a godsend and the only way to get about. Taxi drivers are also a useful source of information as they know London inside-out — they have to, in order to get their licence.

London taxis can be hailed in the street if the yellow 'For Hire' or 'Taxi' sign above the windscreen is lit, hired from taxi ranks, or called by telephone: for numbers, see 'Taxi' in the S-Z section of the London Telephone Directory. Charges vary according to the distance covered and are recorded on the meter; additional charges are made for extra people, luggage, and night journeys. It is customary to tip about 10-15% of the fare, or perhaps a little more if the driver has been particularly helpful. For journeys over six miles — for example, from Heathrow Airport to Central London — you should negotiate a fare in advance.

# Heathrow Airport — London *tel:* 01-759 4321

Heathrow Airport now has four Passenger Terminals in separate parts of the airport. Terminals 1, 2 and 3 are situated in the central area of Heathrow. Terminal 4 is situated at the south east of Heathrow's perimeter road. The central area is linked to the M4 via a motorway spur and the Bath Road (A4) via twin tunnels. Terminal 4 is linked to the Great South West Road (A30) and the M25 via the A3113 and the airport's Southern Perimeter Road.

**Tourist Information Centre**    London Regional Transport and The London Visitor and Convention Bureau (*tel* 01-759 4321) run a travel office with a separate Tourist Information counter in the Heathrow Central Underground Station. There are also information and sales desks near the arrival points in each Terminal.

Heathrow Terminals            7.15am — 9.30pm
   1,2,3 Underground Station
Heathrow Terminal 1 arrivals 7.15am — 9pm
Heathrow Terminal 2 arrivals 7.45am — 3pm
Heathrow Terminal 3 arrivals 6.45am — 5.30pm
Heathrow Terminal 4 arrivals 6.30am — 9.30pm

**Where to leave your car**

### Short-term parking (covered)
Car Parks are sited at all passenger terminals. Car parks 1, 2 and 3 are managed for the BAA by National Car Parks Ltd (*tel:* 01-745 7160) and car park 4 by Europarks Ltd (*tel:* 01-745 7072). No reservations necessary.

### Open-air Long-term parking
Heathrow Airport long-term car parks for Terminals 1, 2 and 3 are managed by National Car Parks Ltd on behalf of the British Airports Authority and are situated on the Northern Perimeter Road. Terminal 4 is managed by Europarks Ltd and is off the Southern Perimeter Road. Entering the airport from the M4 spur or the A4 follow signs to the long-term car parks. A free coach will take passengers to the terminals and return to the relevant car park following arrival at Heathrow. During the hours midnight — 06.00 special direct line telephones are in use at the pick-up points, enabling passengers to contact the coach base to arrange for collection.
   **For a period exceeding 3 hours it is more economical to use these car parks.**

**Public Transport**

### Underground
The extension of the Piccadilly line tube, opened in 1977, provides a direct link from all Heathrow terminals to the West End of London. Departures from the airport start at about 5am on Monday to Saturday and at about 7am on Sunday; the last train leaves at just before midnight, Monday-Saturday, and just before 11pm on Sunday. The first train to Heathrow leaves King's Cross station at about 6am on Monday to Saturday and at about 7.30am on Sunday; the last train leaves just after midnight, Monday-Saturday, and at about 11.30pm on Sunday.

### Buses and Coaches
An extensive bus and coach service operates from Heathrow Central to local and major destinations in Britain which include:

### Airbus (express services):
**A1 to Victoria Station:** stopping at Cromwell Road (Earls Court Road), Cromwell Road (Forum Hotel), Hyde Park Corner (Knightsbridge).
**A2 to Euston Station:** stopping at Holland Park Avenue (Kensington Hilton), Notting Hill Gate, Bayswater Road, Marble Arch, Bloomsbury, Russell Square.
   This bus service runs every 20-30 minutes from 6.30am to 9.30pm.

**'Flight Line' 767** provides a half-hourly (hourly during winter months) link between Heathrow and

London's Victoria Coach Station, from where connections to all parts of Britain can be made.

### Heathrow/Gatwick Road Links

A luxury express service, **Speedlink**, now operates between Heathrow and Gatwick Airport every 20 minutes with a journey time of 50 minutes. First/last bus from Heathrow 0610/2310, first/last bus from Gatwick 0600/2200. *Tel:* 01-668 7261.

*Jetlink 747* Regular fast daily service linking Gatwick with Heathrow Airport and Watford, Hemel Hempstead, Luton, Luton Airport and Stevenage.

Although airbuses and tubes do not operate during the night, there is an all-night bus service — No 97 — which runs at regular intervals from midnight to 5am between central London and Heathrow.

Regular coach services are operated on behalf of British Rail connecting Woking BR Station; also to/from Reading BR Station; bookings can be made at the passenger terminals, railway stations and appointed travel agencies.

Airline buses operate at frequent intervals between Heathrow and certain town terminals in Central London.

*Taxi*
London taxis operate between London and Heathrow Airport.

**Hotels — General Information**

In all the arrival terminals there are reservation desks operated by Hotel Bookings International Ltd.

**Car Hire**

*Avis Rent-a-car* (*all passenger terminals*), Self-drive *tel:* 01-897 9321. Chauffeur-driven *tel:* 01-897 2621. Open 07.00-22.00hrs. A one-way service to/from over 80 locations throughout the UK is also available.
*Budget Rent-a-car,* Skyway Hotel, Bath Road, Hayes *tel:* 01-759 2216. Open 07.00-21.00 daily. Courtesy service to/from airport.
*Godfrey Davis Europcar* (*all passenger terminals*), 24-hour self-drive and chauffeur-driven service, also a one-way service to/from over 270 locations throughout the UK *tel:* 01-897 0811/5.
*Hertz Rent-a-car* (*all passenger terminals*), Central reservation office *tel:* 01-679 1799.
*Kenning Car Hire* (Local and One-Way Car & Van Hire), Sheraton Skyline Hotel, Bath Road, Hayes. *Tel:* 01-759 9701. (Use Sheraton Skyline Hotel courtesy coach from all terminals.)
Also at Hatton Cross, Gt South West Road, Feltham (opposite Hatton Cross Underground Station). *Tel:* 01-890 1167.

**Facilities for disabled travellers**

All terminals have lifts, ramps and specially designed toilets. If special assistance is required, contact the airline being used.

**Queen's Building Roof Gardens**

The Queen's Building Roof Gardens have been designed for the benefit of the public visiting the airport. Refreshment facilities are available. Open daily from 10.00hrs until dusk. Admission charge.

# Gatwick Airport — London

*Tel:* (0293) 28822 or 01-668 4211.
Twenty-eight miles south of London, Gatwick is
the second most important airport in Britain.
Access is available from the A23 and the M23.
Essential traffic direction signs are situated both
inside and outside the airport. Many major airlines
operate from Gatwick. For information on flight
enquiries telephone (0293) 31299. The Airport is
also open to aircraft diverted from Heathrow
Airport London, and the charter service of other
airline companies.

**Tourist Information**

This is provided by the Airport Information desk,
situated in the International Arrivals Hall, and is
open 24 hours a day, seven days a week.

**Where to leave your car**

All car parks on the airport are managed by
National Car Parks Limited as concessionaires to
the British Airports Authority. There is no need to
reserve space although enquiries can be made: *tel:*
(0293) 28822 ext 2395, or (668) 4211 ext 2395
(from London area only).
*Method of payment* Drivers must retain car park
tickets for payment at the kiosk appropriate to the
car park. A receipt and timed coded card is given
which is fed into a card reader at the exit and
raises the barrier. 15 minutes is given to leave the
multi-storey car park and 2 hours is given to leave
the open-air long-term car park.

**Parking**

*Short-term:*
The terminal car park, consisting of three multi-
storey car parks connected by passenger walkways
to the Airport Terminal, provides spaces for 3,000
cars.
*Long-term Open-air Car Park:*
This open-air car park (10,800 spaces) situated to
the south of the airport complex, is connected by
a free bus service to the terminal.

**Public Transport**

*Bus/Coach* services. Regular services to/from
Gatwick are provided by the following: Green
Line Coaches/London Country Bus Services
*tel:* 01-668 7261.
*Services include:*
Flightline 777 London (Victoria Coach Station) —
Gatwick.
This bus service runs every 30 minutes.

**Gatwick/Heathrow Road Links**

A luxury express service, **Speedlink**, now operates
between Gatwick and Heathrow Airport every 20
minutes with a journey time of 50 minutes.
First/last bus from Heathrow 0610/2310, first/last
bus from Gatwick 0600/2200. *Tel:* 01-668 7261.
*Jetlink 747* Gatwick-Heathrow
Regular fast daily service linking Gatwick with
Heathrow Airport and Watford, Hemel Hempstead,
Luton, Luton Airport and Stevenage.

Full details of all Bus and Coach services are available from the Green Line enquiry desk in the airport terminal building, open daily, 07.30-20.30.

*British Rail* — There is direct covered access by escalator and lift to the Airport Terminal concourse from the adjacent railway station. British Rail's non-stop Gatwick Express service links London (Victoria) to Gatwick Airport with trains every 15 minutes from 05.30-22.00hrs. The journey time is approximately 30 minutes. Other services run hourly throughout the night. A daily, fast service at hourly intervals runs for much of the day between Reading and Gatwick Airport calling only at Guildford and Redhill. (This is in addition to the Reading-Tonbridge service operating hourly and stopping at intermediate stations.) At Reading there are excellent rail connections with the West Country, the Midlands and Wales. There are direct hourly trains to the Airport for much of the day from Chichester, Hastings, Bexhill, Eastbourne, Lewes, Portsmouth and Worthing. There are also three trains an hour from Brighton. Through services also operate direct to/from Gatwick Airport and Watford, Milton Keynes, Stafford, Liverpool and Manchester.

Full details of these and all other rail services are available from the British Rail Travel Centre at Gatwick Airport Station, situated in the station concourse, or from your local station.

**Hotels —
General Information**

In the terminal building there is a reservation desk operated by Hotel Plus.

**Car Hire**

Self-drive and chauffeur-driven cars may be hired from the following companies who have desks in the arrivals hall:

| | |
|---|---|
| Avis Rent-a-car Ltd | (0293) 29721 |
| Godfrey Davis Europcar | (0293) 31062 |
| Hertz Rent-a-car Central Reservations | 01-679 1799 |
| Kennings Car Hire | (0293) 549024 |

*Not on Airport premises*
Budget Rent-a-car have a desk in the Gatwick Moathouse *tel:* Horley (0293) 773731.
Continental Car Rental, Edgeworth Park, Balcombe Road, Horley, Surrey *tel:* (0293) 771583.

**Facilities for
Disabled Travellers**

The terminals have lifts, ramps and specially designed toilets. You are advised to contact your airline if you need any special assistance. A leaflet describing facilities for the disabled at Gatwick Airport is available from: Airport Services, British Airports Authority, Gatwick Airport, Gatwick, West Sussex RH6 OHZ.

**Spectators
Viewing Area**

The viewing area is signposted through the International Arrivals section. It is open daily 09.00hrs to dusk. Admission charge. Catering facilities are available. Parking facilities in the Multi-storey Car Parks.

# Stansted Airport — London

*Tel:* Bishop's Stortford (0279) 502387. This is London's developing airport, 35 miles north east with fast access via the M11 motorway.

**Where to leave your car**
Short and long-term parking available opposite Passenger terminal entrance.

**Car Hire**
Self-drive cars may be hired from Godfrey Davis Ltd (adjacent to terminal building) (0279) 812727.

# Sightseeing Tours

An excellent way to get to know London — particularly if this is your first visit — is to join one of the many sightseeing bus or coach tours.

London Transport's **Official Sightseeing Tours** on double-decker red buses start from Piccadilly Circus (Haymarket), Marble Arch (Speakers Corner), Baker Street Station, and Victoria Station. The 18-mile route (lasting about 1½ hours) passes most of London's landmarks including St Paul's, Westminster Abbey, and The Tower. These guided tours leave every half-hour from each point from 10am to 5pm daily (except Christmas Day). Buy your tickets in advance from any London Transport or LVCB Information Centre at a special low rate; or just pay as you board the bus. A special tour includes direct entrance (no boring queueing) to Madame Tussaud's Waxworks. The buses are open-top in summer. Details from London Transport, 55 The Broadway SW1 (tel: 01-222 1234).

**Culture Bus** (tel: 01-629 4999). Daily (except 24 and 25 December), every 20 minutes from 9am to 6.30pm. The distinctive yellow Culture buses follow a circular route in Central London passing many places of interest, with over 20 carefully-chosen stops. Once you've paid, you can hop on and off all day. Tickets bought in advance for the Culture bus can be used instead on one of **London Pride's** Grand Guided Tours (tel: 01-437 9580), which start from the Trocadero, Piccadilly Circus W1: a 90-minute guided tour of the capital, with full commentary.

Other sightseeing bus/coach tours are run by: Evans Evans Tours Ltd (01-930 2377); Frames Rickards (01-837 3111); Golden Tours (01-937 8863); London Tour Company (01-734 3502); London Cityrama (01-720 5971); Travellers Check-In (01-580 8284); Harrods Sightseeing (01-581 3603); London Crusader (01-437 0124); and Thomas Cook Ltd (01-499 4000).

**Boat trips on the River Thames**

A holiday in London cannot be complete without the unique views offered by a boat trip on the Thames. Passenger boat services operate a full programme during the summer months and a restricted one in the winter. From Westminster Pier (01-930 4097), Charing Cross Pier (01-839 3312), and Tower Pier (01-488 0344), services operate downstream to Greenwich, and from Westminster and Charing Cross Piers downstream to the Tower. Upstream services operate from Westminster Pier to Kew, Richmond, and Hampton Court, and from Tower Pier to Westminster. Check departure times with the enquiry numbers given with each Pier, or telephone the **River Boat Information Service** on 01-730 4812 (weekdays, 9am-5.30pm).

**London canal trips**

London also has two canals — the Grand Union and the Regent's Canal. Boat trips operate mainly on the Regent's Canal: the Regent's Canal Waterbus goes from Camden Lock to Little Venice, via London Zoo (01-200 0200); Jason's Canal Cruises (01-286 3428) run luncheon and evening trips along the picturesque part of Regent's Canal using a pair of traditional narrow-boats; there are cruises on the *Jenny Wren* through the Zoo and Regent's Park, and on the *My Fair Lady*, a luxury cruising restaurant (01-485 4433); the *Port A Bella Packet* narrow-boat cruises on the Grand Union and Regent's Canals (01-960 5456). Telephone for full details and itineraries.

**Seeing London by bicycle**

A different way to get about London is to use a bicycle. Traffic, especially in Central London, is often congested and the cyclist has a freedom denied the motorist. There are many firms in London who offer a cycle hire service and who are able to meet the needs of both the casual and experienced cyclist, whether it be for a traditional three-speed or a fast and sophisticated ten-speed bike. Most firms can also supply items of cycling equipment and can provide information on sights to see. *Rent-a-Bike*, Kensington Student Centre, Kensington Church Street W8 (01-937 6089), the largest cycle hire company in Britain, is open seven days a week and offers daily, weekly, and monthly (or longer) periods of rental. The old-established firm of *Savile's Cycle Stores Ltd*, 97-99 Battersea Rise SW11 (01-228 4279), is open from Monday to Saturday, excluding Wednesdays and public holidays. It offers an initial weekly period of rental followed by a daily rate thereafter.

**London on foot**   If you want to discover London by foot — one of the best ways to get to know any city — several firms organise guided walking tours. Information from:

City Walks 01-937 4281
Cockney Walks 01-504 9159
Footloose in London 01-435 0259
London Walks 01-882 2763
Regent Canal Walks 01-586 2510
Royal London Walking Tours 01-740 7100
Streets of London 01-882 3414
London Pub Walks 01-883 2656
Exciting Walks 01-624 9981
Discovering London 0277 213704
Citisights 01-241 0323
(archaeological walks)

If you want to explore London on your own, the Silver Jubilee Walkway covers ten miles of historic London. This walkway was created in 1977 to commemorate the 25th anniversary of the Queen's accession to the throne. The entire route is signposted by silver plaques in the shape of a crown set into the pavement. Parliament Square is a good place to start.

**Pedestrians**   At a Zebra street-crossing (one with flashing orange beacons and black-and-white stripes on the road) you have absolute right-of-way when you have stepped off the kerb — but do use this sensibly and make sure drivers have seen you before you cross.

At Pelican crossings (two lines of studs with traffic lights to halt the traffic), you have to push a button to make the signals stop the traffic for you. When the signal shows a green man, cross. If this signal starts to flash while you are crossing, carry on, you will have plenty of time to reach the other side; do not start to cross when this is flashing nor, of course, when the red man is showing.

Be aware of the bus lanes where buses may travel in the opposite direction to the main flow of traffic.

# Shopping in London

The capital's well-known shopping areas are mostly in the West End, with such world-famous names as Oxford Street, Regent Street, Bond Street, Piccadilly and Knightsbridge. In some cases, shops along a particular road specialise in certain types of goods. Other roads have a more general mixture of shops, where, in a short distance, almost anything can be purchased.

**Oxford Street**   Justifiably famous, Oxford Street is the backbone of London's shopping area. There are no particular specialities, but it is the home of many of London's big department stores and has many clothes, shoe, and fashion shops.

The busiest stretch is between Marble Arch and Oxford Circus, and not far from Marble Arch is **Marks & Spencer's** largest branch, a favourite with shoppers from all over the world for reasonably-priced good quality clothing and other goods. Nearby is **Selfridges**, London's second-largest department store and especially popular for its food hall, restaurants, kitchenware and cosmetics departments. Other department stores along Oxford Street include **D H Evans**, **Debenhams**, and **John Lewis**.

Other inexpensive clothing stores include **British Home Stores** and **C&A**, while nearly every fashion and shoe store chain has at least one branch in Oxford Street. The new **HMV** record shop can lay claim to being one of the largest and most comprehensive of its kind anywhere in the world.

**Regent Street**

More department stores and fashion shops are to be found in Regent Street, which crosses Oxford Street at Oxford Circus. The department stores include **Dickins & Jones**, and **Liberty & Co**, world-famous for its classic fabrics and patterns. Classic British-style clothing will be found at shops such as **Jaeger**, **Austin Reed** and **Aquascutum**. Also on Regent Street is the well-known **Hamleys** toy store and **Garrard**, the Queen's jeweller.

**Bond Street**

New Bond Street runs down from Oxford Street to Burlington Gardens, where it becomes Old Bond Street, and continues to Piccadilly. This is one of London's most expensive streets, where leading names in fashion, jewellery, and beauty salons alternate with premises of famous art dealers. Fashion shops such as **Yves Saint Laurent**, **Ted Lapidus**, **Gucci**, **Kurt Geiger**, and **Magli** are the sort of establishment where anyone who has to ask the price can't afford it. **Asprey & Co** specialises in the fine, rare, and beautiful in leather, gold, silver, jewellery, and antiques, and there is one department store — **Fenwick** — which sells mainly women's fashions. **Elizabeth Arden**, **Max Factor**, and **Yardley** each have a beauty salon and there are a number of photographic shops in New Bond Street, notably **Dixons** and **Wallace Heaton**.

**Piccadilly**

There seem to be more airlines and tourist boards represented in Piccadilly than shops, but those that are here are some of the most important names in London. On Piccadilly Circus is the old-established clothes and sportswear store of **Lillywhites**.

Almost opposite the Royal Academy is **Hatchards**, an excellent general bookshop, and **Fortnum & Mason**, which stocks the finest food and drink as well as a variety of other goods. **Swaine, Adeney, Brigg & Sons** nearby is the place to go for high-quality leather goods, umbrellas and riding equipment. Burlington Arcade, off Piccadilly, has some of the most elegant small shops in London, where ties, woollen goods, and antique and modern jewellery can be bought.

**Simpson** is a first-class tailor and outfitter in Piccadilly, but the well-heeled gentleman will buy his clothing in streets off either side of Piccadilly. He will have his shirts hand-made in Jermyn Street, and his suits supplied from a Savile Row or Sackville Street tailor. Those who can't afford such things will go to **Moss Bros**, in Bedford Street, off the Strand, where good-quality men's dress clothing for any occasion can be hired or bought.

**Tottenham Court Road**

Running up from New Oxford Street to Euston Road, Tottenham Court Road was once thought of as the furniture centre for London. Today it is predominantly known for its hi-fi and electrical equipment shops such as the many branches of **Lasky** and **Lion House**, which has a hi-fi department store on the corner of Store Street. There are still, however, a number of good furnishing stores, the largest being **Heal & Son Ltd**. Newer and smaller, but no less striking, is **Habitat**, whose popular furniture and furnishings are of a modern design. Other interesting shops on Tottenham Court Road are **Paperchase**, which has a unique range of cards, posters, wrapping paper and other stationery, and **The Reject Shop** which stocks a wide range of seconds in pottery and household goods.

**Charing Cross Road**

Charing Cross Road is at the southern end of Tottenham Court Road and is the home of a great variety of new and second-hand bookshops as well as shops selling music and musical instruments. Of the bookshops, **Foyles** must be the most famous, and **Macari's** is one of the many shops stocking musical instruments, though these days most of their trade is in guitars, electric keyboards, and synthesizers. Shaftesbury Avenue, which crosses Charing Cross Road at Cambridge Circus, also has many music shops.

**Covent Garden**

Since the old Flower Market closed in 1974 Covent Garden has blossomed in another way — as one of the best and most popular shopping areas in London. There are shops and stalls of every kind, most selling goods of individual, and excellent, quality. The atmosphere of the market is enhanced by musicians and other street entertainers.

**Knightsbridge**

Though the Knightsbridge, Brompton Road and Sloane Street area has some of the most luxurious fashion boutiques, antique shops and department stores in London, they all tend to be overshadowed by the magnificence of **Harrods**, the largest department store in Europe. Equally notable, but not as comprehensive, is the **Harvey Nichols** department store in Sloane Street. It is a luxurious store particularly noted for women's and children's wear as well as all kinds of furniture and furnishings. Also popular is **The Scotch House**, which specialises in Scottish woollens, knitwear, and woven tartans.

**Kensington High Street**

At the western end of Hyde Park, the two roads of Kensington High Street and Kensington Church Street make up this lively and fashionable off-centre shopping area. The department store **John Barker** specializes in household goods. Going down Kensington High Street, chain clothing stores like **C&A**, **Marks & Spencers**, **British Home Stores**, and individual fashion shops mingle with supermarkets and exotic restaurants. Kensington Church Street is a haven for antique collectors at its eastern end, and at its western end for those looking out for the most up-to-date in clothing.

**King's Road**

Fashions may come and fashions may go, but the King's Road seems able to transcend them all, remaining the most fashionable thoroughfare in London. It is best-known for clothes shops, but there are also sophisticated antique, furnishing and fashion shops. The shoppers in the King's Road are usually every bit as fascinating and diverse as the shops themselves.

## Street Markets

Nothing beats a street market for a particular kind of atmosphere. They are usually good places for such things as fruit, vegetables and inexpensive household effects. Some of London's street markets specialise in such things as antiques, but bargains are few and far between.

**Berwick Street Market**
*Berwick Street, W1*

Fruit and vegetable stalls predominate here, but shellfish, clothing, and household goods are also available, and some of the stalls are attached to neighbouring shops. The market is especially crowded at lunchtimes, as shoppers queue up at stalls which are reputed to sell some of the best quality fruit and vegetables in London.
*Monday-Saturday*

**Brixton Market**
*Electric Avenue, SW9*

As this market is set in an area with a large West Indian population, it is not surprising that many of its stalls are stocked with Caribbean fruit and vegetables. There are also second-hand clothes and household goods stalls.
*Monday-Saturday (Wednesday am only)*

**Camden Lock Market**
*Camden, NW1*

Antiques, bric-à-brac, period and Asian clothes are generally available, and there are also craft and food stalls.
*Saturday and Sunday*

**Camden Passage**
*Camden Passage, N1*

This is a rich and varied mixture of antique shops and stalls, most of the latter appearing on Wednesdays and Saturdays. The arcades of the market become very crowded on Saturdays, and only those arriving early can hope to find a bargain. The goods on display are liberally sprinkled with bric-à-brac and Victorian curios, but Camden Passage is as good a place as any for a wide variety of antiques, with dealers specialising in furniture, jewellery, prints, pottery, books, pub mirrors, period clothing, and silverware.
*Wednesday and Saturday*

**Chapel Market**
*White Conduit Street, N1*

This market is very popular with the locals at weekends. Fruit and vegetables are always available, and there are usually stalls selling fish, groceries, and household goods.
*Tuesday-Sunday am*

**Church Street and Bell Street**
*Lisson Grove, NW8*

A mixture of stalls is to be found in these adjacent markets. Antiques are well represented, with some excellent stalls. There are also clothes, household and food stalls.
*Tuesday-Sunday*

**Club Row**
*Sclater Street, E1*

Part of the East End's famous Petticoat Lane complex of street markets, Club Row has stalls selling general household items.
*Sunday am*

**Columbia Road Market**
*Shoreditch, E2*

An enormous variety of flowers, plants, and shrubs make this market a Mecca for all gardening enthusiasts.
*Sunday am*

**East Street Market**
*Walworth, SE17*

This is an old established general market with some bric-à-brac stalls. Plants, shrubs, and fruit are usually available on Sundays.
*Tuesday and Thursday-Sunday am*

**Jubilee Market**
*Covent Garden, WC2*

Partly under cover, this small general market opened in Covent Garden at about the time that Covent Garden Wholesale Market moved to Nine Elms in the 1970s. There are fruit, vegetables, and bric-à-brac stalls, but the greater part of this market contains souvenirs, clothes, craft, jewellery, and record stalls.
*Monday-Sunday*

**Leadenhall Market**
*Gracechurch Street, EC3*

Formerly purely a wholesale market, today Leadenhall is open to the general public and, while still specialising in meat and poultry, also offers fish, vegetables, and plants. The Victorian arcade, containing cafes and pubs in contrast to the rows of carcasses which are suspended on tiers of hooks outside the shops, is noted for its old-time market atmosphere, and is a favourite haunt for City office workers, whether intent on buying, or simply watching the world go by.
*Monday-Friday*

**Leather Lane**
*Holborn, EC1*

Fruit, groceries, vegetables, clothing, household goods of all descriptions — particularly crockery — are always on display here. The sight of an entire dinner service being expertly tossed in the air is a regular occurrence.
*Monday-Friday*

**Lower Marsh and The Cut**
*Lambeth, SE1*

This busy general market nestles in the shadow of Waterloo Station and becomes very popular during the lunch period.
*Monday-Saturday*

**New Caledonian Market**
*Bermondsey Square, SE1*

This is primarily a dealers' antique market. An enormous selection of articles is on view, set out on closely packed stalls, but those in search of a bargain need to be early risers as a great deal of the trading takes place between 5am and 7am

(when the market officially opens). Although something of a closed community, run principally by dealers for dealers, private collectors and casual visitors are made very welcome. Bric-à-brac, silver, jewellery, clocks, pottery, and porcelain are always available, and furniture, coins, and medals are also featured, but stallholders tend to avoid specialisation, displaying oddments and curios of all descriptions.
*Friday am*

**Northcote Road**
*Battersea, SW11*

A fruit and vegetable market situated near Clapham Junction. It is at its busiest on Saturdays, and at that time the atmosphere can be very lively indeed.
*Monday-Saturday*

**North End Road**
*Fulham, SW6*

This general market specialises in fruit and vegetables, and flowers and plants are on sale during the summer months. Other stalls in this cheerful market offer clothes, and household goods.
*Monday-Saturday (Thursday am only)*

**Petticoat Lane**
*Middlesex Street, E1*

The street acquired the name Petticoat Lane during the 17th century because of the number of old clothes dealers who congregated here. Despite the fact that it officially became known as Middlesex Street as long ago as 1846 the old name has lived on, at least as far as the Sunday market is concerned. It is one of the most famous of all London markets, and opens around 9am, but all the stallholders begin to set up their premises about 7.30am before an interested audience of sightseers. Despite its present-day cosmopolitan atmosphere, engendered by the Indian, West Indian, and Jewish communities which are prevalent in the area, Petticoat Lane still retains its essential Cockney character. The maze of stalls occupies every available corner, and there is very little in the way of household goods and clothes of every description that cannot be purchased.
*Sunday am*

**Portobello Road**
*Notting Hill, W11*

Portobello Road has been noted for its antique shops and stalls since the 1950s. It reached the height of its fame during the late '60s and early '70s when it became the centre of London's hippy community. A general market with fruit, vegetable and meat stalls operates all the week, but it is on Saturdays that all the stalls and arcades are opened. The stalls and shops, of which there are more than 2,000, contain all kinds of furniture, clothes, jewellery, ancient gramophones and records, books, bottles, coins, medals, toys, a great deal of Victoriana, and an endless selection of junk. Buskers, street singers, and street performers jostle with and cajole the crowds. It is rare to find a genuine bargain in the antique stalls at the lower end of the road these days, since all the traders are experts, but real finds can sometimes be made amongst the piles of junk on the stalls beyond the Westway Flyover.
*Monday-Saturday*

**Ridley Road**
*Hackney, E8*

One of the better known of London's East End markets, the stalls here are patronised by the local Jewish and West Indian communities. It is a general market, with many fruit and vegetable stalls, and becomes very crowded on Saturdays.
*Monday-Saturday*

**Roman Road**
*Tower Hamlets, E3*

A busy market with stalls on either side of the road offering a good variety of wares.
*Monday-Sunday (Monday, Wednesday, Friday and Sunday am only)*

**Shepherd's Bush**
*W12*

Stalls specialising in West Indian food, and household goods will be found in the market here. It extends as far as Goldhawk Road beside a railway viaduct.
*Monday-Saturday (Thursday am only)*

**Walthamstow**
*The High Street, E17*

This extensive general market straggles along either side of Walthamstow's main street. It is particularly busy towards the end of the week.
*Monday-Saturday (Wednesday am only)*

**Wembley Market**
*Wembley Stadium,*
*NW10*
*(See also page 68)*

A large open-air market with accommodation for up to 500 stalls is held here every Sunday between 9am-2pm on part of the stadium car park. A large variety of goods is sold, and usually there is free parking.
*Sunday*

**Wentworth Street**
*Tower Hamlets, E1*

This general market is engulfed by Petticoat Lane on Sundays. For the rest of the week if caters for locals, and has some excellent stalls selling Jewish and West Indian foods.
*Daily*

**Whitechapel Road**
*Tower Hamlets, E1*

Stalls line the pavements of this famous East End thoroughfare, multiplying on Saturdays.
*Monday-Saturday*

**Whitecross Street**
*Islington, EC1*

A busy market which caters, to a large extent, for lunch-time shoppers. It is particularly crowded on Wednesdays and Fridays.
*Monday-Saturday*

**Woolwich Market**
*Beresford Square, SE18*

This small market is very popular and has a wide variety of stalls.
*Monday-Saturday (Thursday am only)*

## Trade Markets

**Billingsgate Market**
*North Quay,*
*West India Docks,*
*Isle of Dogs, E14*

The first official mention of this historic wholesale fish market was made as long ago as the end of the 13th century, when a royal charter was granted to the Corporation of London for the sale of fish. A market is known to have been held on Billingsgate's old site in Lower Thames Street in the City of London at least 400 years earlier. In 1982, the traders moved to a new site in London's Docklands.

From about 5am the market becomes a hive of activity and the air is pervaded by a pungent aroma of fish and the uninhibited language of the porters. By 8am most of the business is over and about 300 tons of fish will have changed hands.

**Borough Market**
*Stoney Street, SE3*

This market occupies buildings beneath the railway arches of the viaduct serving London Bridge Station to the south of Southwark Cathedral.

It operates from Monday to Saturday, with traders commencing business as early as 3am. Activity builds up in a crescendo of noise and bustle between 6 and 7 am, and most of the business has been completed by the middle of the morning.

**Covent Garden**
*Nine Elms, SW8*

The original Covent Garden (the area to the east of Charing Cross Road) owes its name to the fact that the monks of Westminster Abbey had a 40 acre walled garden here. It grew to become the most important fruit, vegetable, and flower market in the country, and in 1830 the first specially-built market premises were erected on the site. These buildings were rapidly outgrown, and by the middle of the 20th century wholesalers had taken over all the streets in the area. Traffic congestion had become a serious problem by this time, and it was decided that the only solution was to move the market to specially-built premises at Nine Elms. The move was made in 1974, to the sorrow of many people, as Covent Garden had a unique and irreplaceable character.

The market has now settled into its new home at Nine Elms, and there is no doubt that the vast building makes up in increased efficiency what it lacks in character.

**Smithfield Market**
*Charterhouse Street, EC1*

Smithfield is London's principal wholesale meat market, and is one of the largest meat, poultry, and provision markets in the world. The total area covered by all the market buildings is over eight acres.

Smithfield, which is derived from 'Smoothfield', was originally an open space located just outside the old city walls.

Up until the middle of the 19th century all cattle sold at Smithfield were driven through the narrow and congested streets of central London. At one time the number of beasts flowing in and out of the market amounted to 70,000 a week. It was not until 1867 that a government statute placed restrictions on the droving of cattle through the capital's thoroughfares. It was at this time that the present Central London Meat Market was constructed. It was designed by Sir Horace Jones and is a Renaissance-style building consisting of iron and glass arcades fronted with red brick and flanked by domed towers. To the west of the cattle market is the Poultry Market building, which was built in 1963 to replace a Victorian structure that was destroyed by fire in 1958.

**Spitalfields Market**
*Commercial Street, E1*

Named after the priory of St Mary Spital which was founded here in 1197, Spitalfields refers both to the area and to the wholesale market, which trades in fruit, vegetables, and flowers. The New Market buildings were opened in 1928 by Queen

Mary. The buildings have been extensively modernised, and now provide stands for 150 wholesale merchants. There are extensive underground chambers, used principally for ripening bananas, beneath the market. Trading begins at 5.30am every weekday and is generally completed by 9am.

### Fine Art Auctioneers

The three big names in London are Sotheby's, Christie's and Phillips, all of which have international connections and hold sales all over the world. The public is admitted to previews and sales except on very rare occasions when admission is by ticket only, and all three auction houses welcome people bringing objects for free inspection and estimation of value.

**Christie, Manson & Woods Ltd**
*8 King Street, SW1*

Founded in 1766, Christie's holds as many as three or four sales a day in its King Street salerooms. Over 150,000 pictures, pieces of furniture, silver, porcelain, jewellery, books, arms and armour, and *objets d'art* are sold each year, two-thirds of them for less than £300. There are a number of specialist sales, and sales in the lower price range are held at Christie's South Kensington.

**Phillips**
*7 Blenheim Street (off New Bond Street), W1*

Phillips was founded in 1796, and today regular sales are held for antiques of all sorts and works of art. In addition there are a great number of specialist sales ranging from coins and stamps to musical instruments and suits of armour.

**Sotheby, Parke, Bernet & Co**
*34 New Bond Street, W1*

Sotheby's, founded in 1744, has over the last few years seen some of the most important art sales ever. Apart from its London offices, Sotheby's has 64 other auction rooms, representative offices in 27 countries, and their overall turnover in 1985-86 was a staggering £475,000,000. Sotheby's can claim a number of firsts which have become standard practice in many international auction houses, for instance the introduction of specialised sales, the use of closed-circuit television and TV satellite for transatlantic bidding, and the use of a computer to convert the bids instantly into six different currencies.

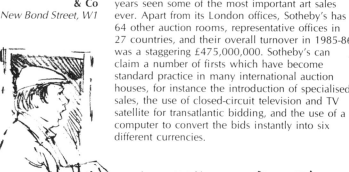

Covent Garden

# Sport

Spectator sport remains popular in London, despite television, and the tarnished reputation of fans of some sports. To be at the finals of a football tournament, or at a cricket test match, or urging your horse to be first past the post is very exciting.

**Association Football**

The Football Association (FA) was not founded until 1863, and the first FA Challenge Cup Final was played at the Oval, Kennington, in 1872. Today London has 12 teams in the four divisions of the Football League, and it has had at least one team in the top category, Division One, every year since 1904. In addition, London boasts Britain's foremost football stadium — Wembley. (See page 68). The football season runs from August to May.

## London's Football Clubs

**Arsenal**
*Arsenal Stadium, Highbury, N5*

**Brentford**
*Griffin Park, Braemar Road, Brentford*

**Charlton Athletic**
*The Valley, Floyd Road, Charlton, SE7*
*(Now playing at Crystal Palace)*

**Chelsea**
*Stamford Bridge, Fulham Road, SW6*

**Crystal Palace**
*Selhurst Park, Whitehouse Lane, SE25*

**Fulham**
*Craven Cottage, Stevenage Road, Fulham, SW6*

**Millwall**
*The Den, Cold Blow Lane, New Cross, SE14*

**Orient**
*Leyton Stadium, Brisbane Road, Leyton, E10*

**Queen's Park Rangers**
*South Africa Road, W12*

**Tottenham Hotspur**
*748 High Road, Tottenham, N17*

**West Ham United**
*Boleyn Ground, Green Street, Upton Park, E13*

**Wimbledon**
*Plough Lane Ground, 45 Durnsford,*
*Wimbledon, SW19*

**Athletics**

London has witnessed many great moments in athletics history, including the staging of the 14th Olympic Games at Wembley in 1948. The White City stadium has also been the scene of many memorable events. Built at the beginning of this century, it was the venue for the 4th Modern Olympic Games and was London's principal athletic stadium for more than half a century.

In 1964 the Crystal Palace National Sports Centre opened and the White City finally ended its long and honourable association with athletics. The purpose-built Sports Centre has an all-weather track and covered accommodation for spectators, and stages all manner of athletics competitions.

**Crystal Palace National Sports Centre**
*Crystal Palace Park, Sydenham, SE19*

**New River Sports Centre**
*White Hart Lane, Wood Green, N22*

**Parliament Hill Fields**
*Gospel Oak, NW3*

**Victoria Park**
*Victoria Park, E9*

**West London Stadium**
*Wormwood Scrubs, W12*

## Cricket

Cricket is widely played in London, on commons and playing fields, but the two major venues are Lord's Cricket Ground in St John's Wood and the Oval in Kennington.

Lord's is probably the best-known ground in the country and is the home ground for two clubs — Middlesex County Cricket Club and the famous Marylebone Cricket Club, perhaps even better known by its initials, MCC. Until recently the MCC was effectively the governing body for the game, and its collection of cricket memorabilia forms the Lord's Cricket Museum (See page 82).

The game of cricket accompanied the British to the colonies and it became equally popular in Australia, New Zealand, the West Indies, India and Pakistan. It is these countries who play England in the Test Matches, which are played here and in their own countries. A Test Match is usually five days long and there can be as many as six in a series, played on various pitches throughout the country. Both Lord's and the Oval are traditional venues for Test Matches, the latter being the site of the first-ever Test in 1880.

The Oval is the home ground of Surrey County Cricket Club, and today it is usually the venue for the final Test in a series.

Lord's, too, has Test Matches, and many other countries as well as the six Test countries are being drawn into international cricket by the new Prudential Cup competition. Begun in 1975, it takes place every four years, with the final being played at Lord's in June. The many other matches played at Lord's include county cricket, the finals of the Gillette Cup and the Benson and Hedges Cup, and the annual match between Eton and Harrow.

**Lord's Ground**
*St John's Wood Road, NW8*

**The Oval**
*The Oval, Kennington, SE11*

**Greyhound Racing**

'Going to the dogs' has always been a popular pastime, especially with East End Londoners. Pure-bred greyhounds chase after an artificial hare on an electrified rail at speeds of up to 40mph. Races, either on the flat or over hurdles, are over varying distances and attract a good deal of betting and prize money. The more famous tracks are at Harringay and Walthamstow. Several of the tracks have restaurants overlooking the races.

**Catford**
*Greyhound Stadium,*
*SE6*

**Hackney Wick**
*Waterden Road, E15*

**Harringay**
*Green Lanes, N4*

**Walthamstow**
*Chingford Road, E4*

**Wembley**
*Stadium Way*

**Wimbledon**
*Plough Lane, SW19*

**Horse Racing**

Horse racing is as much a part of the social calendar as it is a sport. Many go to the races to see and to be seen. There is plenty of excitement for those who go for the actual racing, and of course there is the possibility of winning a bet. The flat-racing season is from March to November, and steeplechasing takes place between August and June.

**Ascot Racecourse**
*Ascot, Berkshire*

**Epsom Racecourse**
*Epsom, Surrey*

**Kempton Park Racecourse**
*Sunbury-on-Thames,*
*Greater London*

**Sandown Racecourse**
*Esher, Surrey*

**Windsor Racecourse**
*Windsor, Berkshire*

**Rugby Union Football**

Wherever one is in London, there is likely to be a rugby game worth watching. Fixtures to look out for at Twickenham are internationals (which are well publicised), the Oxford *v* Cambridge match in early December, the RFU 'John Player' Club Competition final in April, and the Inter-Services Championships played during March and April. Apart from the major clubs listed below there are a number of Old Boys' Clubs and teams which compete for the Hospitals Cup, as well as the many college and school teams acting as nurseries for future great players.

**Blackheath RFC**
*Rectory Field, Charlton Road, Blackheath, SE3*

**Harlequin RFC**
*Stoop Memorial Ground, Craneford Way, Twickenham, Greater London*

**London Irish RFC**
*Pavilion, The Avenue, Sunbury-on-Thames*

**London Scottish RFC**
*Richmond Athletic Ground, Richmond, Surrey*

**London Welsh RFC**
*Old Deer Park, Kew Road, Richmond, Surrey*

**Metropolitan Police RFC**
*Police Sports Club, Ember Court, Embercourt Road, East Molesey, Surrey*

**Richmond RFC**
*Richmond Athletic Ground, Richmond, Surrey*

**Rosslyn Park RFC**
*Priory Lane, Upper Richmond Road, Roehampton, SW15*

**Saracens RFC**
*The Pavilion, Bromley Sports Ground, Green Road, Southgate, N14*

**Wasps RFC**
*Repton Avenue, Wembley, Greater London*

**Speedway**    This highly-specialised motorcycling sport, which developed from dirt-track racing in open fields, is now usually held within large football or greyhound stadiums. The fearless riders need a great deal of skill and daring to execute the long, broadside drifts on the sweeping curves at each end of the track, sending showers of the loose shale surface into the air.

**Hackney Wick**
*Waterden Road, E15*

**Wimbledon**
*Plough Lane, SW19*

**Tennis**    In the last week of June and the first week in July, the All England Lawn Tennis and Croquet Club hosts, in effect, the world tennis championships on grass, though the event is called simply the Lawn Tennis Championships Meeting.

The Wimbledon complex, to which improvements have been made since its opening in 1922 by King George V, consists of 30 grass courts with their cherished and world-famous Cumberland turf, 9 hard courts and two indoor courts. The complex includes a post office, bank, and restaurants.

**All England Lawn Tennis and Croquet Club**
*Church Road, Wimbledon, SW19*

# Pageantry, Ceremonies and Events

The most famous events in London's ceremonial calendar are the grand royal pageants, such as Trooping the Colour, which are brilliantly colourful and which attract huge crowds. But London has hundreds of other events, some very big, like the Lord Mayor's Show, and some tiny, like the Ceremony of the Lilies and Roses. For further information on all these events, telephone the London Visitor and Convention Bureau — (01) 730 3488. (See also list of events at Earls Court and Olympia, page 68.)

### Changing of the Guard ceremonies

**Buckingham Palace**    This famous ceremony takes place in front of Buckingham Palace daily from the end of April to the end of June, and on alternate days from August to March. If the weather is very wet, or if there is some other ceremony on that day, then there may be no change, or the times may be altered. The Guard is changed at 11.30am, but onlookers are advised to be in place outside the palace well before that to get a good viewing position. The Guard is drawn from troops of the Brigade of Guards, the Queen's personal bodyguard. The new guard, usually accompanied by a band, marches to the palace from Wellington Barracks.

**Mounting the Guard**
Horse Guards,
Whitehall

This ceremony, which takes about half an hour, takes place at 11.00am Monday to Saturday, and at 10.00am on Sunday. The mounted guardsmen, drawn from the Household Cavalry, ride from Hyde Park to Whitehall.

**St James's Palace**

The detachment of the Queen's Guard which patrols St James's Palace marches to Buckingham Palace at 11.15am and returns to St James's Palace at 12.10pm. This ceremony does not take place if there is no guard-change at Buckingham Palace.

**Tower of London**

If there is a guard-change at Buckingham Palace, the Guard at the Tower is changed at 11.30am.

**Ceremony of the Keys**

For 700 years the main gate at the Tower has been locked by the Chief Yeoman Warder of the Tower and an escort of Guards. The ceremony starts at 9.50pm. Permits are essential for this ceremony; they can be applied for from the Resident Governor, Queens House, H M Tower of London, EC3 4AB. At least four weeks advanced booking is necessary.

**Gun Salutes**

Royal Salutes take place annually at midday in Hyde Park on February 6 (the Queen's Accession Day), April 21 (the Queen's Birthday), June 2 (Coronation Day), June 10 (the Duke of Edinburgh's Birthday), August 4 (Queen Mother's Birthday). The salutes (of 41 guns) are fired by the King's Troop, Royal Horse Artillery. On the same days, 62-gun salutes are fired at the Tower of London by the Honourable Artillery Company. These salutes take place at 1.00pm.

# Major events

## January

**Model Engineer Exhibition**
Wembley Conference Centre, Wembley.

**6th January**

**Royal Epiphany Gifts Service**
Chapel Royal, St James's Palace

A 700 year-old ceremony in which officers of the royal household offer up gifts of gold, frankincense and myrrh. The gold is subsequently exchanged for currency and distributed for charitable purposes.

**early January**

**Old Bailey in Session**
Central Criminal Court, Old Bailey

The opening session of the Central Criminal Court, Old Bailey, is attended by the Lord Mayor of London, who leads a procession from the Mansion House to the Old Bailey attended by the sheriffs, swordbearer, common crier and City marshal.

**Court of Common Council Service**
Church of St Lawrence Jewry, Gresham St

The Lord Mayor of London and his officers walk in procession from the Guildhall to attend a service at the Church of St Lawrence Jewry, Gresham Street, prior to the first sitting of the newly-elected Court of Common Council which presides over the City of London.

**30th January**

**Charles I Commemoration Ceremony**
Trafalgar Square

Each year members of the Society of King Charles the Martyr and the Royal Stuart Society commemorate the execution of Charles I on 30th January 1649. They walk in procession from St Martin-in-the-Fields to the equestrian statue of the King which stands in Trafalgar Square near the entrance to Whitehall.

# February

**Stampex**
Royal Horticultural Halls SW1
National Stamp Exhibition

**Sunday nearest first day of new Lunar calendar**

**Chinese New Year**
Gerrard St

London's 'Chinatown' is decorated for this event, and a procession led by a 'lion' weaves through the area receiving gifts from shops. This celebration has evolved in recent years to become one of London's most colourful and exciting ceremonies.

**Ash Wednesday**

**Cakes and Ale Sermon**
St Paul's Cathedral

Members of the Stationers Company walk in procession from Stationers' Hall to St Paul's Cathedral where their chaplain preaches a sermon in accordance with the wishes of John Norton, a member of the Worshipful Company of Stationers who died during the reign of James I. Cakes and ale are distributed before or after the service.

**3rd February
(St Blaise's Day)**

**Blessing of the Throats**
St Ethelreda Church, Holborn

Throat sufferers congregate at the Church of St Ethelreda, in Holborn, for a service commemorating St Blaise, Bishop of Dalmatia, who saved the life of a child with a fishbone lodged in its throat while on his way to a martyr's death during the 3rd century.

**on the Saturday nearest to 22nd February**

**Scout and Guide Founders' Day Service**
Westminster Abbey

Scouts and guides gather in Westminster Abbey on the shared birthday of Lord Baden-Powell, founder of the Scout and Guide Movement, and his widow. Wreaths are laid on the Baden-Powell memorial.

**Shrove Tuesday
(occasionally March)**

**Pancake Race**
Lincoln's Inn Fields, Paternoster Square

| | |
|---|---|
| on or near 20th | **Sir John Cass Commemoration Service** |

on or near 20th
**Sir John Cass Commemoration Service**
St Botolph's Church, Aldgate

This service commemorates a City Sheriff who founded the school named after him in 1709.

first Sunday in February
**The Clown Service — Grimaldi Commemoration Service**
Holy Trinity Church, Dalston

Joseph Grimaldi was one of the most famous clowns of all time, and there is a memorial to him in this church. The service is attended by clowns in full costume.

# March

(on or near 21st, Spring Equinox)
**Druid's Observance Ceremony**
Tower Hill

Members of the Druid Order gather to celebrate the spring equinox here.

(or April)
**Oxford & Cambridge Boat Race**
Putney — Mortlake

The Boat Race, a contest between two crews of eight rowers and one coxswain representing the universities of Oxford and Cambridge, is one of the most famous sporting events in the world. The first Boat Race took place at Henley-on-Thames in 1829, but in 1845 the event was moved to its present location in London. The course runs on the Thames from Putney to Mortlake, a distance of over 4 miles, and it takes place annually on a Saturday shortly before Easter.

on or near 28th March
**Oranges & Lemons Children's Service**
St Clement Dane's Church, Strand

A service to mark the restoration of the bells of St Clement Danes in the Strand, the 'St Clements' of the well-known nursery rhyme 'Oranges and Lemons'. The service is attended by children of the St Clement Danes Primary School and each child receives an orange and a lemon.

# Easter

Maundy Thursday
**Distribution of the Royal Maundy Money**
Alternate locations including Westminster Abbey and Southwark Cathedral

This ancient ceremony of royal humility, which dates back to the time of Edward III, once included the reigning monarch washing the feet of the poor. The last sovereign to perform this rite was James II. William III delegated the washing to an aide, and the last foot-washing took place in 1754, after which the ceremony consisted of giving specially-minted Maundy pennies. Today the Queen distributes two purses, one containing the Maundy Money, the other containing money which represents the now discontinued gifts of food and clothing, to senior citizens selected from London parishes. The ceremony is held at various alternate locations including Westminster Abbey and Southwark Cathedral.

**Good Friday** — **Hot-Cross Buns Service**
St Bartholomew-the-Great Church, Smithfield

Under the terms of an ancient charity, the morning service at St Bartholomew-the-Great, Smithfield, is concluded by the distribution of money and hot-cross buns to 21 local widows.

**Easter Monday** — **Harness Horse Parade**
Regent's Park

An extensive display of private and commercial horse-drawn vehicles, featuring all types of horses from shire horses drawing brewers' drays to the pony and trap, which takes place on the Inner Circle, Regent's Park.

**second Wednesday after Easter** — **Spital Sermon Procession**
Guildhall to St Lawrence Jewry Church

The Lord Mayor of London walks in procession with aldermen and other City dignitaries from the Guildhall to the Church of St Lawrence Jewry where a bishop nominated by the Archbishop of Canterbury preaches the Spital Sermon. These sermons have an Easter theme and were preached at St Paul's Cross in the Cathedral churchyard prior to the Great Fire.

# April

**on or near 5th April** — **John Stow's Quill Pen Ceremony**
St Andrew Undershaft Church, Leadenhall St

The memorial service for John Stow, who wrote **The Survey of London** in 1598, takes place each year at the Church of St Andrew Undershaft, Leadenhall Street, attended by the Lord Mayor and other dignitaries. During the service the Lord Mayor places a fresh quill in the hand of Stow's statue, which depicts him at work on his **Survey**.

**Spring Flower Show**
Royal Horticultural Society Halls, Vincent Square, SW1

# May

**21st May** — **Ceremony of the Lilies and Roses**
Tower of London

Representatives of Eton College and King's College, Cambridge, both founded by Henry VI, join in a ceremony at the Wakefield Tower, Tower of London on the anniversary of the King's murder. Lilies from Eton and roses from King's are placed on the spot where Henry was killed in 1471.

**29th May** — **Oak Apple Day**
Royal Hospital, Chelsea

The Chelsea Pensioners honour Charles II, the founder of the Royal Hospital, on the anniversary of his escape after the Battle of Worcester (1651). His statue is decorated with oak leaves and branches — in memory of the fact that the King hid in an oak tree.

**(May to July)**

**Royal Academy Summer Art Exhibition**
Royal Academy, Piccadilly

**Royal Windsor Horse Show**
Windsor

**Association Football Cup Final**
Wembley

**Chelsea Flower Show**
Royal Hospital, Chelsea

The Royal Hospital Gardens have been the setting for the Flower Show since 1913. Entire landscapes are created for the show, and new strains of flowers are often unveiled here.

**(April or May)**

**London Marathon**
Greenwich to Westminster

This event has now established itself as one of the highlights of the London year. Thousands of runners, from the very young to the very old and from the fit to the not-so-fit, compete in a good-humoured race through London.

# June

**second Saturday in June**

**Trooping the Colour**
Buckingham Palace to The Mall to Horse Guards Parade

Held on the Queen's official birthday, at Horse Guards Parade, off Whitehall, Trooping the Colour is probably the most spectacular military display in the country. The 200-year-old ceremony, with its roots stretching back to medieval times, begins with the Queen riding from Buckingham Palace, wearing the uniform of one of the regiments of which she is Colonel-in-Chief, to Horse Guards Parade, where the Brigade of Guards and the Household Cavalry await her, massed on the parade ground. Her Majesty takes the salute which is followed by a display of marching and the 'trooping' or carrying of the colours of a selected regiment. Originally the colours were 'trooped' so that the men of the regiment could learn to recognise their own colours. The Queen then leads a contingent of Guards back to Buckingham Palace. The sovereign's official birthday is always held in summer when the chances of good weather are at their best.

**about 24th June**

**The Knollys Red Rose Rent**
Seething Lane to Mansion House

This ceremony commemorates the fining of Sir Robert Knollys in the 14th century for building a footbridge between two of his properties on either side of Seething Lane. In recognition of his recent military service in France the fine imposed was the presentation of a red rose from his garden to the Lord Mayor every Midsummer Day. Today churchwardens of All Hallows-by-the-Tower carry a red rose to the Mansion House on an altar cushion where it is presented to the Lord Mayor together with a bouquet of roses for the Lady Mayoress.

**Epsom Races — The Derby**
Epsom

**Royal Ascot Races**
Ascot

**(2 weeks end June/ beginning July**

**Lawn Tennis Championships**
Wimbledon

**(occasionally July)**

**Cricket — Test Match**
Lord's Cricket Ground

**Grosvenor House Antiques Fair**
Park Lane

**(early June)**

**Beating Retreat — Household Division**
Horse Guards Parade

**(mid June)**

**Royal Artillery**
Horse Guards Parade

An impressive military display of marching and drilling bands. Each event is held over three days.

# July

**on or near last Monday in July**

**Swan Upping**
London Bridge to Henley

The Vintners' and Dyers' Livery Companies have the right, shared with the monarch, of keeping swans on the River Thames between London Bridge and Henley. Swan Upping takes place when the cygnets (or young swans) are about two months old, and entails the Queen's Swan Keeper and the Swan Wardens and Swan Markers of the two companies inspecting all the adult swans and establishing the ownership of the cygnets. These are duly marked by the officials, who wear traditional livery, and operate from skiffs rowed by assistants in striped jerseys and hats.

**late July/early August**

**Doggett's Coat and Badge Race**
London Bridge to Albert Bridge

This, the oldest rowing event in the world, was instituted in 1715 by Thomas Doggett, an Irish actor, in honour of the accession to the throne of George I. Today, under the patronage of the Fishmongers' Company, six Thames watermen race against the tide from London Bridge to Albert Bridge. The winner of what is sometimes called the 'Watermen's Derby' receives a scarlet livery with silver buttons and a large silver badge on the left arm.

Mid July/mid August    **Henry Wood Promenade Concerts**
Royal Albert Hall SW7

Founded in 1895 by Sir Henry Wood, this series of concerts is famous the world over.

**Royal International Horse Show**
Wembley

**Cricket: Benson and Hedges Cup Final**
Lord's Cricket Ground

**Vintners' Procession**
Vintners' Hall to St James, Garlickhythe

After the installation of a Master Vintner, the wine porters sweep a path for the following procession.

# August

**Greater London Horse Show**
Clapham Common

**Notting Hill Carnival**
Portobello Road area

A noisy, friendly, colourful event, with a large contribution by London's Caribbean population.

# September

28th September or
preceding Friday    **Admission of Sheriffs**
Mansion House to Guildhall

The two sheriffs elected by the livery companies on Midsummer Day go in full procession together with the Lord Mayor, senior City officials, and their fellow liverymen, from the Mansion House to the Guildhall. Here the sheriffs are presented with their chains of office.

on or near
29th September    **Election of the Lord Mayor**
Guildhall to Mansion House

The election of the Lord Mayor of London has taken place on Michaelmas Day since 1546. After a service in St Lawrence Jewry, the current Lord Mayor goes in procession to the Guildhall, where he and his aldermen make the final selection from the candidates nominated by the livery companies. After the ceremony the Lord Mayor and his successor ride in the state coach to the Mansion House to the accompaniment of the city bells.

on or near 15th
September 11am-noon    **Battle of Britain Week**
Greater London and Westminster Abbey

Flypast of aircraft over London and Thanksgiving service in Westminster Abbey on Sunday.

**Last Night of the Proms**
Royal Albert Hall

(Autumn Equinox)    **Druids Observance Ceremony**
Primrose Hill, Regent's Park

**Royal National Rose Society Show**
Royal Horticultural Society Hall, Vincent Square

# October

**21st October**

**Trafalgar Service and Parade**
Trafalgar Square
A naval parade in memory of the Battle of
Trafalgar, 1805, including a march from the Horse
Guards Parade to Trafalgar Square followed by a
service and the laying of wreaths at the foot of
Nelson's Column.

**late October/
early November**

**State Opening of Parliament**
Buckingham Palace to House of Lords,
Westminster
In one of London's most colourful pageants, the
Queen rides in the Irish State Coach from
Buckingham Palace to the Palace of Westminster
via the Mall and Whitehall. At Westminster, the
Queen and other members of the royal family are
greeted by a gun salute fired by the King's Troop
of the Royal Horse Artillery. The royal party then
enters the Houses of Parliament through the great
arch under the Victoria Tower, and the Queen
enters the Robing Room. Later Her Majesty
emerges wearing the royal robes and the crown,
and is conducted, amidst a procession of great
officers of state, heralds, and the sound of
trumpets, to the House of Lords where she
ascends to the throne. The Lords, in their
ceremonial robes, are already present and the
Speaker and members of the House of Commons
are now summoned by the official called Black
Rod. After their arrival the Queen makes her
speech outlining the government's proposed
legislation for the new parliamentary session.
A few hours before the Queen arrives, Yeomen of
the Guard search the vaults of the Houses of
Parliament. This exercise has been carried out
each year since the unsuccessful Gunpowder Plot
of 1605. The actual ceremony of the State Opening
of Parliament is not open to the public, but many
thousands of people line the processional route.

**Horse of the Year Show**
Wembley

**1st Sun, 3pm**

**Costermonger's Harvest Festival**
St Martin-in-the-Fields
This service, originating in the 19th century, is
attended by the Pearly Kings and Queens in their
traditional button-covered costumes.

**late October**

**Quit-Rents Ceremony**
Royal Courts of Justice, Strand
This public ceremony, one of the oldest still
carried out in London, is held at the Royal Courts
of Justice, and involves the City Solicitor making
token payments for two properties. The Queen's
Remembrancer receives the rents, which take the
form of two faggots of wood, a billhook, and a
hatchet of land in Shropshire, and six horseshoes
and sixty-one nails, for a forge which once stood
in the Strand. The ceremony is so old that its
origins are obscure.

# November

**first Sunday in November**

**RAC Veteran Car Run**
Hyde Park Corner to Brighton

Cars built between 1895 and 1904 take part in this run which starts from Hyde Park Corner and finishes at Madeira Drive, Brighton. The event dates originally from 1896 when the law compelling motorists to have a man with a red flag walking in front of them was abolished and jubilant drivers destroyed their flags and roared off to Brighton. The first organised Run was held in 1933. All the cars taking part in the event are beautifully cared-for, and many of the drivers and passengers dress in period costume.

**2nd Saturday in November**

**Lord Mayor's Show**
Guildhall to Royal Courts of Justice, Strand

This is the day when the new Lord Mayor publicly takes office. He rides to the Royal Courts of Justice in a ceremonial 18th-century coach, drawn by six horses, attended by a bodyguard of Pikemen and Musketeers, and preceded by a colourful procession of floats depicting some theme related to London's history. This ceremony is at least 600 years old and is the City's most spectacular showpiece. On the following Monday the Lord Mayor gives a lavish banquet at the Guildhall, attended by the Prime Minister and the Archbishop of Canterbury.

**8th November**

**Installation of the Lord Mayor**
Mansion House to Guildhall

The current Lord Mayor and the Lord Mayor-Elect attend a luncheon at the Mansion House together with liverymen of each of their companies. They then go in procession to the Guildhall where they officially change places and transfer the insignia of office. The two Lord Mayors then return to the Mansion House to the accompaniment of peals of bells from the City churches.

**on the Sunday nearest to 11th November**

**Remembrance Day Service**
Cenotaph, Whitehall

A service at the Cenotaph, in Whitehall, to remember the dead of both World Wars, is attended by the Queen, members of the royal family, representatives of the armed services, ex-servicemen's associations and leading politicians. A gun salute is followed by two minutes' silence after which wreaths are laid at the Cenotaph.

**on or near 22nd November**

**Festival of St Cecilia**
St Sepulchre's, Holborn

A service is held at St Sepulchre's, Holborn, in honour of St Cecilia, the patron saint of music. Well-known organists and choirs from Westminster Abbey, St Paul's and Canterbury Cathedral combine to provide a feast of church music in a 16th-century ceremony which was revived in 1946 after having died out in the 19th century.

# December

around 16th onwards

### Christmas Tree and Carol Singing
Trafalgar Square

Every year a giant Christmas tree is donated to London by the people of Oslo, Norway. It is set up in Trafalgar Square and becomes the focal point for evening carol services.

### Christmas Decorations
Regent St/Oxford St

Sunday before
Christmas

### Tower of London Parade
Tower of London

The Yeomen Warders in full uniform are inspected before and after morning service.

### New Year's Eve Celebrations
Trafalgar Square

On New Year's Eve the square is the scene of tumultuous celebrations as hundreds see the new year in, many of them demonstrating their joy by dousing each other in the fountains.

## Occasional Ceremonies

### Nosegays for Judges
Central Criminal Court

Whenever a High Court judge hears cases at The Central Criminal Court (The Old Bailey) between May and September, nosegays are presented to all presiding judges. This ceremony dates from the days when evil smells from Newgate Jail pervaded the court during the summer months and judges were given bunches of strong smelling herbs to protect their sensitive noses.

### Beating the Bounds
Tower of London

Once every three years a service is held on Ascension Day (May) at the Tower of London in the Chapel Royal of St Peter Vincula attended by all the dignitaries of the Tower. After the service the Chaplain leads a procession to each boundary stone where he shouts 'Cursed is he who moveth his neighbour's landmark' and the Chief Warder orders the choirboys to beat the stone with their willow wands. This curious custom dates from the Middle Ages and similar ceremonies are still held in a number of parishes throughout the country. Its purpose (it is thought) was to teach young boys their local parish boundaries.

CHRISTMAS CAROLS IN TRAFALGAR SQUARE

**AA**

# *Pocket Guide to* LONDON

# DRIVING AND PARKING IN LONDON

car hire, parking regulations, parking,
exhibition centres, Wembley, car tour, etc

# Driving a car in London

Parking and traffic congestion in central London is a problem and driving can be difficult. Many one-way street systems have been introduced which do create difficulties for the visitor. However, for those unfamiliar with the complexities of London traffic, the two agencies listed below will provide a driver to meet the client at a specific point and drive or guide him in his own car into or across central London or the suburbs. Charges, including expenses, must be paid to the driver at the end of the assignment.

**European Chauffeurs Ltd**
40-42 Oxford Street, W1, *tel* 01-580 7183/7193

**Universal Aunts Ltd**
250 Kings Road, SW3, *tel* 01-351 5761

For those who still wish to drive themselves and are unfamiliar with conditions in the capital, the best advice is to obtain a copy of the **Highway Code**. When driving in London avoid the rush-hour traffic, which is at its height around 08.00-09.30hrs and 16.00-18.30hrs. Areas to avoid are Buckingham Palace and The Mall between 11.00hrs and 12.00hrs when the changing of the Guard at the Palace causes traffic delays. Additionally, no cars are allowed to use Oxford Street between 07.00hrs and 19.00hrs from Monday to Saturday.

## Car hire

Most of the major car hire firms in London are represented at **Car Hire Centre International**, 93 Regent Street, W1, *tel* 01-734 7661.

## Street Parking

Parking zones

Street parking in central London is controlled by the Greater London Council's parking policy of meter zones known as the Inner London Parking Area. There are also parking zones in outer London, most of which include meters. The controlled zones are indicated by signs at their boundary points, giving the hours of operation. Special regulations may also apply in areas near to the wholesale markets and where Sunday street markets are held. Street parking other than at officially designated places is prohibited during the specified hours. In many zones, some parking places may be reserved exclusively for residents or other classes of users specified on nearby plates.

Parking meters

Parking meters take 5p, 10p, 20p and 50p coins but there are differences in charges and variations in the length of time for which parking is allowed. The car must be parked within the limits of the parking bay, indicated by the white lines on the road. It must also face in the same direction as the traffic flow, unless angle parking is indicated by road markings. Payment must be made on arrival, although unexpired meter time paid for by a a previous occupant of the space may be used. After the initial payment has been made, additional parking time may not be bought by making any further payments.

Infringement of these rules results in penalties in the form of expensive '**parking tickets**', which you will find attached to the windscreen of the car.

**Waiting restrictions**

The usual system of yellow lines should indicate these, but their omission does not necessarily mean there is no effective restriction. In addition, any vehicle waiting on a road may be judged to be causing 'unnecessary obstruction', without proof that other vehicles or persons may have actually been obstructed, and a prosecution could ensue. Enforcement is mostly by the use of fixed penalty notices (parking tickets). There are also teams engaged in the removal of offending vehicles to a police pound, and in an experimental area (West End/S. Kensington), immobilization by fixing a wheel clamp has been introduced.

**Parking at night**

Cars, motor cycles and goods vehicles under 30 cwt unladen weight can park without lights provided that:

a    The road is subject to a speed limit of 30 mph or less.

b    No part of the vehicle is within 15 yards of a road junction.

c    The vehicle is parked close to the kerb and parallel to it, and except in one-way streets, with its nearside to the kerb, or in a parking place. Vehicles 30cwt or more unladen weight, or carrying eight or more passengers, must show two white lights to the front and two red lights with an illuminated number plate to the rear, in any night parking situation.

Similarly, if the road is not subject to a 30mph speed limit, any vehicle left standing on the highway at night must conform to the lighting regulations as above.

**The Royal Parks**

There is some free parking on the roads in Hyde Park and Regent's Park. The times may be unusual, but are shown by the normal yellow lines and plates. Read the plates very carefully.

### Disabled Persons — Orange Badge Scheme

Certain disabled drivers or disabled passengers, including registered blind people, may apply for parking concessions under the Orange Badge Scheme. Application must be made direct to the appropriate County or District Council except in the GLC area where the London Boroughs are the issuing authority.

The badges are valid throughout the country except for the following areas of Central London: the Cities of London and Westminster, the Borough of Kensington and Chelsea and any part of the Borough of Camden, south of and including Euston Road. In these areas, the Boroughs concerned operate their own concessionary schemes.

# Car Parking in Central London

The following is a list of car parks within the Inner London area. They are operated mainly by National Car Parks Ltd, except where indicated. National Car Parks are easily spotted by their large yellow NCP signs. The classification of areas is by means of the postal district lettering/numbering system *e.g.* E1, EC1 etc, with a brief description of the district covered. The majority of the car parks listed are shown on the map and can be located by means of the grid reference given alongside.

Most of these car parks are open during normal business hours, or for a slightly longer period at each end of the working day.

It is not possible to quote charges, but the rates in the West End or City of London usually start at around £1.80 for the first two hours, rising to approximately £10 for a 9 hour period, and £13 for a 24-hour period. Cheaper night rates are available between 18.00 and 09.00. In outer areas the charges are lower, depending on the distance from the central area.

**When parking your car, always remember to secure it against theft and not leave any valuable property inside.**

Information about traffic conditions, parking, and motoring in general can always be obtained from the many AA Centres in London — or phone their central number (01) 954 7373.

## Main Operators' Addresses

Apcoa Parking — UK, 111 Windmill Rd, Sunbury-on-Thames, Middx TW16 7EF *tel* Sunbury 89812

*(ECP)* Euro Car Parks Ltd, Lower Ground, National Theatre, York Road, Southwark, London SE1 *tel* 01-928 3940

*MLCP* M L Car Parks Ltd, 44A Elmsdale Road, E17 *tel* 01-509 0127

National Car Parks Ltd, 21 Bryanston St, Marble Arch, London W1A 4NH *tel* 01-499 7050 (for London Airports: Heathrow *tel* 01-897 3626, Gatwick *tel* 01-688 4211 ext 2396)

Sterling Guards Ltd, Empress Place, SW6 1TT *tel* 01-381 4321/8 (Earls Court and Olympia only)

Details of small operators are given in the text.

## Abbreviations used in text/type of car park

| | |
|---|---|
| C,Ch & L | Cars, coaches & lorries |
| M/S | Multi-storey |
| S | Surface |
| U/C | Under cover |
| U/G | Underground |
| P | Petrol facilities |
| * | Open 24 hours |
| Mdnt | Open until Midnight |

| Page | Map Ref | | Type | Capacity |
|------|---------|---|------|----------|
| | | **E1  Stepney, Whitechapel** | | |
| 12 | N8 | Shoreditch High Street (one-way, north/south direction), near junction Commercial Street | S*, C & L | 300 |
| 12 | N7 | Rodwell House, Middlesex Street | U/G* | 180 |
| 12 | N7 | Spitalfields, Whites Row | M/S* | 450 |
| 12 | N7 | Steward Street | S Sun only | 100 |
| | Not on Map | Fieldgate St, (off Whitechapel Rd; south side) (entrance in Fieldgate St via Plumber's Row) (MLCP) | S | 120 |
| | | **EC1  Finsbury** | | |
| 12 | L7 | Aldersgate Street | M/S* | 850 |
| 11 | K8 | Bowling Green Lane | S | 150 |
| 12 | L8 | Charterhouse Square | S | 100 |
| 11 | K7 | Cowcross Street, Caxton House | U/G | 65 |
| 11 | K8 | Great Sutton Street | U/C | 40 |
| 11 | K8 | Gloucester Way, Rosebery Ave | S | 140 |
| 11 | K8 | Sans Walk/St James's Row | S | 62 |
| 11 | K8 | Saffron Hill, St Cross St | M/S | 400 |
| 11 | K8 | Skinner Street | U/G | 250 |
| 11 | K7 | Smithfield Central Market | U/G C, L | 450 |
| 11 | K7 | Smithfield Surface, Hosier Lane | S | 50 |
| 11 | K7 | Smithfield Street | S | 100 |
| 11 | K7 | Snowhill (off Farringdon Street) | U/C | 128 |
| 11 | K8 | Warner Street (off Farringdon Road) | S | 250 |
| | | **EC2  Moorgate, Liverpool St** | | |
| 12 | L7 | Barbican Centre | U/G | 500 |
| 12 | M8 | Clere Street | S | 60 |
| 12 | M8 | Curtain Rd (entrance in Worship St) | S Mon-Fri 07.30-18.30 Sun 08.00-14.00 | 100 |
| 12 | M7 | Finsbury Square | U/G, P (07.00-18.00) | 285 |
| 12 | L7 | London Wall | U/G | 250 |
| 12 | N8 | Rivington Street | S | 60 |
| | | **EC3  Aldgate, Tower Hill** | | |
| 12 | M6 | Tower Hill, Lower Thames Street | U/G C & Ch | 210 |
| | | **EC4  St Paul's, Cannon Street, Ludgate Circus** | | |
| 12 | L6 | Baynard House, Queen Victoria Street | U/G* | 300 |

| Page | Map Ref | | Type | Capacity |
|---|---|---|---|---|
| 12 | L6 | Distaff Lane, (off Cannon Street) | U/C | 100 |
| 12 | L7 | Paternoster Row, Ave Maria Lane | U/G* | 265 |
| 11 | K7 | Seacoal Lane, Hillgate House | U/G* | 180 |
| 11 | K7 | Shoe Lane, International Press Centre | U/G | 80 |
| 12 | M6 | Swan Lane | M/S | 450 |
| 12 | L6 | Upper Thames Street, Vintry | M/S | 485 |
| 12 | L6 | Walbrook, Bucklersbury House *Mamos Motors Ltd 01-248 5874* | U/G | 40 |
| | | **N1   Islington** | | |
| 12 | L9 | Britannia Walk, (off City Road) | S | 100 |
| 12 | L9 | Pitfield St, (off Old Street) | S | 100 |
| | | **NW1   Camden Town, Euston, Marylebone** | | |
| | Not on Map | Arlington Road | S | 60 |
| 10 | H8 | Euston Station | U/G* | 235 |
| 9 | F7 | Marylebone Road, Dorset House | U/G* | 180 |
| 8 | E8 | Park Road, Regent's Park | U/G | 97 |
| 10 | I9 | St Pancras Station | S | 50 |
| | | **NW6   Kilburn** | | |
| | Not on Map | Kilburn Square, off Kilburn High Road | U/G | 120 |
| | | **NW8   St John's Wood** | | |
| 8 | D9 | Acacia Garage, Kingsmill Terrace (Royal British Legion Attendants Co Ltd 01-722 1404) | M/S* | 250 |
| 8 | E7 | Church Street, Penfold Street (*APCOA*) | U/G | 150 |
| | | **SE1   Elephant and Castle** | | |
| 6 | L4 | Elephant and Castle | U/G | 150 |
| 6 | L4 | Skipton Street | S | 110 |
| | | **SE1   Waterloo — Royal Festival Hall — National Theatre Complex** | | |
| 5 | J5 | Doon Street (*ECP*) (entrance in Upper Ground) | S, C & Ch 08.00-Mdnt | 50 |
| 5 | J5 | Royal Festival Hall, (*ECP*) Belvedere Road | S 08.00-Mdnt | 140 |
| 5 | J5 | Jubilee Gardens (overflow) (*ECP*) | S 08.00-Mdnt | 100 |
| 11 | J6 | National Theatre, (*ECP*) South Bank | U/G 08.00-02.00 | 410 |
| 5 | J5 | Waterloo Station Approach (British Rail SR) | S* | 117 |

| Page | Map Ref | | Type | Capacity |
|------|---------|--|------|----------|
| | | **SE1  Southwark, Bermondsey** | | |
| 11 | K6 | Barge House Street, off Upper Ground | S | 52 |
| 6 | M5 | Snowsfields | M/S* | 500 |
| | | **SW1  Westminster, Victoria** | | |
| 4 | I4 | Abingdon Street (entrance: Gt College Street) | U/G* | 250 |
| 4 | H5 | Arlington Street, Arlington House | U/G* | 108 |
| 4 | H5 | Bury Street | S | 45 |
| 3 | F4 | Cadogan Place, off Sloane Street | U/G* | 349 |
| 4 | H2 | Dolphin Square Garage, Grosvenor Road | U/G* P. Servicing | 250 |
| 3 | F4 | Knightsbridge, Park Tower Hotel | U/G* | 90 |
| 2 | E4 | Knightsbridge Green, Raphael Street | U/G | 65 |
| 3 | F4 | Pavilion Road | M/S* | 311 |
| 4 | H4 | Rochester Row | M/S* | 299 |
| 3 | G3 | Semley Place, Ebury Street | M/S* | 422 |
| 4 | I5 | Trafalgar Square, Spring Gardens (*MLCP*) | U/G* | 340 |
| 3 | F4 | Wilton Place, Berkeley Hotel | U/G 06.30-23.00 | 80 |
| | | **SW3  Chelsea** | | |
| 2 | E3 | Cale St, St Lukes | S, C | 150 |
| 2 | E3 | King's Road (near Smith Street) | S & U/C | 120 |
| | | **SW5  Earls Court** | | |
| 1 | C3 | Cromwell Road, London International Hotel | S, U/C | 40 |
| 1 | B2 | Earls Court Exhibition (Operator: Sterling Guards) | S & U/C | 1,300 |
| | | **SW6  Fulham** | | |
| 1 | B2 | 47/67 Lillie Road, West Centre Hotel | U/G* | 140 |
| | | **SW7  South Kensington** | | |
| 2 | E4 | 70/71 Ennismore Gardens (Kingston House Garage *tel* 01-589 6726) | U/G Mon-Fri (07.30-23.00 Sat & Sun 08.00-23.00) | 60 |
| 1 | D3 | Cromwell Road, The Forum Hotel | U/G* | 95 |
| | | **SW8**  *South Lambeth* | | |
| 4 | I2 | Vauxhall Bridge Foot, Vauxhall Station | S C, Ch & L* | 100 |
| | Not on Map | Wandsworth (Arndale Centre), Buckhold Road | M/S | 1,060 |

| Page | Map Ref | | Type | Capacity |
|------|---------|---|------|----------|
| | | **SW17   Tooting** | | |
| | Not on Map | Upper Tooting Road, Castle Hotel | S | 75 |
| | | **W1   West End** | | |
| 9 | G6 | Adams Row, Britannia Hotel | U/G* | 175 |
| 3 | G5 | Audley Square, South Audley Street | M/S* | 310 |
| 10 | H6 | Brewer Street, Piccadilly Circus | M/S* | 450 |
| 9 | G8 | Carburton Street, Regent Crest Hotel | U/G* | 65 |
| 3 | G5 | Carrington Street, Shepherd Market | M/S | 310 |
| 9 | G7 | Cavendish Square | U/G Mon-Sat 07.00-23.00 | 545 |
| 9 | G7 | Chandos Street, Queen Anne Mews (APCOA) | U/G* | 390 |
| 3 | G5 | Chesterfield House, Chesterfield Gdns | U/G | 50 |
| 9 | F7 | Chiltern Street, Paddington Street | M/S* | 395 |
| 10 | H7 | Cleveland Street | U/G | 84 |
| 9 | G7 | Clipstone Street (MLCP) | U/G* | 347 |
| 9 | F7 | Cramer Street | S | 200 |
| 8 | E7 | Crawford Street | S & U/C | 60 |
| 10 | H6 | Dean Street, off Shaftesbury Avenue | S | 70 |
| 10 | H6 | Denman Street | U/G* | 143 |
| 10 | H6 | Dufours Place, Broadwick Garage (APCOA) | U/C | 75 |
| 9 | F7 | Gloucester Place, Portman Square Garage | M/S* | 443 |
| 9 | F6 | Gt Cumberland Place, Bilton Towers | U/G* | 160 |
| 9 | G6 | Grosvenor Hill | M/S | 216 |
| 10 | H6 | Kingly Street (enter from Beak Street) | S | 35 |
| 9 | F6 | (Marble Arch) Bryanston Street, Cumberland Garage | M/S* | 310 |
| 9 | F6 | Marriot Hotel (off Duke Street) | U/G | 85 |
| 10 | H6 | Old Burlington Street Burlington Garage | M/S | 477 |
| 3 | G5 | Old Park Lane, Brick Street | U/G | 65 |
| 9 | F6 | Orchard Street (enter from Duke Street) (Selfridge Garage Ltd, 01-493 5181) | M/S* P | 700 |
| 9 | F6 | Park Lane | U/G* | 1,000 |
| 3 | G5 | Park Lane, Hilton Hotel | U/G* | 235 |
| 10 | H6 | Poland Street (APCOA) | M/S Mon-Sat 06.00-Mdnt Sun & Bank Hols closed | 150 |

| Page | Map Ref | | Type | Capacity |
|---|---|---|---|---|
| 9 | G7 | Portland Place, Weymouth Mews | U/G | 35 |
| 9 | F6 | Portman Square, Churchill Hotel | U/G | 51 |
| 10 | H6 | Wardour Street (*APCOA*) | M/S* | 160 |
| 9 | G7 | Welbeck Street | M/S | 392 |
| | | **W2  Paddington,  Bayswater** | | |
| 1 | C5 | Bayswater Road, Kensington Gardens | S C & Ch | 240 |
| 7 | C6 | Bishop's Bridge Road Colonnades, Porchester Terrace North | U/G* | 152 |
| 8 | E7 | Edgware Road, Burwood Place (Water Gardens; Flats) | U/G | 300 |
| 8 | E7 | Harrow Road, London Metropole Hotel | M/S* | 80 |
| 8 | E6 | Kendal Street | U/G* | 45 |
| 7 | C6 | Queensway (*MLCP*) | U/G* | 300 |
| 7 | C6 | Queensway, Arthur Court (north end of Queensway) | U/C* | 85 |
| | | **W6  Hammersmith** | | |
| | Not on Map | Hammersmith Broadway (Queen Caroline St) | S Mon-Sat 08.00-22.00 | 300 |
| | Not on Map | King's Mall, Glenthorne Road (*eastern end*) | M/S Mon-Sat 08.00 18.30 | 960 |
| | | **W8  Kensington** | | |
| 1 | B4 | Hornton Street, Kensington Town Hall (*APCOA*) | U/G* | 410 |
| 1 | C4 | Royal Garden Hotel, Kensington | U/G* | 160 |
| 1 | C4 | Young Street | M/S* | 250 |
| | | **W12  Shepherds Bush** | | |
| | Not on Map | Shepherds Bush Centre, Charecroft Way | Roof top part U/C | 300 |
| | | **W14  West Kensington** | | |
| 1 | A3 | Holland Road, Royal Kensington Hotel (*380 Kensington High Street*) | U/G | 70 |
| 1 | A3 | Maclise Road (Olympia) (*Sterling Guards*) | M/S* | 750 |
| 1 | A4 | Olympia Way | S | 300 |
| 1 | B3 | Warwick Road, (*west side*) | S* C Ch & L | 350 |
| 1 | B3 | Warwick Road, Fenelon Place | S 08.00-18.00 | 170 |
| 1 | A3 | Warwick Road, Radnor Terrace (TA Centre) | S | 200 |

Note: *All Warwick Road car parks are on the west side and north of junction West Cromwell Road, and are listed in sequence of approach*

| Page | Map Ref | | Type | Capacity |
|------|---------|--|------|----------|
| | | **WC1  Bloomsbury, Holborn** | | |
| 10 | I7 | Bloomsbury Square | U/G* | 450 |
| 10 | I8 | Brunswick Square | U/G* | 443 |
| 10 | I7 | Coptic Street | S P Mon-Fri 08.00-1830 | 40 |
| 10 | I7 | Museum Street | M/S* | 250 |
| 10 | H7 | Ridgmount Place | S | 35 |
| 10 | I8 | Russell Court, Woburn Place | U/G | 110 |
| 10 | I8 | Russell Square, Imperial Hotel | U/G | 140 |
| 10 | I7 | Tottenham Court Road, Adeline Place YMCA | M/S* | 450 |
| 10 | I8 | Woburn Place, Royal National Hotel | U/G 07.00-20.00 | 150 |
| | | **WC2  Leicester Square, Strand** | | |
| 10 | I6 | Bedfordbury | U/G | 62 |
| 10 | I7 | Drury Lane, Parker Street | U/G 06.00-24.00 | 450 |
| 10 | I6 | Savoy Place, Victoria Embankment (*Adelphi Garage tel 01-836 4838*) | U/C* | 70 |
| 10 | I6 | Swiss Centre, Leicester Square | U/G | 90 |
| 10 | I6 | Trafalgar Square, St Martin's Street | S | 180 |
| 10 | I6 | Upper St Martin's Lane | M/S | 220 |
| 4 | I5 | Villiers Street (*Charing Cross Garage Ltd, tel 01-839 1189/ 1406*) | U/C Mon-Sat 07.30-Mdnt P | 110 |
| 10 | I6 | Whitcomb Street (*APCOA*) | M/S* | 300 |

KENSINGTON ROAD

# Car Parking
# Main approach routes
# into London

This section provides information about parking at railway or underground stations on the outskirts of London, to assist visitors who may prefer to park their car and continue their journey by railway or underground train to the centre. In some cases where no reasonable facilities exist at the station, other types of car park have been included, but these are usually adjacent.

It is not a comprehensive list of suburban off-street parking: neither does it include details of parking-meter zones in suburban areas.

Stations are grouped into sectors, commencing from North-West and continuing in clockwise order. The order of priority is then the route number of the main approach road into London, followed by the name of the station and relevant information.

**Opening times** The hours of opening of BR station car parks vary according to the opening and closing hours of the station, which are subject to the current timetable. London Regional Transport (LRT) car parks are open from the time of the first train to the time of the last train. Where parking facilities operated by London Borough Councils (LB) or companies are shown, details are given within the text alongside the entry for the station. Car parks open 24-hrs are indicated by an asterisk*.

**Charges** Charges are displayed at all British Rail and London Regional Transport car parks.

Some car parks operated by London Boroughs and other operators are free of charge but this policy could be varied at short notice. There is no standard rate of charges. This depends on the locality and availability of the car park. At some car parks charges are raised above the standard rate during the morning peak hours or a car park is closed completely to discourage commuter parking. On Saturdays some car parks double the weekday charges.

| App-roach Route | Station | Operator Location | Opening Times | Type Capa-city |
|---|---|---|---|---|
| **NORTH WEST** | | | | |
| M40/A40 | Hillingdon | LRT | | Open 285 (free) |
| A40 | South Ruislip | (1) LRT and BR-LMR | | Open 42 |
| | | (2) LB Hillingdon Long Drive (*adjacent to station*) | * | Open 86 (free) |

| App-roach Route | Station | Operator Location | Opening Times | Type Capacity |
|---|---|---|---|---|
| M40/A40 | Uxbridge | LB Hillingdon Uxbridge Station | * | M/S Open 1400 |

**NORTH**

| App-roach Route | Station | Operator Location | Opening Times | Type Capacity |
|---|---|---|---|---|
| M1/A1 /A41 | Edgware | (1) LRT | Open 185 + 100 spaces after redevelopment due to start in 1986 | |
| | | (2) NCP | Mon-Sat 08.00-18.30 | Open 65 |
| M1/A1 /A41 | Stanmore | LRT | | Open 457 |
| M1/A1 /A41 | Swiss Cottage | Regency Service Station Finchley Rd, NW3 (50 yds south of station) tel: 01-586 3516/7 Night (answering service) tel: 01-722 5911 | *P | U/G 120 |
| A1/A6 | High Barnet | LRT | | Open 227 |
| A1/A6 | Cockfosters | LRT | | Open 440 |
| A1/A6 | Finchley Central | LRT | | Open 365 |
| A1/A6 | Southgate N14 | LB Enfield Winchmore Hill Road | *Mon-Sat Suns free | M/S 623 |
| A10 /A406 | Arnos Grove N11 | LRT | | Open 291 |

**EAST AND NORTH EAST**

| App-roach Route | Station | Operator Location | Opening Times | Type Capacity |
|---|---|---|---|---|
| M11/A11 /A12 | Blackhorse Road (entrance in Forest Rd) | LRT | | Open 380 |
| M11/A11 /A12 | Leytonstone E11 | LRT Grove Green Rd | | Open 195 |
| M11/A11 /A12 | Stratford E15 | LB Newham, Stratford Bus Station, Great Eastern Rd | Mon-Sat 07.00- 22.00 | M/S 460 |
| A12 | Gants Hill | LB Redbridge Bramley Crescent (off Cranbrook Rd) | * | M/S 321 |
| A12 | Ilford | LB Redbridge Balfour Rd, (off Ley Street) | * | M/S 483 |
| A12 | Newbury Park | LRT | | Open 541 |
| A127 | Upminster | BR-ER and LRT | * (Sat Free) | Open 501 |
| A13 | Barking | LB Barking Salisbury Avenue (Opposite Station) | * | Open 480 |
| A13 | Dagenham Heathway | LB Barking Church Elm Lane (near Station) | | M/S 220 |

**SOUTH EAST**

| App-roach Route | Station | Operator Location | Opening Times | Type Capacity |
|---|---|---|---|---|
| A2 | Bexley | BR-SR | | Open 334 |
| A2/A20 | Blackheath | LB Lewisham | *(No charge) | Open 66 |
| A2/A20 | New Cross | LB Lewisham: Mornington Road | *(Charging time 08.30-18.30) | Open 80 |
| A20 | Sidcup | BR-SR | | Open 160 |

| Approach Route | Station | Operator Location | Opening Times | Type Capacity |
|---|---|---|---|---|
| A20/A21 | Lewisham | LB Lewisham:<br>(1) Molesworth Street | *(Attendant - charging time 08.00-18.30 Mon, Tue, Sat (20.00 Thu & Fri) | M/S 1000<br><br>Open 150 |
| | | (2) Clarendon Rise | *(Charging time 08.30-18.30) | |
| | | (3) Molesworth Street | Pay & Display 08.30-18.30 | Open 180 |
| A21 /A205 | Catford or Catford Bridge SE6 | LB Lewisham: | | |
| | | (1) Adenmore Road | Mon-Sat 08.00-18.30 | Open 150 (free) |
| | | (2) Holbeach Road | * | M/S 500 |
| | | (3) Canadian Ave | *(Attendant — charging time 08.30-18.30) | Open 350 |
| A21 | Bromley | LB Bromley junction London Rd/ Beckenham Lane | *(Attendant — charging time 07.30-21.30 Reducing 17.30) | M/S 707 |
| A21 | Bromley South | LB Bromley junction Westmoreland Road/Masons Hill (opposite Station) | *(Attendant — charging time 07.30-21.30 Reducing 17.30) | M/S 600 |
| A21 | Orpington | LB Bromley Station Road | *(Attendant — charging time 07.15-17.45) | M/S 562 |

**SOUTH**

| Approach Route | Station | Operator Location | Opening Times | Type Capacity |
|---|---|---|---|---|
| A22/A23 | Brixton | LB Lambeth Popes Road SW9 | *Mon-Sat 07.00-22.30 | M/S 488 |
| A22/A23 | South Croydon | BR-SR | *(charging time Mon-Sat 07.45-17.45) | Open 75 (to be extended) |
| A22/A23 | West Croydon | LB Croydon West Croydon (next to station in London Road) | (charging time 07.45-17.45 Mon-Sat) | Open 70 |
| A22/A23 | East Croydon | LB Croydon (1) Dingwall Road | *(After 18.00 charge reduced) | M/S 600 |
| | | (2) Fairfield (Barclay Rd) | *(After 18.00 charge reduced) | M/S 1300 |
| A22/A23 | Purley | (1) BR-SR | * | Open 120 |
| | | (2) LB Croydon: Dale Rd | *(charging time 07.30-09.30 only) | Open 140 |
| A23 | Smitham | LB Croydon Lion Green Rd, Coulsdon | *(charging time 07.45-17.45 Mon-Sat) | Open 180 |

**SOUTH WEST**

| Approach Route | Station | Operator Location | Opening Times | Type Capacity |
|---|---|---|---|---|
| M3/A30 | Feltham | LB Hounslow 2 parks in Bedfont Lane by the level crossing | * | Open 250<br>Open 90 |

| App-roach Route | Station | Operator Location | Opening Times | Type Capacity |
|---|---|---|---|---|
| M3/A308 /A309 | Hampton Court | BR-SR | | Open 250 |
| M3/A316 | Richmond | NCP Richmond Station | Mon-Sat 07.00-Mdnt | M/S 426 |
| A3 | Surbiton | BR-SR | * | Open 540 |
| A3/A24 | Wimbledon | LB Merton Queen's Rd SW19 (_alongside Station_) | _Charging time:_ _06.30-18.30_ | Open 329 |
| A3/A24 | Worcester Park | BR | | Open 120 |
| A24 | Morden | LB Merton | | Open 320 |
| A24 | Morden | LB Merton Kenley Road | Mon-Sat 07.30-20.00 | Open 120 |
| A24 | Morden | LB Merton York Close | Mon-Sat 07.30-21.30 | Open 269 |
| A217 /A297 | Morden | LB Merton Morden Hall Road | Mon-Fri 07.30-21.30 Sat 07.30-19.00 | Open 156 |
| A238 | Raynes Park | LB Merton Coombe Lane | Mon-Sat 08.00-18.30 | Open 120 |
| **WEST** | | | | |
| M4/A4 /A30 | Osterley | LRT | | Open 126 |
| M3/M4 /A30/A4 | Hammer-smith | NCP Queen Caroline Street W6 (_near flyover_) | Mon-Sat 08.00-22.00 | Open 300 |
| M4/A4 /A30 | Hatton Cross | LRT | * | Open 101 |
| M4/A4 /A30 | Hounslow West | LRT | | Open 332 |

# Exhibition Centres

### Earls Court and Olympia

These are the two traditional major exhibition
centres in London, hosting a wide variety of events
throughout the year.

Parking facilities at the exhibitions is limited and
street parking is difficult. It may be worth
considering using public transport.

Parking at Earls Court and Olympia is controlled
by: Sterling Guards Ltd, Empress Place, London
SW6 1TT (_tel:_ 01-602 9788).

Contact the company direct for current details
and advance parking reservations.

**Parking at Earls Court**   Parking is available during shows only, and prices
may vary for different exhibitions. Parking for
1000 cars is available at the rear of Earls Court.
Access is via the front entrance in Warwick Road.
Additional parking for 450 cars is available at
nearby Seagrave Road.

**Parking at Olympia**   There is parking for 400 cars in the multi-storey
car park at the rear of Olympia.

The NCP operate a number of car parks in the
vicinity. For further information see page 61.

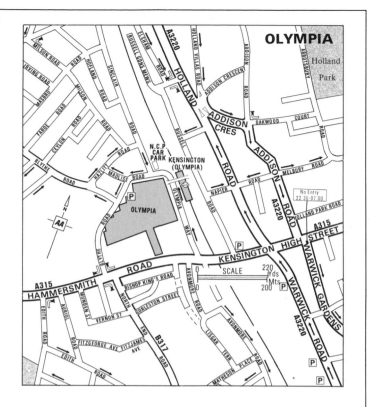

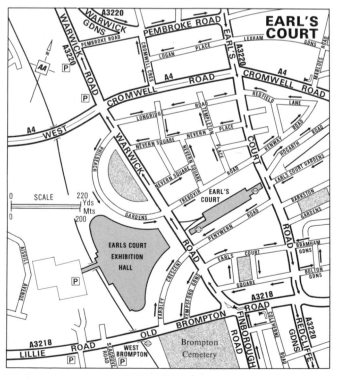

### Forthcoming events

A selection of exhibitions being held throughout each year at the two venues is shown below. Visitors are advised to check the exact date and venue with the organisers before planning a visit.

For enquiries regarding fixtures at either Earls Court or Olympia please contact: Commercial Director, Earls Court and Olympia Ltd, Warwick Road, London SW5 9TA *tel:* 01-385 1200.

| | | |
|---|---|---|
| London International Boat Show | Earls Court | January |
| Cruft's Dog Show | Earls Court | February |
| 'Daily Mail' Ideal Home Exhibition | Earls Court | March |
| Fine Art & Antique Fair | Olympia | June |
| Royal Tournament | Earls Court | July |
| British Music Fair | Olympia | August |
| Personal Computer World Show | Olympia | September |
| 'Daily Mail' International Ski Show | Earls Court | November |
| Caravan Camping Holiday Show | Earls Court | November |
| World Travel Market | Olympia | December |
| The Royal Smithfield Show | Earls Court | December |
| National Cat Club Show | Olympia | December |
| Olympia International Show Jumping | Olympia | December |

### Other exhibition centres in the London area are at:

**The Barbican Centre** (central map, page 12, L7). Barbican, EC2Y 8DS *tel:* 01-588 8211.
**Kensington Exhibition Centre** (central map, page 1, C4). 99 Kensington High Street, W8 *tel:* 01-937 9898.
**Alexandra Palace** (district map, page 169, D5). Wood Green, N22 4AY *tel:* 01-883 6477 (due to re-open Jan 1988).

# Wembley Complex

**District map, page 168, B4.** The Wembley complex is situated 6 miles north-west of Central London and is close to the southern terminal of M1 Motorway. The A40/M40, M4 Motorway and the North Circular Road A406 are also within easy reach.

The main buildings in the 73-acre complex are:-
**Wembley Stadium** 100,000 capacity, famed for its Football and other major sporting activities.

**Wembley Arena** an indoor building with 8,000 seats, where ice-shows, rock concerts, horse shows and many varied sporting events are held.

**Conference Centre** for conferences and exhibitions the Thames Suite provides over 3,000 sq metres of display space and there are many small display and hospitality areas.

WEMBLEY STADIUM

*Wembley Grand Hall* (The main conference area) with a seating capacity of over 2,500, also hosts regular sporting and entertainment events.

*Squash Centre* no membership required. 15 courts including the Championship Court, open seven days a week, 09.30-22.30, *tel:* 01-902 9230.

### Catering at Wembley

Grandstand Restaurant which overlooks the greyhound race course and pitch. Wembley Stadium *tel:* 01-902 8833
Wembley Conference Centre *tel:* 01-902 8833
Starlight Lounge Bar, Wembley Squash Centre *tel:* 01-902 8833

### General Information

Box Office arrangements (all enquiries *tel:* 01-902 1234) Postal enquiries: Wembley Stadium Ltd, Main Box Office, Wembley, Middx HA9 0DW.

### Facilities for the Disabled

Easy access all buildings. In the conference centre there are special ramps and lifts to all floors. Toilet facilities for the disabled are available in the arena, conference centre and stadium. Wheelchair users are advised to telephone in advance to make arrangements for their visits *tel:* 01-902 1234.

### Guided Tour — see page 109

**Sunday Market,** see page 35

### Parking at Wembley

The space available will accommodate up to 5,000 cars or up to 1,000 coaches. Parking charges can vary according to the size and class of events.

### Parking outside the Wembley Area

Limited parking facilities are available at a few underground railway stations, if it is decided to proceed to Wembley by means of rail transport for the final stage of the journey. Parking cannot be booked in advance, neither can accommodation be guaranteed. On Monday to Friday the car parks are used extensively by commuters and on Saturday by shoppers. The stations listed on page 72 have been selected because they have reasonably large car parks. *London Regional Transport car parks are open from the time of the first train to the time of the last train.*

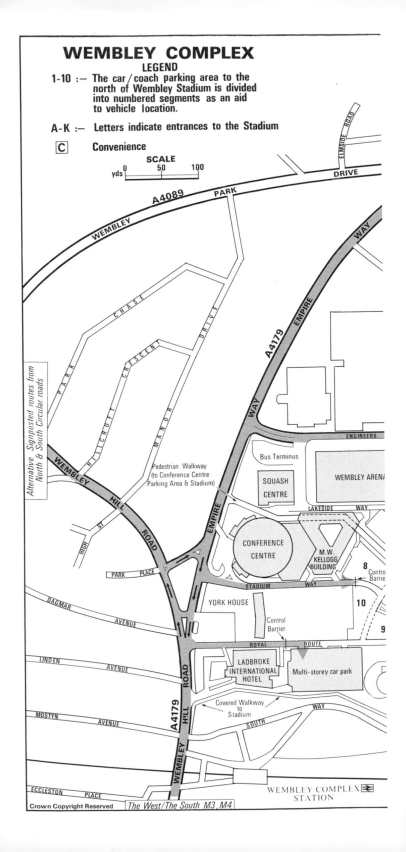

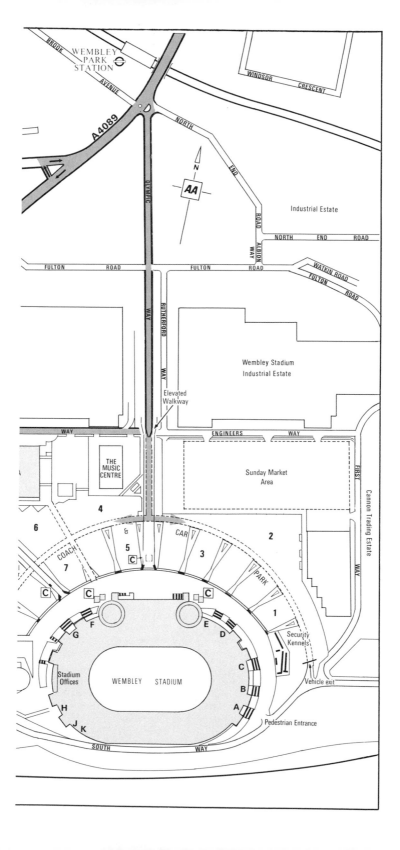

### A40/M40 and the West
Hillingdon Underground Station — Long Lane,
B466 150 yds north of Hillingdon Circus (Western
Avenue A40) open car park, capacity 285, free.
Metropolitan Line to Wembley Park Station.

### M1, A1, A41 and the North
Stanmore Underground Station — London Road,
A410
Open car park, capacity 457, charges as displayed.
Jubilee Line to Wembley Park Station.

### Accommodation
**A selection of hotels and guesthouses (GH) at, or
within a short radius of the Stadium is given
below:**
The widest choice of accommodation is in Central
London, from where there are ample transport
facilities operating at frequent intervals to
Wembley. For further details see page 10.

### *Hotels and guesthouses in the locality*
Within 3 miles:
**Harrow**

| | |
|---|---|
| ★★ | Cumberland Hotel, 1 St John's Road, *tel:* 01-863 4111 |
| ★★ | Harrow Hotel, Roxborough Bridge, 12-22 Pinner Road *tel:* 01-427 3435 |
| ★★ | Monksdene Hotel, 2-12 Northwick Park Road, *tel:* 01-427 2899 |
| GH | Hindes Hotel, 8 Hindes Road, *tel:* 01-427 7468 |
| GH | Kempsford House, 21/23 St John's Road *tel:* 01-427 4983 |

**Harrow Weald**

| | |
|---|---|
| ★★★ | Grims' Dyke Hotel, Old Redding, *tel:* 01-954 4227 |

Within 4 miles
**Ealing W5**

| | |
|---|---|
| ★★★ | Carnarvon Hotel, Ealing Common *tel:* 01-992 5399 |

### Public Transport:
#### *By Rail*
**Wembley Park Station** (Metropolitan and Jubilee
Lines)
**Wembley Complex Station** (*closed on Sundays*)
(British Rail from Marylebone)
**Wembley Central Station** (within ¾ mile). British
Rail from Euston/Broad Street.

#### *By Bus*
London Transport 83, 92 and 182 routes all pass
the complex. Other buses that pass nearby are
routes 18, 79, 226, 245 and Mon-Sat only — 79A,
297, also night service N18.

#### *By Taxi*
Taxi ranks are situated outside the Conference
Centre and Wembley Park Station.

# A tour of the City and West End of London

This circular tour is specially designed for visitors to London who wish to drive through the city and West End in their own vehicles. It may be commenced at any point. It is essential to use the direction of travel indicated as this takes advantage of the one-way systems. The best days to use it are on Saturdays (after 14.00hrs) and Sundays, as traffic conditions and parking during a weekday may be found difficult for those who are unaccustomed to driving in London.

The route follows the principal thoroughfares in the simplest and most straightforward way and includes some of the most notable buildings and other places of interest; it must be emphasised that no more than a passing glance is usually possible — even less for the driver!

Drivers should look well ahead in the route directions to ensure that they are in the correct lane for negotiating turns at traffic junctions. Under average traffic conditions the tour should take about an hour and a half with continuous driving.

**Route directions for a 16.5 mile circular tour of London. Distances between points of interest are given as decimal parts of a mile.**

| | |
|---|---|
| **Hyde Park Corner** | (For Sunday travel see footnote on page 76) |
| 0.5 | Follow Constitution Hill (signposted Green Park) |
| **Buckingham Palace** | At Queen Victoria Memorial bear left into The |
| 0.7 | Mall. At end pass through Admiralty Arch to |
| **Trafalgar Square** | Turn left (one-way) then take right hand lane & keep forward along Cockspur St. Turn right into Pall Mall East (signposted Bank) and keep forward along north side of square. Turn right down east |
| 0.8 | side and forward into Whitehall passing Horse Guards and Downing St (on right) |
| **Parliament Square** | Forward into Millbank (SP Vauxhall) passing Houses of Parliament (on left) & Westminster Abbey (on right). In 0.4m at roundabout take 1st |
| 0.5 | exit (signposted Elephant & Castle) & cross |
| **Lambeth Bridge** | On far side at roundabout take 2nd exit into Lambeth Rd (signed London Bridge) passing |
| 0.6 | Lambeth Palace (on left) |
| **Imperial War Museum** | At traffic signals turn left into St George's Rd (one-way) then turn right & take centre lane |
| 0.3 | |
| **St George's Circus** | At roundabout take 2nd exit into Borough Rd (signed The City) At far end turn left into Borough |
| 0.5 | High St |
| **The Borough** | (St George's Ch on right)  Over X-rds & in 0.3m at traffic signals turn right (Southwark Cathedral 100yds ahead under railway bridge) into St Thomas St (signed Tower Bridge) then turn left (one-way) into Joiner St & at traffic signals turn right into Tooley St passing London Dungeon (on right) and HMS Belfast (on left down Abbots Lane). |

| | |
|---|---|
| 1.2 **Tower Bridge** 0.4 | In 0.2m keep left then turn left & cross On far side keep left (one-way) then turn left into Tower Hill passing the Tower. |
| **Tower of London** 0.5 | Keep forward and at traffic signals turn right into Gt Tower St (SP Barbican) for Eastcheap |
| **Monument** 0.2 | (on left in Fish St Hill) Over X-rds (traffic signals) & immediately at next traffic signals turn sharp right (SP Bank & Holborn) into King William St |
| **Bank of England** | (on right) Keep left and immediately left again (signed Ludgate Circus) into Queen Victoria St passing Mansion House (on left) |

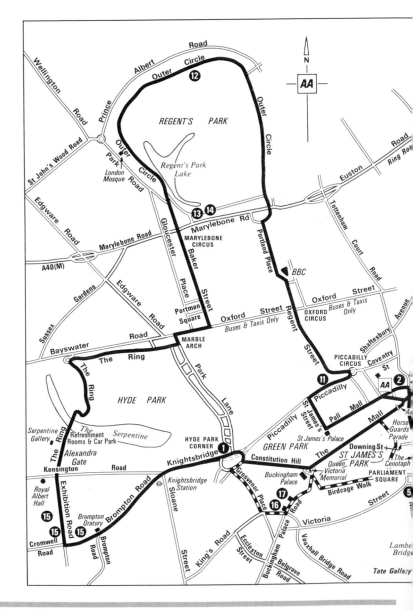

| | | | |
|---|---|---|---|
| **1.** | Wellington Museum | **11.** | Royal Academy of Arts |
| **2.** | National Gallery | **12.** | London Zoological Gardens |
| **3.** | Banqueting House | **13.** | Planetarium |
| **4.** | Houses of Parliament | **14.** | Madame Tussaud's |
| **5.** | Westminster Abbey | **15.** | South Kensington Museums |
| **6.** | Imperial War Museum | | (Geological, Natural History, |
| **7.** | London Dungeon | | Victoria & Albert and Science) |
| **8.** | HMS Belfast | **16.** | The Royal Mews |
| **9.** | Tower of London | **17.** | Queen's Gallery |
| **10.** | St Paul's Cathedral | | |

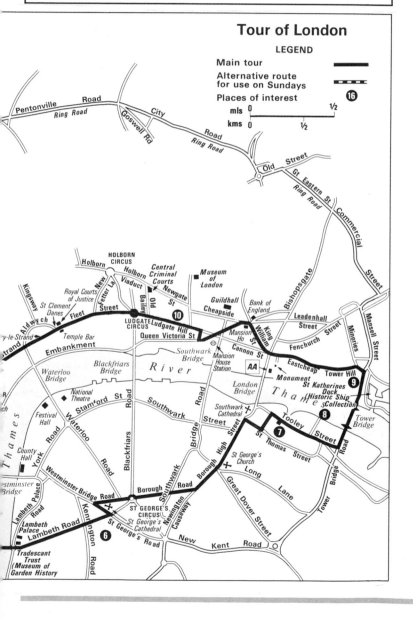

## Tour of London

**LEGEND**

Main tour
Alternative route for use on Sundays
Places of interest

| | |
|---|---|
| 0.2 **Mansion House Sta** | Take right hand lane & turn right (SP Holborn) then turn left. At traffic signals forward |
| 0.2 **St Paul's Cathedral** | Forward into Ludgate Hill (200 yds on right, is Old Bailey, for Central Criminal Courts) |
| 0.3 **Ludgate Circus** | Forward into Fleet Street. Pass Temple Bar & |
| 0.4 **Royal Courts of Justice** | Keep forward into the Strand and take right hand lane (signed Trafalgar Sq) |
| 0.7 **Trafalgar Square** | Bear right across the square (SP Piccadilly Circus) into Cockspur St & forward with one-way traffic keeping left along Pall Mall (signed Hyde Park Corner). At far end (St James's Palace on left) turn right into St James's St. At end turn right into Piccadilly (SP Piccadilly Circus) & keep to left hand lane |
| 1 **Piccadilly Circus** | Turn left and immediately left again into Regent St (signed Oxford Circus) |
| 0.6 **Oxford Circus** | Forward (signed Regent's Park) for Langham Place (Broadcasting House on right) & Portland Place. At T-road turn right into Park Crescent & at traffic signals forward into Park Square East for Outer Circle Regent's Park |
| 0.5 **London Zoological Gardens** | Continue with Outer Circle passing the London Mosque (on right). 0.4m farther branch right leaving park & forward into Baker St (signed West End) |
| 1.3 **Marylebone Circus** | (Planetarium & Madame Tussaud's to left in Marylebone Rd). Over X-rds (signed Oxford Circus). Forward through Portman Square then at next traffic signals turn right into Oxford Street |
| 0.8 **Marble Arch** | Turn left (one-way) then right & forward (signed Hyde Park) into The Ring Rd. In 1m cross Serpentine (Serpentine Gallery on right) then in 0.3m at traffic signals forward into Exhibition Rd. Pass Museums then at traffic signals turn left into Cromwell Rd for Brompton Rd (passing Brompton Oratory, on left) |
| 2.5 **Knightsbridge St** | Keep forward for |
| 0.5 **Hyde Park Corner** | ALTERNATIVE route for use on Sundays between 08.00 and dusk when Constitution Hill and The Mall are closed to vehicles: |
| **Hyde Park Corner** | Follow signs Victoria into Grosvenor Place. In 0.3m at traffic signals turn left into Lower Grosvenor Place (one-way) then at next traffic signals turn left into Buckingham Palace Rd (signed St James's Park) passing Royal Mews & Queen's Gallery (on left). At 2nd traffic signals bear left passing |
| 0.9 **Buckingham Palace** | Turn sharp right then into Birdcage Walk. At end of park turn left into Horse Guards Road |
| 0.7 **Horse Guards Parade** | At T-rd turn right and pass through Admiralty Arch to |
| 0.3 **Trafalgar Square** | then join main tour. |

# GAZETTEER

principal places of interest, including
museums, art galleries, etc

### Africa Centre

King Street, WC2
Central map: page 10, I6
☎ 01-836 1973

The centre is a charity and of
particular interest to those who wish
to learn more about African culture.
There are displays of paintings,
photographs and craftware by African
artists.

*Open: Mon-Fri 9.30-5.30, Sat 10-4.*
*Admission free.*

### Agnew's Galleries

43 Old Bond Street, W1
Central map: page 4, H5
☎ 01-629 6176

Annual exhibitions held here include
a watercolour exhibition devoted to
English watercolours and drawings of
the 18th and 19th centuries in Jan &
Feb, and a selling exhibition of Old
Master paintings from the 14th and
19th centuries. There are also
exhibitions of French and English
drawings from about 1800 to the
present day, work by English painters
of this century and loan exhibitions
in aid of charity. Many works pass
through Agnew's on their way to
famous art galleries and museums.

*Open: all year Mon-Fri, 9.30-5.30*
*(6.30pm Thu, during major*
*exhibitions). (Closed BH).*
*Admission free (admission charge for*
*some loan exhibitions).*

### Banqueting House

Palace of Whitehall, SW1
Central map: page 4, I5
☎ 01-212 4785

Built in 1619 for James I to a design
by Inigo Jones, the Banqueting
House is in a severe classical style,
but the interior is enriched by
Rubens' paintings. It is one of the
most important buildings of its
period. London court life was centred
here during the 17th century and it
was the scene of many historic events,
including the execution of Charles I
in 1649, the restoration of Charles II,
and the offer of the throne to Prince
William of Orange and Princess Mary.

*Open: Tue-Sat 10-5, Sun 2-5 (closed*
*Good Fri & 24-26 Dec). May also be*
*closed at short notice for government*
*functions.*
*Admission charge.*

### Bear Gardens Museum

Bear Gardens, SE1
Central map: page 12, L6
☎ 01-261 1353

This museum stands on the site of
the last bear-baiting ring on
Bankside, close to the site of the
Hope Theatre and Shakespeare's
Globe. It occupies a 19th-century
warehouse and consists of a
permanent exhibition relating to
Elizabethan theatre.

*Open: all year. Sat 10-5.30, Sun 2-6*
*(at other times by appointment).*
*Admission charge.*
*&. (Ground floor only)* ☞
*✗ (ex guide dogs)*

### Bethnal Green Museum of Childhood

Cambridge Heath Road, E2
District map: page 169, 1 E4
☎ 01-980 2415

The principal exhibits here are toys,
dolls and dolls' houses, model
soldiers, puppets, games, model
theatres, wedding dresses, children's
costume and Spitalfield silks — all
housed in a very attractive building.

*Open: Mon-Thu & Sat 10-6, Sun*
*2.30-6. (Closed: Fri, Spring BH Mon,*
*24-26 Dec & New Year's day).*
*Admission free.*
*&. Shop ✗ (ex guide dogs)*

### Bourne Hall Cultural Centre

Spring St, Ewell
District map: page 168, 2 C1
☎ 01-393 9573

An 18th-century house is the setting
for this cultural centre which
comprises museum, art centre,
library, theatre hall and banqueting
rooms. Collections embrace the
human and natural history of the
Epsom and Ewell area, and include
costumes, dolls, toys and early
photography. The Art Gallery has a

continuous temporary exhibition programme.

*Open: all year Mon-Sat, Mon, Wed & Thu 10-5 (8pm Tue & Fri) & 9.30-8 on Sat.*
*Admission free.*
⌨ ᴔ ✹

## Brass Rubbing

Given below are descriptions of three places where brasses (which can be described as commemorative plaques) can be seen and rubbed. Admission is free, but charges are made for rubbing, and for rubbing materials. The churches themselves are described separately.

### All Hallows Church by the Tower

Byward St, EC2
Central map: page 12, M6
☎ 01-481 2928

The church contains 19 original brasses dating from 1389—1591. There is also an exhibition of 26 Medieval facsimile brasses from which visitors can take rubbings. Staff are available to assist.
(All Hallows Church — see page 126).

*Open: daily Mon-Sat 11-5.45, Sun 12.30-5.45 (closed Xmas day).*
*Admission free, charge for making rubbings.*

### St James's Church

197 Piccadilly, W1
Central map: page 10, H6
☎ 01-437 6023

A collection of around 70 facsimile brasses from churches in all parts of Britain, from which rubbings can be made. These include some of Henry VIII's courtiers, such as Anne Boleyn's father — Sir Thomas Bullen — and Sir Humphrey Stafford. Staff are available to assist making rubbings.
(St James's Church — see page 130)

*Open: daily Mon-Sat 10-6, Sun 12-6 (closed Xmas day)*
*Admission free, charge for making rubbings.*

### Westminster Abbey

Broad Sanctuary, SW1
Central map: page 4, 14
☎ 01-222 2085

In the North Cloisters there is a collection of around 100 facsimile brasses. These include facsimiles of original brasses in Westminster Abbey. Some of the facsimiles are taken from the foot supports of larger brasses. These include animals, shields, and coats of arms. Staff are available to assist making rubbings.
(Westminster Abbey — see page 134)

*Open: daily Mon-Sat 9-5. (Closed Xmas day).*
*Admission free, charge for making rubbings.*

## British Crafts Centre

43 Earlham Street, WC2
Central map: page 10, I6
☎ 01-836 6993

The regular programme of special exhibitions and retail displays held here includes wallhangings, furniture, studio ceramics, pottery, wood, jewellery, etc. There are also books and magazines specialising in craft and design. It is an excellent place to see the best of contemporary British crafts.

*Open: all year, Mon-Fri 10-5.30, Sat 11-5. (Closed: Sun & BH).*
*Admission free. ᴔ (ground floor only). ✹*

WESTMINSTER ABBEY.

### British Museum

Great Russell Street, WC1
Central map: page 10, I7
☎ 01-636 1555

Founded in 1753, this is one of the
world's great museums, showing the
works of man from all over the
world from prehistoric to
comparatively modern times. The
imposing building which houses the
museum was designed by Sir Robert
Smirke and completed in the mid
19th century. The galleries are the
responsibility of the following
departments; Egyptian; Greek and
Roman; Western Asiatic; Prehistoric
and Romano-British; Medieval and
Later; Coins and Medals; Oriental;
Prints and Drawings. Since there is
so much to see in the museum,
visitors are advised to equip
themselves with a guide book and
make a selection of exhibits which
they can look at in the time
available. Most visitors wish to see
the superb Elgin marbles, from
temples and other buildings in
Athens. British treasures include the
beautiful 7th-century Sutton Hoo
Treasure and the 12th-century Lewis
Chessmen. Each year, special
exhibitions focus more detailed
attention on certain aspects of the
collections. Programmes on request.
Gallery talks (Mon-Sat) Lectures (Tue-
Sat) and Films (Tue-Fri). Children's
trail at all times.

*Open: all year, Mon-Sat 10-5, Sun
2.30-6. (Closed: Good Fri, May Day,
24-26 Dec & 1 Jan).
Admission free ⌷(licensed) ⅊ Shop
🐕(ex guide dogs)*

ELGIN MARBLES

### Bruce Castle Museum

Lordship Lane, N17
District map: page 169, 3 E5
☎ 01-808 8772

An E-shaped part Elizabethan, part
Jacobean and Georgian building,
with an adjacent circular 16th-
century tower, which stands in a
small park. The museum contains
sections on local history, postal
history and the Middlesex Regiment,
also known as the 'diehards'.

*Open: daily 1-5. (Closed: Good Fri,
Xmas & New Year's day)
Admission free (Donations). Shop 🐕*

### Cabinet War Rooms

Clive Steps, King Charles St, SW1
Central map: page 4, I5
☎ 01-930 6961

The rooms comprise the most
important surviving part of the
underground emergency
accommodation provided to protect
Winston Churchill, his War Cabinet
and Chiefs of Staff of Britain's armed
forces against air attacks in World
War II. Among the rooms are the
Cabinet Room, the Transatlantic

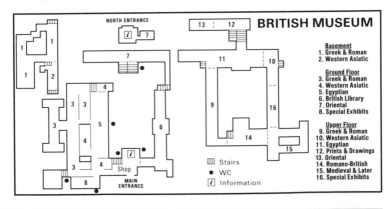

**BRITISH MUSEUM**

NORTH ENTRANCE

13 | 12

□ Stairs
● WC
ℹ Information

**Basement**
1. Greek & Roman
2. Western Asiatic

**Ground Floor**
3. Greek & Roman
4. Western Asiatic
5. Egyptian
6. British Library
7. Oriental
8. Special Exhibits

**Upper Floor**
9. Greek & Roman
10. Western Asiatic
11. Egyptian
12. Prints & Drawings
13. Oriental
14. Romano-British
15. Medieval & Later
16. Special Exhibits

Shop

MAIN ENTRANCE

Telephone Room, the Map Room (where information about operations on all fronts was collected) and the Prime Minister's Room. The more important rooms have been preserved intact since the War, while others have been carefully restored to their wartime appearance.

*Open: Tue-Sun also Etr Mon, Spring BH & Summer BH 10-5.50 (last admission 5.15pm). (Closed Good Fri, May Day BH, Xmas Eve — Boxing Day & New Year's Day). Admission charge.* ও *shop* 米 *(ex guide dogs).*

### Carlyle's House

Cheyne Row, SW3
Central map: page 2, E2
☏ 01-352 7087

Built in 1708, this is a fine example of an 18th-century town house. Here Thomas Carlyle and his wife Jane lived from 1834 to 1865 and entertained among others Dickens, Thackeray, Browning and Tennyson. Many of Carlyle's letters, personal possessions and furniture are preserved here, including an early piano on which Chopin played and the desk where Carlyle wrote his books.

*Open: 29 Mar-Oct, Wed-Sun & BH Mons 11-5.*
*Admission charge.*
*No parties over 20 persons. (NT)*

### Central Criminal Courts

Old Bailey, EC4
Central map: page 12, K7
☏ 01-248 3277

Most of the major trials of this century have been heard here, including those of Crippen, Christie and Haig. On the first two days of each session the judges carry posies of flowers and the courts are strewn with herbs, a custom dating from the time when it was necessary to disguise the stench of Newgate Prison. When the courts are in session visitors may sit in the public galleries. It is often necessary to queue. (Entrance in Newgate Street).

*Open: Mon-Fri, 10.30-1 & 2-4.*
*Admission free.*

### Chelsea Physic Gardens

Hospital Rd, SW3
Central map: page 3, F2
☏ 01-352 5646

This is the second oldest botanic garden in England, about 50 years younger than the one at Oxford. It was set up in 1673 to grow plants for recognition and study for medicinal and general scientific use.

*Open: 13 Apr-19 Oct, Wed, Sun & BH 2-5. Additional opening during Chelsea Flower Show week. Admission charge.* ও *shop*

### Chessington Zoo

Chessington (on A243)
District map: page 168, 4 B1
☏ Epsom (03727) 27227

Situated in 65 acres of lovely Surrey countryside, the zoo has a large and varied collection of animals and birds including gorillas and chimpanzees, as well as a children's zoo and reptile house. During the summer there is a funfair, miniature railway and free circus.

*Open: daily Nov-Mar 10-4; Apr-Oct 10-5 (Closed Xmas day).*
*Admission charge.*
*⌑ (licensed)* 져 ও *shop* 米

### Chiswick House

Burlington Lane, W4
District map: page 168, 5 C3
☏ 01-995 0508

Considered to be the finest example of Palladian architecture in Great Britain, this domed mansion was built between 1725 and 1730.

*Open: mid Mar-mid Oct, daily 9.30-6.30, mid Oct-mid Mar, Sun & Wed-Sat 9.30-4.*
*Admission charge.*
*⌑ (AM)*

### Church Farm House Museum

Greyhound Hill, NW4
District map: page 168, 6 C5
☏ 01-203 0130

A gabled house, dating from 1660s, which is now a museum of local interest. Attractions here include a period furnished kitchen and dining room. There is a programme of changing exhibitions.

*Open: all year, Mon-Sat 10-1 & 2-5.30 (Tue 10-1 only), Sun 2-5.30. (Closed: Good Fri, 25 & 26 Dec, 1 Jan).*
*Admission free.*
&#9855;*(garden only) shop* ✘

## Claremont, Esher

Entrance by Claremont Lane A244
District map: page 168, 7 B1
☎ *(0372) 67841*

This mansion was designed in 1772 by Henry Holland and Capability Brown for Clive of India to replace an earlier house. The façade has a columned portico; there are fine fireplaces and plaster ceilings inside. Now a co-educational school run by Christian Scientists.

*Open: Feb-Nov, 1st wknd in month 2-5.*
*Admission charge.*
*Shop* ✘

## Claremont Landscape Garden, Esher

Entrance on edge of Esher (W of A307)
District map: page 168, 8 A1

This, the earliest surviving example of an English landscape garden, has recently been restored. It has a lake with an island pavilion, grotto, turf amphitheatre, viewpoint and avenue.

*Open: daily ex Xmas & New Year's day, Apr-Oct 9-7 or sunset; Nov-Mar 9-4.*
*Admission charge.*
*(NT) (The house is not NT property).*

## Commonwealth Institute

Kensington High St, W8
Central map: page 1, B4
☎ *01-603 4535*

Life in the countries of the Commonwealth is depicted here by a large number of exhibitions. Also library, art gallery, and arts centre.

*Open: Mon-Sat 10-5.30, Sun 2-5*

*(Closed Good Fri, May Day, 24-26 Dec & 1 Jan)*
*Admission free in daytime, evening admission fee payable.*
  &#9851;*(licensed)* &#9855; *shop*
✘ *(ex guide dogs)*

## Courtauld Institute Galleries

Woburn Sq, WC1
Central map: page 10, H8
☎ *01-387 0370 & 01-580 1015*

These galleries contain the most important collection of Impressionist paintings in Britain, including work by Monet, Renoir, Degas, Cezanne, Van Gogh, Gauguin and Toulouse-Lautrec. There are also Old Master paintings and drawings, including works by Peter Bruegel, Michaelangelo and Rubens, as well as works by the Bloomsbury Group.

*Open: all year Mon-Sat 10-5, Sun 2-5. (Closed Etr, Xmas and most BH)*
*Admission charge.*

## Cricket Memorial Gallery

Lord's Ground, NW8
Central map: page 8, D8
☎ *01-289 1611*

Founded about 1865 the collections here include cricket bygones and paintings of cricket. There is also a library of cricket literature, enriched by the notable book collections of A L Ford and Sir Julien Cahn.

*Open on match days Mon-Sat 10.30-5, other times by appointment. Admission charge. Library open free of charge to students by appointment with the Curator.*
&#9855; *(ground floor and grounds only) shop* ✘

## Cuming Museum

155/157 Walworth Rd, SE17
Central map: page 6, L3
☎ *01-703 3324 ext 32*

Roman and medieval finds from the suburb of Southwark, south of London Bridge, are among the exhibits to be seen here. Also on display are examples of the local 'Delft' pottery industry, items associated with Dickens and Michael

Faraday (born locally in 1791), and the equipment of a family dairy firm which served the neighbourhood for over 150 years.

*Open: all year Mon-Fri 10-5.30 (7pm Thu), Sat 10-5.*
*Admission free.*
*Shop* ✕

## Cutty Sark Clipper Ship

Greenwich Pier, SE10
District map: page 169, 9 E3
☎ 01-858 3445

Probably one of the most famous ships in the world, the Cutty Sark was launched in 1869, and was built for speed — she once covered 363 miles in a day. Her cargoes were tea, and latterly wool. In 1922 she was converted into a nautical training school, and in 1957 was transferred to dry dock at Greenwich. In her holds are displays explaining her history and a collection of ships' figureheads.

*Open: daily 10.30-5, Sun 2.30-6pm in summer. (Closed 24-26 Dec & 1 Jan)*
*Admission charge.*
*Ġ (tween-deck only) shop* ✕

## Dickens' Old Curiosity Shop

13-14 Portsmouth St, WC2
Central map: page 11, J7
☎ 01-405 9891

Established in the 17th century, this half-timbered shop is one of the oldest in London. It is said to be the shop immortalized by Dickens in his novel of the same name. Inside is a desk containing items owned by Dickens.

*Open: April-Oct, Mon-Fri 9-5.30; Nov-Mar, Mon-Fri 9.30-5.30; Sat, Sun & BH 9.30-5*
*Admission free.*

## Dickens House

48 Doughty St, WC1
Central map: page 11, J8
☎ 01-405 2127

Dickens lived here during his twenties and here completed

*Pickwick Papers* and wrote *Oliver Twist* and *Nicholas Nickleby*. Pages of the original manuscripts of his early books and others are on view, together with valuable first editions in the original paper parts of his works; his special marriage licence; his family Bible which contains a personal record of his sons and daughters, and many other personal relics. Entrance includes Suzannet Rooms.

*Open: daily 10-5, last admission 4.30 pm. (Closed Sun, BH, Good Fri & Xmas wk).*
*Admission charge.*
*Ġ (ground floor only) shop* ✕

## Dr Johnson's House

17 Gough Sq, EC4
Central map: page 11, K7
☎ 01-353 3745

Gough Square was built in about 1700 and this house has changed very little since that time. Dr Johnson lived here (1749-1759) and it was here that he completed his famous English dictionary (a first edition is on display) and wrote *The Rambler* and *The Idler* . The house was opened as a museum in 1914 and contains a fine collection of prints as well as letters and other relics.

*Open: May-Sep daily 11-5.30; Oct-Apr 11-5 (Closed Sun, BH, Xmas Eve & Good Fri).*
*Admission charge.*
*Shop* ✕

## Dulwich Picture Gallery

College Rd, SE21
District map: page 169, 10 E2
☎ 01-693 5254

Few art galleries are as beautiful to look at as this; it was specially designed by Sir John Soane in 1811 and was the first public picture gallery in England. Among the notable paintings here are works by Gainsborough, Poussin, Raphael, Rembrandt, Rubens and Watteau.

*Open: all year Tue-Sat 10-1 &2-5 Sun 2-5 (Closed Mon).*
*Admission charge.*
*Ġ shop* ✕

### Eltham Palace

Off Court Rd, Eltham, SE9
District map: page 169, 11 F2
☎ 01-859 2112 (ext 255). Advisable
to contact Admin Officer before visit.

The palace is especially noted for the
great hall with its 15th-century
hammer beam roof. An old bridge
spans the moat.

Open: Nov-Mar Thu & Sun 10.30-4;
Apr-Oct Thu & Sun 10.30-6.
Opening arrangements subject to
possible alteration.
Admission free.
(AM)

### Fenton House

Hampstead Grove NW3
District map: page 168, 12 C4
☎ 01-435 3471

This is an elegant William and Mary
house, built around 1693, and set in
a walled garden. Collections housed
here include notable Oriental,
Continental and English china,
needlework, furniture and the
fascinating Benton Fletcher
Collection of early keyboard
instruments. Concerts are held here
in summer.

Open: Mar, Sat & Sun 2pm-6pm,
31 Mar-Oct Sat-Wed 11-6
(last admission 5pm).
Admission charge.
(NT)

### Forty Hall

Forty Hill, Enfield
District map: page 169, 13 E5
☎ 01-363 4046

Built in 1629 for Sir Nicholas
Raynton, Lord Mayor of London, this
mansion was modified in the early
18th century. Contemporary plaster
ceilings and a screen can be seen
here, as can 17th-and 18th-century
furnishings and paintings, ceramics
and glass.

Open: all year Tue-Fri 10-6 (5pm
Oct-Etr) Sat & Sun 10-6 (5pm Oct-
Etr).
Admission free.
🖵 🚻
shop 🏋

### Geffrye Museum

Kingsland Rd, E2
Central map: page 12, N9
☎ 01-739 8368

A collection of furniture and
woodwork from the Elizabethan
period to 1939, including a
reconstruction of John Evelyn's closet
of curiosities, is contained in these
former almshouses, which were built
in the early 18th century.

Open: Tue-Sat 10-5, Sun 2-5 & BH
Mon 10-5 (Closed Mon, Good Fri,
24-26 Dec & New Year's day).
Admission free.
🖵 ⓱ (ground floor only) shop 🏋

### Geological Museum

Exhibition Rd, SW7
Central map: page 2, 04
☎ 01-589 3444

This is the national museum of earth
sciences. On show here are exquisite
fossils from the earliest periods of life
on Earth, beautiful gemstones, and
examples of every kind of geological
formation. Its exhibits include a
piece of the Moon and the largest
exhibition on basic earth science in
the world — The Story of the Earth.
This is split into four main sections:
the Earth in Space, which includes
an exhibit showing that an observer
150 million light years away, looking
through an immensely powerful
telescope, would see dinosaurs
roaming around in a Jurassic
landscape; The Earth's Interior and
Crust; Geological processes; and
Geological Time. There is also a
famous collection of fine gem-stones,
showing them in their parent rock, in
natural crystal form and in their final
cut state. The regional geology of
Great Britain, and ore deposits of the
world are also displayed. Permanent
exhibitions, British Fossils and Britain
Before Man and an exciting new
exhibition called Treasures of the
Earth can also be seen.

Open: all year Mon-Sat 10-6, Sun
2.30-6. (Closed Good Fri, May Day,
24-26 Dec & 1 Jan).
Admission free.
⓱ (ex mezzanine floor)
shop 🏋

### Gipsy Moth IV

Greenwich Pier, King Williams Walk, SE10
District map: page 169, 14 E3
☎ 01-858 3445

The yacht in which Sir Francis Chichester sailed single-handed round the world in 1966-67, starting the fashion for 'Round the World' sailing races.

*Open: daily Apr-Oct 10.30-6.
Admission charge.*

### Grange Museum

Neasden Lane, NW10
(centre of roundabout)
District map: page 168, 15 C4
☎ 01-452 8311

Dating from around 1700, this building originally formed part of the outbuildings of a large farm and was later converted into a 'gothic' cottage. Permanent collections inside tell the story of the area that is now the London Borough of Brent. There are also temporary exhibitions, a local history library and a display on the British Empire Exhibition for which Wembley Stadium was built. Two period rooms of late 19th century and early 20th century, and a reconstructed draper's shop form part of the display.

*Open: all year (ex BH) Mon-Fri 12-5 (8pm Wed), Sat 10-5.
Admission free. Parties by advanced booking only.*
& *(ground floor & gardens only)*
*shop*

### Guildhall

Basinghall St, EC2
Central map: page 12, L7
☎ 01-606 3030

Parts of this magnificent building date from 1411. Particularly fine is the crypt, which is the largest of its kind in London. It was severely damaged in the Great Fire of 1666 (after which Wren restored it) and during the Blitz. Restoration work, completed in 1954, was carried out to designs by Sir Giles Scott. Here the Court of Common Council,

which administers the city, meets and entertains. The Guildhall Library contains an unrivalled collection of books, manuscripts, and illustrations on all aspects of London. The Guildhall Clock Museum, with 700 exhibits, illustrates 500 years of time-keeping.

*Open: Guildhall May-Sep, Mon-Sat 10-5, BH & Sun 2-5; Guildhall Library Mon-Fri 9.30-5. (Closed: BH); Guildhall Clock Museum Mon-Fri 9.30-5. (Closed BH).
Admission free.*
& *(ground floor only)*

### Guinness World of Records

The Trocadero, Piccadilly Circus, W1
Central map: page 10, H6
☎ 01-439 7331

This museum has been specially designed to bring to life many of the records within the famous Guinness Book of Records. It has six theme areas, corresponding with the sections of the book: the Human World, the Animal World, Our Planet Earth, Structures and Machines, the Sports World, the World of Entertainment and British Innovation and Achievement.

*Open: daily from 10am (last admission 10pm). (Closed Xmas day).
Admission charge.*
& *shop*

GUILDHALL

## Gunnersbury Park Museum

Popes Lane, W3
District map: page 168, 16 B3
☎ 01-992 1612

This 19th-century former Rothschild mansion, set in a fine park, is now a museum of local interest for the London Borough of Ealing and Hounslow, showing archaeological discoveries, transport items, costume and topographical and social material. Rothschild coaches are on display. The Victorian kitchens are open to the public on certain summer weekends.

*Open: Mar-Oct (end of British Summer Time) Mon-Fri 1-5, Sat, Sun & BH 2-6; Nov-Feb, Mon-Fri 1-4, Sat, Sun & BH 2-4 (Closed: Good Fri & 24-26 Dec).*
*Admission free*
Å (ground floor only) shop Nursery ✗

## Hall Place

Bexley (near junction of A2 & A233)
District map: page 169, 17 F2
☎ Crayford (0322) 526574

A 15th-16th-century mansion building with contrasting elevations of chequered flint and brick, Hall Place is surrounded by ornamental gardens, with topiary in the form of Queen's Beasts, rose, rock, water, herb and peat gardens. There are also conservatory houses and recreation facilities.

*Open: House Mon-Sat 10-5, Sun 2-6 (summer), Mon-Sat 10-5, Sun 2-dusk (winter); Gardens Mon-Fri 7.30-dusk, Sat & Sun 9-dusk.*
*Admission free.*
⌑ (weather permitting) Å (gardens only) ✗

## Ham House

Ham St, Ham (annexe of Victoria & Albert Museum)
District map: page 168, 18 B2
☎ 01-940 1950

An outstanding Stuart house, built in 1610, redecorated and furnished in the 1670s by the Duke and Duchess of Lauderdale. Much of this furniture is still in its original rooms today.

*Open: Tue-Sun & BH Mons, 11-5 (Closed Good Fri, 5 May & 24-26 Dec & 1 Jan).*
*House: admission charge, Grounds: free.*
✗ (NT) and Victoria & Albert Museum

## Hampton Court Palace

Hampton Court
District map: page 168, 19 B2
☎ 01-977 8441

Built by Cardinal Wolsey in the early 16th century, Hampton Court was to have been his personal palace, but he gave it to Henry VIII in a vain attempt to stave off his downfall. It has since been added to and altered by many monarchs, and it has been the setting for many historic events. Sir Christopher Wren was commissioned by William and Mary to convert it to a palace on the lines of Versailles, and much of the exterior dates from this time. The last monarch to live here was George II, after which it became a series of 'grace and favour' residences. Today it is full of priceless paintings, tapestries and furniture, some of which were saved from a fire which caused great damage in 1986. The gardens and grounds, which include the famous maze, set the palace off to perfection.

*Open: Gardens and grounds. See page 146; Kitchens, cellars and Tudor tennis courts Apr-Sep Mon-Sat 9.30-6, Sun 11-6.*
*Admission free.*
*State apartments open: Apr-Sep Mon-Sat 9.30-6, Sun 11-6; Oct-Mar, Mon-Sat 9.30-5, Sun 2-5. (Closed Good Fri, 24-26 Dec & Jan 1)*
*Admission charge.*
Å ⌑ Shop

THE CLOCK COURT, HAMPTON COURT PALACE

## HMS Belfast

Symons Wharf, Vine Lane, Tooley St, SE1
Central map: page 6, M5
☎ 01-407 6434

This 11,000 ton cruiser, which is now part of the Imperial War Museum, is permanently moored in the Pool of London as a floating naval museum. She was launched in 1938, but was damaged by a mine in November 1939 and did not re-enter active service until November 1942. She played an active role for the rest of the war, including duty on the famous Russian convoys.

*Open: daily 20 Mar-Oct 11-5.50 last admission 5.20; Nov-19 Mar 11-4.30 last admission 4. (Closed Good Fri, May Day, 24-26 Dec & 1 Jan). Admission charge.*
*☞ (summer only) shop* ✲

## Highgate Cemetery

Swains Lane, N6
District map: page 169, 20 D4
☎ 01-340 1834

One of the private cemeteries which sprang up in the 1830s. The Eastern part is well known for the grave of Karl Marx. The Western part, decaying and overgrown through years of neglect, provides a marvellous backdrop for the magnificent tombs, vaults and buildings. Other famous Victorians buried here include George Eliot, Faraday and Charles Dickens's family.

*Open: Eastern cemetery daily Apr-Sep 10-5, Oct-Mar 10-4 (Last admission ½ hour before closing); Western cemetery guided tours on the hour daily, Apr-Sep 10-4, Oct-Mar 10-3.*
*Admission free (Donations)*

## Hogarth's House

Hogarth Lane, Great West Road, W4
District map: page 168, 21 C3
☎ 01-994 6757

William Hogarth lived in this 17th-century house for 15 years. Many of his engravings and drawings are on show here, as are other mementoes of the life and times of this great artist.

*Open: all year Mon, Wed-Sat 11-6, Sun 2-6 (4pm Oct-Mar). (Closed: Tue & Good Fri, 1st two weeks Sep, last 3 weeks Dec & New Year's Day) Admission free.*

## Horniman Museum

London Road, SE23
District map: page 169, 22 E2
☎ 01-699 2339

Displays from different cultures and large natural history collections, including living creatures, can be seen here, and there is also an exhibition of musical instruments from all parts of the world. Extensive library and lectures and concerts in spring and autumn. Special exhibitions. Educational Centre programmes.

*Open: all year Mon-Sat 10.30-6, Sun 2-6. (Closed: 24-26 Dec).*
*Admission free.*
*☞ shop* ✲*(ex guide dogs)*

## Houses of Parliament

SW1
Central map: page 4, I4
☎ 01-219 3090 & 3100

From Edward the Confessor to Henry VIII, the Palace of Westminster was the principal residence of the monarch. Almost all of the old palace was destroyed in a fire in 1834, the only substantial survivor being the superb Westminster Hall (see below). The Commons and the Lords had sat in various parts of the palace (including the Hall) since the time of Henry VIII. Immediately after the fire a competition was held for a building to replace it, and this was won by Sir Charles Barry. Although the basic design was Barry's, much of the detailed work was done by Augustus Pugin, and together they created a gothic masterpiece which is now one of the most famous buildings in the world. Although most people now know it as the Houses of Parliament, it is still, strictly, the Palace of Westminster. The two principal chambers are set either side of a central hall and corridor — the House of Lords to the south and the House of Commons to the north. The clock tower, 320ft high, contains Big Ben, the hour bell weighing 13½ tons, while the Victoria tower stands 340ft high. The House of Commons suffered bomb damage in 1941 and a new chamber was constructed to the design of Sir Giles Gilbert Scott and opened in 1950.

*To gain admission to the Strangers' Galleries join the queue at St Stephen's entrance from approx 4.30 pm Mon-Thu, approx 9.30am Fri (House of Commons) or from approx 2.30pm Tue & Wed, from 3pm Thu & occasionally 11am Fri (House of Lords) or by arrangement with an MP (House of Commons) or Peer (House of Lords).*
*Free, although guides require payment if employed.*
*&. (by arrangement)*
*Bookstall ✗ (ex guide dogs)*

### also Westminster Hall

☎ *01-219 3090*

Built 1097-99 by William Rufus, it is the oldest remaining part of Westminster Palace. The glory of the hall is the cantilever, or hammerbeam roof, the earliest and largest of its kind in existence, built between 1394 and 1401. The Hall has been the setting for many momentous national events, including the trial of Charles I in 1649, and the lying in state of monarchs and statesmen.

*Open: Mon-Thu am by arrangement with an MP only.*
*Free, although guides require payment if employed.*
*&. (by arrangement)*
*✗ (ex guide dogs)*

### IBA Broadcasting Gallery

70 Brompton Road, SW3
Central map: page 2 E4
☎ *01-584 7011*

This permanent exhibition recreates nearly a century of television and radio. A multiscreen audio-visual presentation shows how ITN covers an important and developing story in the course of a day's news programmes. Different stages of a typical production can be seen in a *son et lumiere* display. There is also a working exhibition of Victorian parlour entertainment and replicas of experimental models used by pioneers.

*Open: Tours, Mon-Fri at 10, 11, 2 & 3 (tours take approx. one hour). Children under 16 only allowed access if part of an organised group. Admission free.*

### Imperial Collection

(Crown Jewels of the World) Central Hall SW1
Central map: page 4, I4
☎ *01-222 0770*

This sparkling collection includes over 150 reproductions of crowns, tiaras, orbs, sceptres, swords, garters, jewellery etc, together with reproductions of the most famous diamonds in the world. Many pieces on show are the only copies, as the originals were lost or destroyed in wars or revolutions. Among replicas from 15 countries can be seen the Crown of Charlemagne of the Holy Roman Empire; the Vatican Crown; crowns and jewellery from Bavaria, Austria, Hungary, Prussia and Germany.

*Open: Jan-Sep, Mon-Sat 10-6; Oct-Dec, Mon-Sat 11-5 (Closed Good Fri & Xmas day)*
*Admission charge.*
*Shop*

### Imperial War Museum

Lambeth Road, SE1
Central map: page 5, K4
☎ *01-735 8922*

Housed in the buildings of the

former lunatic asylum universally known as 'Bedlam', this museum illustrates and records all aspects of the two World Wars and other military operations involving Britain and the Commonwealth since 1914. Extensive renovation and redevelopment will entail gallery closures from 1986, and a major interim exhibition of the two World Wars is being mounted while the work is in progress. Various reference departments, open by appointment only.

*Open: all year, daily Mon-Sat 10-5.50, Sun 2-5.50. (Closed: Good Fri, May Day, 24-26 Dec, New Year's Day).*
*Admission free.*
*& Shop ✗ (ex guide dogs)*

## The Inns of Court

There used to be 12 Inns of Court, but only three still exist in their traditional capacity — Gray's Inn, Lincoln's Inn and Temple. To pass through the gateways of any of these is to step back in time — their peace and tranquillity is anachronistic, more in keeping with their monastic origins than the secular hubbub outside their walls.

*Gray's Inn*

Gray's Inn Road, WC2
Central map: page 11, J7
☎ 01-405 8164

A late 17th-century gatehouse opens from Holborn into the confines of Gray's Inn Square. Of particular interest are the 16th-century Hall, with its contemporary windows, the Library, with a statue of Francis Bacon, the most famous member of the Inn, and the chapel. The gardens here are lovely. They are said to have been laid out by Sir Francis Bacon — famous Elizabethan statesman and essayist — who kept chambers here from 1577 to 1626. The ancient catalpa trees in the garden are reputed to be the ones that Bacon planted.

*Open: Gardens May-Sep, Mon-Fri 12-2.30 (buildings by prior application to the Undertreasurer).*
*Admission free.*
*✗ (children not admitted)*

*Lincoln's Inn*

Chancery Lane, WC2
Central map: page 11, J7
☎ 01-405 1393

The buildings here date mainly from the 16th and 17th centuries. The Gatehouse was built in 1518, and still has its original oak doors. Old Hall dates from 1506, but was extensively restored in 1928. Inigo Jones is often said to have designed the 17th-century chapel. The complex is dominated by Victoria New Hall and Library dating from 1843.

*Open: Chapel and gardens, Mon-Fri 12-2.30 (Closed Etr, Xmas and 1 Jan) Other buildings open by application to the Treasurer of the Inn.*
*Admission free.*
*✗*

*Temple*

Fleet Street, EC4
Central map: page 11, J6/K6
☎ 01-353 7323 *(Prince Henry's Room)*
☎ 01-353 8462 *(Inner Temple Hall and Church)*
☎ 01-353 4355 *(Middle Temple Hall)*

Originally, the Temple was the English headquarters of the Knights Templar. The entrance from Fleet Street is through Inner Temple Gateway. Above this is Prince Henry's Room, which retains its original panelling and ceiling. It contains an exhibition relating to Samuel Pepys. The oldest building in the complex is Temple Church, one of only four round churches surviving in England. Middle Temple Hall is a superb example of Tudor architecture.

*Open: Prince Henry's Room (Inner Temple Gateway) Mon-Fri 1.45-5 (Sat 4.30) (Closed BH).*
*Temple Church, daily 10-4 (except for services)*
*Middle Temple Hall, Mon-Fri 10-11.30, 3-4.00 (Closed Xmas, week after Etr, Aug-mid Sep)*
*Inner Temple Hall: Mon-Fri 10-11, 1.45-4 (opening subject to porter being available)*
*Admission free*
*✗*

### Interpretative Centre, St Mary Magdalene Churchyard Nature Reserve

Norman Road, E6
District map: page 169, 23 F4
☎ 01-519 4296

Displays relating to natural history and history of an interesting churchyard nature reserve.

*Open: Tue-Thu & Sun 2-5.*
*Admission free*
*Shop* ✘

### Jewish Museum

Woburn House,
Tavistock Square, WC1
Central map: page 10, H8
☎ 01-388 4525

Many of the objects on display here reflect Anglo-Jewish history from the 13th century until today. All aspects of ritual and domestic life are covered in a museum which shows, among other things, that Jewish people are an integral and enriching part of British life and culture.

*Open: Tue-Fri 10-4; Sun 10-12.45.*
*(Closed: Jewish & PH).*
*Admission free*

### Keats House

Keats Grove, NW3
District map: page 169, 24 D4
☎ 01-435 2062

In fact, this was originally two Regency houses. Keats lived in one with his friend Charles Brown, while next door lived his nurse and lover, Fanny Brawne. It was here that he wrote his greatest poetry, including *Ode to a Nightingale*, which was composed in the garden. The little group lived here between 1818 and 1820. Today the combined houses are furnished in period style and contain many manuscripts, letters and relics.

*Open: all year, Mon-Sat 10-1 & 2-6,*
*Sun & BH 2-5. (Closed: Good Fri, Etr*
*Sat, May Day, Xmas & New Year's*
*day).*
*Guided tours by appointment*
*Admission free.*
ᙇ *(ground floor only) shop* ✘

### Kensington Palace State Apartments & Court Dress Collection

W8
Central map: page 1 C5
☎ 01-937 9561

The Palace was acquired by William III in 1689 and remodelled and enlarged by Sir Christopher Wren. Queen Victoria was born and brought up here, and it remains a royal residence. Contained within the state apartments are pictures and furniture from the royal collection. The redecorated Victorian rooms and the room devoted to the Great Exhibition can be seen. Also on view is a colourful new museum, the Court Dress Collection. Its exhibits provide a glimpse into a bygone age, with displays of costumes worn at court from 1750 to the present day.

*Open: Mon-Sat 9-5, Sun 1-5. Last*
*admission 4.30pm (Closed Good Fri,*
*24-26 Dec & 1 Jan)*
*Admission charge.*
ᙇ *(ground floor only) shop* ✘
*(Dept of Environment)*

### Kenwood, Iveagh Bequest

Hampstead Lane, NW8
District map: page 169, 25 D4
☎ 01-348 1286

This fine mansion was remodelled by Robert Adam between 1767 and 1769. Further changes and additions were made later in the 18th century. The house and grounds, which form part of Hampstead Heath, were bequeathed to the nation by Lord Iveagh in 1927. Adam's Library is especially notable, and there is much excellent furniture. Outstanding, however, are the works of art, including paintings by Rembrandt, Hals, Vermeer, Reynolds and Gainsborough. Also on display are collections of 18th-century shoe buckles and jewellery. Summer exhibition. Concerts.

*Open: daily; Apr-Sep 10-7; Feb, Mar*
*& Oct 10-5; Nov-Jan 10-4.*
*Admission free (Charges for special*
*exhibitions).*
   ᙙ ᙇ *(ground floor & garden only)*
*Shop* ✘

### Kew Bridge Engines Trust, The Pumping Station, Kew

Bridge Rd, Brentford (entrance in Green Dragon Lane)
District map: page 168, 26 B3
☎ 01-568 4757

London's living steam museum, containing model engines, steam engines and six beam engines, five working, plus traction engines and a museum of London's water supply. Old workshops and forges help to re-create a working site which was operational from 1820 to 1945. Various events throughout the year.

*Open: all year daily 11-5. Engines in steam Sat, Sun & BH Mon (Closed Xmas wk).*
*Admission charge.*
*⌨ & (ground floor only) shop.*

### Kew Gardens

Royal Botanic Gardens, Kew
District map: page 168, 27 B3

See page 152

### Kew Palace

Kew
District map: page 168, 28 B3

A Dutch-gabled 17th to 18th-century house containing souvenirs of George III. Queen Charlotte died here in 1818. It stands in the Royal Botanical Gardens at Kew. (See page 152)

*Open: Apr-Sep daily 11-5.30*
*Admission charge*
*(Dept of Environment).*

### and Queen Charlotte's Cottage

Built in 1772 for the Queen, wife of George III. It is a perfect rural retreat — timber-framed and with a thatched roof — and stands in the most 'natural' seeming part of Kew Gardens. The interior remains as it was in the 18th century when royalty were in residence.

*Open: Apr-Sep 11-5.30 Sat, Sun & BH.*
*Admission charge*
*(Dept of Environment).*

### Lancaster House

Stable Yard SW1
Central map: page 4, H5

Built in the 19th century by the 'Grand Old Duke of York' and originally called 'York House', Lancaster House is now used as a centre for government hospitality.

*Open: Etr-mid Dec (ex during government functions). Sat, Sun & BH 2-6.*
*Admission charge*
*(Dept of Environment).*

### Leighton House

12 Holland Park Road, W14
Central map: page 1, B4
☎ 01-602 3316

Leighton House is a uniquely opulent and exotic example of High Victorian taste. Built for the President of the Royal Academy, Frederic, Lord Leighton, by George Aitchison, the main body of the house was completed in 1866. The fabulous Arab Hall, with its rare middle-eastern tiles, fountain and gilded decoration, is a 19th-century Arabian Nights' creation finished in 1879. Fine Victorian paintings by Lord Leighton and his contemporaries hang in the rooms, and there are three galleries for exhibitions of modern and historic art.

*Open: all year, Mon-Sat 10-5 (6pm during temporary exhibitions). (Closed BH).*
*Gardens open Apr-Sep 11-5.*
*Admission free.*
*卉 & (ground floor) ✗*

### Light Fantastic

The Trocadero Centre,
13 Coventry St, W1
Central map: page 10, H6
☎ 01-734 4516

The largest hologram in the world is part of this laser light show of over 100 holograms. Holograms are three-dimensional shapes which appear to float through space.

*Open: all year, daily 10am-10pm. (Closed 25 Dec).*

### Linley Sambourne House

18 Stafford Ter., W8
Central map: page 1, B4
☎ *01-994 1019 (The Victorian Society)*

The home of Linley Sambourne (1845-1910), chief political cartoonist of *Punch*. The magnificent interior has survived almost unchanged, and the fixtures and fittings have been preserved together with many of Sambourne's own pictures.

*Open: Wed 10-4, Sun 2-5 Mar-Oct*
*Admission charge.*
*Shop* ✗

### Livesey Museum

682 Old Kent Road, SE15
District map: page 169, 29 E3
☎ *01-639 5604*

This museum holds one major exhibition every year, dealing mainly with Southwark's past and present. A permanent exhibition of Southwark street furniture can be seen.

*Open: when exhibition is in progress, Mon-Sat 10-5*
*Admission free.*
& *(ground floor only) shop* ✗

### Lloyd's of London

Lime St, EC3
Central map: page 12, M6
☎ *01-623 7100*

The world's leading insurance market moved into a new headquarters building of advanced design in Lime Street in May 1986. It incorporates a purpose-built exhibition encompassing Lloyd's 300 years in the City as well as a viewing area.

*Open: all year, Mon-Fri 10-2*
*(4.30pm for booked groups). (Closed PH and occasional other days).*
*Admission free.*
✗

### London Diamond Centre

10 Hanover St, W1
Central map: page 9, G6
☎ *01-629 5511*

A unique exhibition of and about diamonds where visitors can see diamond cutters and polishers practising their craft, a goldsmith creating jewellery exclusively for the London Diamond Centre and many other interesting aspects about the craft and industry. A feature is a walk-in diamond mine and a video on diamond mining. Another part of the exhibition displays a collection of replicas of some of the world's most historic diamonds, and shapes in which diamonds can be cut.

*Open: Mon-Sat 9.30-5.30 (Oct-Apr Sat 9.30-1.30).*
*Other times by arrangement.*
*Admission charge (includes a free memento in the form of a brilliant cut stone (not a diamond) in a presentation case, which value far exceeds the admission fee).*
*Shop* ✗

### The London Dungeon

28/34 Tooley St, SE1
Central map: page 6, M5
☎ *01-403 0606*

The London Dungeon can lay claim to the bizarre fact that it is the world's only medieval horror museum. Vast dark vaults house strange and horrifying scenes of man's inhumanity to man in Britain's dark past.

*Open: all year, Apr-Sep 10-5.30, Oct-Mar 10-4.30. (Closed Xmas).*
*Admission charge.*
⌨ & *shop* ✗

### The London Experience

The Trocadero Centre, Piccadilly Circus, W1
Central map: page 10, H6
☎ *01-439 4938*

A multi-screen audio visual display in sound, vision and light, which takes visitors back through time to experience London's past history. Scenes include the Plague, the Great Fire of London, the hunt for Jack the Ripper, London through the wars, and its pageantry, markets and people.

*Open: daily 10.20am-10.20pm. (Closed Xmas day)*
*Admission charge.*

## London Planetarium

Marylebone Rd, NW1
Central map: page 9, F7
☎ 01-486 1121
(Laserium 01-486 2242)

Here the night skies are projected in all their beauty onto the inside of the dome to an accompanying commentary. An exhibition called 'The Astronomers' includes wax figures of such notable scientists as Einstein and Galileo in three-dimensional representations of their discoveries. Laser light concerts most evenings.

*Open: all year daily (ex 25 Dec) star shows 11-4.30.*
*Admission charge.*
  ⌂ shop ✗

## London Silver Vaults

Chancery Lane, WC2
Central map: page 11, J7
☎ 01-242 3844

A fine collection of antiques and modern silverware in an underground location. Visitors can browse and traders are happy to talk about their wares, look up hallmarks and explain histories.

*Open: Mon-Fri, 9-5.30, Sat 9-12.30.*
*Admission free.*

## London Toy & Model Museum

October House, 21-23 Craven Hill, W2
Central map: page 7, D6
☎ 01-262 9450/7905

This Victorian building houses a fine collection of commercially-made toys and models with an emphasis on trains, cars and boats. Pleasant garden and extensive garden railway.

*Open: Tue-Sat 10-5.30 Sun 11-5.*
*(Closed PH ex BH Mons).*
*Admission charge.*
  ⌂ ♿ (ground floor & gardens only)
shop ✗

## London Transport Museum

The Piazza, Covent Garden, WC2
Central map: page 10, I6
☎ 01-379 6344

Housed in the former Flower Market in Covent Garden, this museum tells the story of the development of London's transport from its earliest beginnings right up to the present day. Vehicles include steam locomotives, trams, buses, trolleybuses, railway coaches and horse buses. There are also extensive displays using working and static models, posters and audio-visual material. One can 'drive' a modern bus, a tram and a tube train. A reference library is available by appointment.
Film shows and other activities at weekends.

*Open: daily 10-6, last admission 5.15pm. (Closed Xmas).*
*Admission charge.*
  ⌂ (daily) ♿ shop ✗
(ex guide dogs)

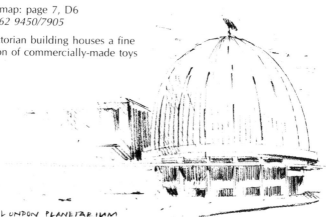

LONDON PLANETARIUM

### London Zoo (Regent's Park)

NW1
Central map: page 9, F9
☎ 01-722 3333

Set in Regent's Park, the zoo is one of the most comprehensive collections of animals in the world, with over 8000 animals on view. Creatures from every corner of the globe can be seen here, varying from tiny marsupials to huge mammals, from insects to dolphins and from brilliantly-coloured tropical fishes to reptiles and amphibians. Among the many world firsts that the zoo can claim are a reptile house opened in 1849, an aquarium in 1853 and an insect house in 1889. In recent years many new pavilions have been built including a giant walkthrough aviary designed by Lord Snowdon. More improvements are on the way; the Mappin Terraces, revolutionary at the time they were built, are being entirely re-developed. The zoo makes every effort to keep its charges in surroundings that are as near like their natural habitats as possible; its success in this can, perhaps, be judged from the high number of breeding successes. Although it is a fine place simply to watch creatures at close hand, the zoo also has a serious scientific function, and to this end much research work is carried out. The London and Whipsnade Zoos are supported by the most professionally complete veterinary and research services to maintain high animal management standards.

*Open: Mon-Sat 9-6 (Mar-Oct) 10-dusk in winter, Suns & BH close at 7 or dusk, whichever is earlier (Closed Xmas day).*
*Admission charge.*
*⌸ (licensed) ⏑ ♿ (ground floor & gardens only) shop ✗*

### Madame Tussaud's

Marylebone Rd, NW1
Central map: page 9, F7
☎ 01-935 6861

Founded in Paris, Madame Tussaud's Wax Exhibition settled in London in 1835. Exhibits include new versions of the tableaux and Chamber of Horrors, historical figures, HRH the Prince of Wales, kings, queens, sportsmen and other famous figures.

*Open: all year 10-5.30 (Closed Xmas day)*
*Admission charge.*
*⌸ ♿ shop ✗*

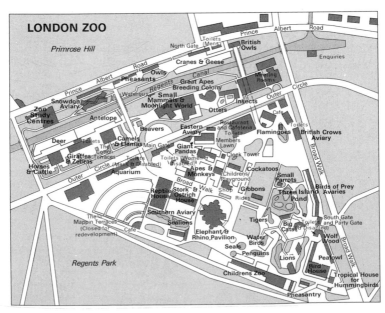

## Mall Galleries

The Mall, SW1
Central map: page 4, I5
☏ 01-930 6845

These are exhibition galleries of the Federation of British Artists, where thirteen Art Societies administered by the organisation hold their annual exhibitions.

*Open: all year, daily 10-5.*
*Admission charge (gallery friends free).* ♿

## Mansion House

EC4
Central map: page 12, M6
☏ 01-626 2500 ext.324

This Palladian building, designed in 1739-53 by George Dance the Elder, is the official residence of the Lord Mayor of London. The principal rooms are the Egyptian Hall, or dining room, and the Salon, which contains 19th-century tapestries and an enormous Waterford glass chandelier.

*Open: Tours Tue, Wed & Thu 11 & 2. For tickets apply to: Diary Secretary to the Lord Mayor. Tours last 1 hour.*
*Admission free.*
✘

## Marble Hill House

Marble Hill Park, Richmond Rd, Twickenham
District map: page 168, 30 B2
☏ 01-892 5115

An example of English Palladian architecture standing in a wooded park near the River Thames, Marble Hill House was built in 1724-9 for Henrietta Howard, mistress of George II and later Countess of Suffolk. It contains Georgian paintings and furniture, and there are Italian paintings in the Great Room by G P Panini.

*Open: Mon-Thu, Sat & Sun 10-5 (4pm Nov-Jan). (Closed 24 & 25 Dec).*
*Admission free.*
   ⊞ *(Apr-Sep)* ♿ *(ground floor & gardens only) shop* ✘

## Museum of Artillery in the Rotunda

Repository Rd, SE18
District map: page 169, 31 F3
☏ 01-856 5533 ext 385

At one time this singular circular structure, which was designed by John Nash, stood in St James's Park. Today it contains a varied collection of artillery.

*Open: all year, Apr-Oct Mon-Fri 12-5, Sat & Sun 1-5, Nov-Mar, Mon-Fri 12-4 Sat & Sun 1-4 (Closed Good Fri, 24-26 Dec & 1 Jan).*
*Admission free.*
⊓ ♿ *(ground floor only) shop*

## Museum of London

London Wall, EC2
Central map: page 12, L7
☏ 01-600 3699 ext 240

This museum is devoted entirely to London and its people, presenting by way of exhibitions and tableaux the story of its development and life. Open-plan and arranged in chronological order, the museum affords a continuous view from prehistoric times to the 20th century. The exhibits include an audio-visual reconstruction of the Great Fire of 1666, an 18th-century prison cell, a

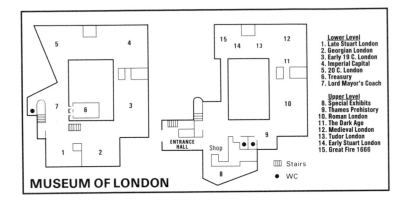

**MUSEUM OF LONDON**

Lower Level
1. Late Stuart London
2. Georgian London
3. Early 19 C. London
4. Imperial Capital
5. 20 C. London
6. Treasury
7. Lord Mayor's Coach

Upper Level
8. Special Exhibits
9. Thames Prehistory
10. Roman London
11. The Dark Age
12. Medieval London
13. Tudor London
14. Early Stuart London
15. Great Fire 1666

▥ Stairs
● WC

music hall, a barber's shop from Islington, sculptures from the Temple of Mithras, a 1930 Ford, Selfridge's lift, a medieval hen's egg and a Roman bikini.

*Open: Tue-Sat 10-6, Sun 2-6 (Closed BH & Xmas).*
*Parties by arrangement.*
*Admission free.*
  *⌖ (licensed) ♿ shop ✖*

### Museum of Mankind

6 Burlington Gdns, W1
Central map: page 10, H6
☎ 01-437 2224 ext.43

Housed here are the exhibitions, library and offices of the ethnography department of the British Museum. Its collections embrace the art and material culture of tribal village and other pre-industrial societies from most areas of the world excluding Western Europe. There are also archaeological collections from the Americas and Africa. A few important pieces are on permanent exhibition, but the museum's policy is to mount a number of temporary exhibitions usually lasting for at least a year. These are always fascinating. A separate store in Shoreditch contains the reserve collection which can be made available for serious study by arrangement. Film shows and educational services are also available.

*Open: all year Mon-Sat 10-5, Sun 2.30-6. (Closed Good Fri, May Day, 24-27 Dec & 1 Jan).*
*Admission free.*
*Shop ✖ (ex guide dogs)*

### Museum of the Order of St John

St John's Gate, St John's Lane, EC1
Central map: page 11, K8
☎ 01-253 6644 ext 35

This museum is housed in a 16th-century gatehouse, the former entrance to the medieval Priory of the Order of St John of Jerusalem. It is now the headquarters of the modern order, whose charitable foundations include St John's Ambulance and the Ophthalmic hospital in Jerusalem. Also to be seen are the Norman crypt and 15th-century Grand Priory Church. The exhibits include paintings, silver, furniture and historical medical instruments, certificates, textbooks and memorabilia of notable early St John personalities and pioneers. Special features are St John's role in the development of medical transport and its service in the Boer and two World Wars.

*Open: all year, Tue & Fri 10-6, Sat 10-4. Guided tours Sat 11 & 2.30. (Closed: Etr, Xmas wk & BH).*
*Admission free (Donations).*
*♿ (ground floor only) shop ✖*

### Musical Museum

368 High St, Brentford (7mW of London off A315)
District map: page 168, 32 B3
☎ 01-560 8108

A unique collection of working musical instruments from small musical boxes to huge orchestrations. Instruments are played during tours, which last an hour, when silence must be maintained. Evening concert is fortnightly.

*Open: Apr-Oct, Sat & Sun 2-5 (1½ hr tour).*
*Admission charge.*
⌂ shop ✂

## National Army Museum

Royal Hospital Road, SW3
Central map: page 3, F2
☏ 01-730 0717

A permanent chronological display of the history of the British, Indian and Colonial forces from 1485 is contained here. Among the exhibits are uniforms, weapons, prints, photographs, manuscripts, letters, glass, china, silver and relics of British commanders and mementoes of Britain's soldiers. There is a special display of the orders and decorations of the Duke of Windsor and also those of five great field marshals — Lords Roberts, Gough, Kitchener and Wolseley and Sir George White VC. The picture gallery includes portraits by Beechy, Romney and Lawrence, battle scenes and pictures of Indian regiments. The reading room, with its thousands of books and archives, is open Tue-Sat 10-4.30 to holders of readers' tickets, obtainable by written application to the Director.

*Open: all year Mon-Sat 10-5.30, Sun 2-5.30. (Closed: Good Fri, May Day, 24-26 Dec & 1 Jan).*
*Lectures etc for school parties.*
*Admission free.*
ᛔ shop ✂

## National Gallery

Trafalgar Sq, WC2
Central map: page 10, I6
☏ 01-839 3321 & recorded information 01-839 3526

Founded by vote of Parliament in 1824, but first opened in the present building in 1838, the gallery houses the national collection of masterpieces of European painting from the 13th to 19th century. Among the outstanding works here are van Eyck's *Arnolfini Marriage*, Velazquez's *The Toilet of Venus*, Leonardo da Vinci's cartoon *The Virgin and the Child with SS Anne and John the Baptist*, Rembrandt's *Belzhazzar's Feast*, Titian's *Bacchus and Ariadne*, and many more. British works are also shown here, although the national collection of these is in the Tate Gallery. Not to be missed in the British collections are Constable's *Haywain* and Gainsborough's *Mr and Mrs Andrews*. Among the earlier works is the *Wilton Diptych*, dating from the 14th century and showing Richard II being presented to the Madonna. Lunchtime lectures and guided tours daily; quizzes and worksheets are available for children. Constantly changing programme of exhibitions, usually highlighting certain aspects of the collection. The view from the gallery's portico gives a splendid vista over Trafalgar Square.

*Open: daily Mon-Sat 10-6, Sun 2-6 (Closed Good Fri, May Day, 24-26 Dec & 1 Jan).*
*Admission free.*
⌸ (licensed) ᛔ shop ✂

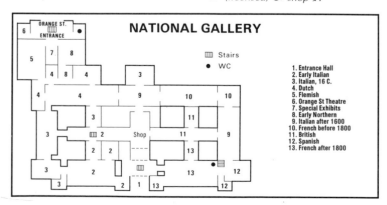

**NATIONAL GALLERY**

▥ Stairs
● WC

1. Entrance Hall
2. Early Italian
3. Italian, 16 C.
4. Dutch
5. Flemish
6. Orange St Theatre
7. Special Exhibits
8. Early Northern
9. Italian after 1600
10. French before 1800
11. British
12. Spanish
13. French after 1800

## National Maritime Museum

Romney Rd, SE10
District map: page 169, 33 E3
☎ 01-858 4422 (Information Desk ext 221)

Part of this collection is housed in the 17th-century Queen's House, which was designed by Inigo Jones. The collection illustrates man's relationship with the sea, and exhibits include some of the finest seascapes ever painted. There are also galleries devoted to Lord Nelson and Captain Cook.

*Open: all year daily Mon-Fri 10-5 (6pm summer), Sat 10-5.30 (6 in summer), Sun 2-5.30 in winter (Closed Good Fri, May Day, 24-26 Dec & 1 Jan).*
*Admission charge.*
*⌨ (licensed) ᐃ (ground floor only) shop ✗ (ex guide dogs).*

## National Museum of Labour History

Limehouse Town Hall, Commercial Rd, E14
District map: page 169, 34 E3
☎ 01-515 3229

The prime concern of this large and rare collection is to portray the development of democracy over the last 200 years. The visual history from the late 18th century to 1945 is portrayed in two sections, from autocracy to democracy and the turn to socialism 1881 to 1945.

*Open: Tue-Sat 9.30-5, Sun 2.30-5.30.*
*Admission free.*
*Shop ✗*

## National Portrait Gallery

2 St Martin's Place, WC2
Central map, page 10, I6
☎ 01-930 1552

This gallery contains the national collection of portraits of the famous and infamous in British history, including paintings, sculptures, miniatures, engravings, photographs, and cartoons. The works are arranged more-or-less in chronological order, and are accompanied by furniture, maps, weapons and other items to set them in their historical context. Beginning in medieval times, they range in quality from masterpieces to works of a mundane nature. Special exhibitions several times a year.

*Open: all year Mon-Fri 10-5, Sat 10-6, Sun 2-6. (Closed: Good Fri, May Day, 24-26 Dec & 1 Jan.)*
*Admission free (charges for special exhibitions).*
*Shop ✗*

## National Postal Museum

King Edward Building, King Edward St, EC1
Central map: page 12, L7
☎ 01-606 3769 & 01-432 3851

What is probably the finest and most comprehensive collection of postage stamps in the world is contained here. Included are the RM Phillips collection of 19th-century Great Britain (with special emphasis on the One Penny Black and its creation); the Post Office Collection; a world-wide collection including practically every stamp issued since 1878; and the philatelic correspondence archives of Thomas de la Rue and Co, who furnished stamps to over 150 countries between 1855 and 1965. Within these collections are thousands of original drawings and unique proof sheets of every British stamp since 1840. Special exhibitions; visits for up to 40 people may be arranged with a guide and film show.

*Open: Mon-Thu (ex BH) 10-4.30, Fri 10-4.*
*Admission free.*
*ᐃ (ground floor only) shop ✗*

## Natural History Museum

Cromwell Road, SW7
Central map: page 2, D4
☎ 01-589 6323.

Some of London's great museums are regarded with affection by the British people, and the Natural History museum is certainly one of these. Its exhibits, which include the famous dinosaurs, are housed in a vast and elegant Victorian building. In the Hall of Human Biology visitors can

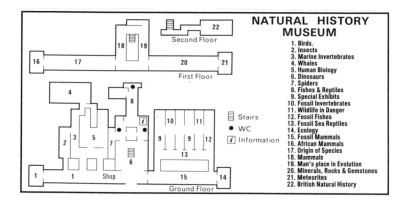

**NATURAL HISTORY MUSEUM**

1. Birds.
2. Insects
3. Marine Invertebrates
4. Whales
5. Human Biology
6. Dinosaurs
7. Spiders
8. Fishes & Reptiles
9. Special Exhibits
10. Fossil Invertebrates
11. Wildlife in Danger
12. Fossil Fishes
13. Fossil Sea Reptiles
14. Ecology
15. Fossil Mammals
16. African Mammals
17. Origin of Species
18. Mammals
19. Man's place in Evolution
20. Minerals, Rocks & Gemstones
21. Meteorites
22. British Natural History

learn more about the way their bodies work, while 'British Natural History' shows over 2,000 native plants and animals. The exhibition 'Whales and their Relatives' explores the life of sea mammals. Other permanent exhibitions include 'Man's Place in Evolution', 'Origin of Species', 'Dinosaurs and their Living Relatives' and 'Introducing Ecology'. In other parts of the Museum there are many traditional displays of living and fossil plants and animals, minerals, rocks and meteorites from the national collections. Exhibits of special interest include a life-size model of a blue whale, the Cranbourne meteorite, a specimen of a coelacanth (a fish known as a living fossil) and the British bird pavilion where visitors can hear recordings of many different bird songs.

As the museum is currently reorganising its public displays, some of the galleries may be temporarily closed. There are public films and lectures on Tue, Thu and Sat. Leaflet available on request.

*Open: daily, Mon-Sat 10-6, Sun 2.30-6. (Closed: Good Fri, May Day, Xmas, New Year's day.)*
*Admission charge as from April 1987.*
*🖃 ⟨ (ex British Natural History Exhibition) shop ✖*

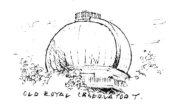
OLD ROYAL OBSERVATORY

## North Woolwich Old Station Museum

Pier Road, E16
District map: page 169, 35 F3
☎ 01-474 7244

This is an imposing restored station building with three galleries of photographs, models, and an original turntable pit. Each Sunday a locomotive is in steam.

*Open: Mon-Sat 10-5, Sun & BH 2-5. (Closed: Xmas.)*
*Admission free.*

## Old Royal Observatory

Greenwich Park, SE10
District map: page 169, 36 E3
☎ 01-858 1167

Set in Greenwich Park (see page 145), which was laid out to plans by Le Nôtre, famous French gardener of the time of Louis XIV, the Observatory is part of the National Maritime Museum. There are exhibits of astronomical, horological and navigational interest.

*Open: all year daily Mon-Fri 10-5 (6pm summer), Sat 10-5.30 (6 in summer), Sun 2-5.30 (5 in winter). (Closed Good Fri, May Day, 24-26 Dec & 1 Jan.)*
*Admission charge.*
*Planetarium gives shows during school holidays, Tue, Thu, Fri 2.30 & 3.30; special programmes on Sat in summer (Information from Schools Liaison Officer 01-858 4422).*
*⟨ (ground floor only) shop ✖ (ex guide dogs)*

### Old St Thomas's Operating Theatre

The Chapter House, St Thomas's St, SE1
Central map: page 6, M5
☎ 01-407 7600 Ext 2739

This is the only early 19th-century operating theatre to survive in England. The exhibits tell the history of surgery during the 19th century at Guy's and St Thomas's Hospitals.

*Open: Mon, Wed, Fri 12.30-4 (Tue & Thu by appointment only) (Closed BHs mid Dec-end Jan & two weeks in August).*
*Admission charge.*

### Orleans House Gallery

Riverside, Twickenham
District map: page 168, 37 B2
☎ 01-892 0221

The original Orleans House, in which Louis Phillippe, Duc d'Orléans, King of the French 1830-48, lived in exile in the early 19th century was demolished in 1927. All that survives is the octagonal room, designed by James Gibbs in c1720. It has exquisite plasterwork.

*Open: Tue-Sat 1-5.30 (4.30pm Oct-Mar) Sun & BH 2-5.30 (Oct-Mar 2-4.30). (Closed 25-26 Dec and Good Fri). Woodland gardens open all year, daily 9-dusk.*
*Admission free.*
*&. (ground floor only)* ✗

### Osterley Park House

Osterley (off A4, Great West Rd)
District map: page 168, 38 B3
☎ 01-560 3918

An Elizabethan mansion transformed into an 18th-century villa, this elegant building has neoclassical interior decoration designed by Robert Adam. (Osterley Park, see page 154).

*House: open all year daily ex Mon 11-5. (Closed Good Fri, May Day, 24-26 Dec & 1 Jan).*
*Admission charge.*
*⌨ &. (gardens only)* ✗ *NT & V & A Museum*

### Passmore Edwards Museum

Romford Road, E15
District map: page 169, 39 F4
☎ 01-519 4296

Greater London and Essex archaeology, biology, geology and history are illustrated here by a series of displays and exhibits.

*Open: Mon-Wed & Fri 10-6, Thu 10-6, Sat 10-1 & 2-5, Sun & BH 2-5.*
*Admission free.*
*&. (ground floor only) shop* ✗

### Percival David Foundation of Chinese Art

53 Gordon Square, WC1
Central map: page 10, I8
☎ 01-387 3909

A unique collection of Chinese ceramics, dating from between the 10th and 18th centuries is housed here. It encompases the Sung, Yuan, Ming and Ch'ing dynasties. It was presented to London University by Percival David in 1951.

*Open: Mon 2-5, Tue-Fri 10.30-5, Sat 10.30-1.*
*Admission free.*

### Pollock's Toy Museum

1 Scala St, W1
Central map: page 10, H7
☎ 01-636 3452

The museum occupies two little houses joined together: the rooms are small and connected by narrow winding staircases. The collection is wide-ranging and covers items from all over the world. It includes a 19th-century toy theatre workshop, toy

theatre with performances and slide shows, dolls, optical and mechanical toys, young girl's nursery, folk toys, English tin toys and teddy bears.

*Open: Mon-Sat 10-5 (Closed Good Fri, Etr Mon, Spring BH Mon, Summer BH Mon & Xmas).*
*Admission charge.*
&#9855; *(ground floor only) shop* &#10013;

## Priory Museum

The Priory, Church Hill, Orpington
District map: page 169, 40 F1
&#9990; *(0689) 31551*

This is a 13th-to 14th-century clergy house with the addition of a 15th-century manor house. It is now a museum of local interest and special exhibitions are held during the year.

*Open: all year (ex Thu & Sun) 9-6 (5pm Sat) (Closed PH)*
*Admission free.*
&#9855; *(ground floor only)* &#10013;

## Public Record Office Museum

Chancery Lane, WC2
Central map: page 11, K7
&#9990; *01-405 0741*

This is the chief repository for the national archives. The Search Rooms contain records from the Norman Conquest to the present day. There is an exhibition of records illustrating major events in British history. Famous documents which can be seen include the Domesday Book, William the Conqueror's survey of 1086. Also on display are letters from Cardinal Wolsey and Guy Fawkes, and Shakespeare's will. A series of special temporary exhibitions is held.

*Open: all year Mon-Sat 10-5.*
*Admission charge.*
&#9855; *shop* &#10013;

## Queen Elizabeth's Hunting Lodge and Museum

Epping Forest, Rangers Rd, Chingford
District map: page 169, 41 F5
&#9990; *01-529 6681*

A picturesque Tudor building dating from about 1543, the lodge houses a museum relating the life of animals, birds and plants in Epping and man's association with them.

*Open: all year Wed-Sun & BH Mons, 2-6 (or dusk).*
*Admission charge.*
&#9855; *(ground floor only) shop* &#10013;

## Queens Gallery

(Buckingham Palace) Buckingham Palace Rd, SW1
Central map: page 3, G4
&#9990; *01-930 3007 ext 430 or 01-930 4832 ext 321*

Items from the Royal Collection are housed here in a building originally designed as a conservatory by John Nash in 1831, and later converted by Blore into a chapel in 1843. After suffering severe bomb damage in 1940, the building was eventually reconstructed in 1962, partly as the Private Chapel of Buckingham Palace and partly as an art gallery.

*Open: all year, Tue-Sat & BH Mon 11-5, Sun 2-5 (ex for short periods between exhibitions).*
*Admission charge.*
&#9855; *(ground floor only) shop* &#10013; *(ex guide dogs)*

## Rangers House

Chesterfield Walk, SE3
District map: page 169, 42 E3
&#9990; *01-853 0035*

The Suffolk collection of Jacobean and Stuart portraits is housed in this 18th-century villa, former home of Philip Stanhope, 4th Earl of Chesterfield. The collection contains a set of portraits by William Larkin, among the finest to survive from the Jacobean period, and a small collection of Old Masters. Three first floor rooms house the Dolmetsch collection of musical instruments on loan from the Horniman Museum. Also chamber concerts and poetry readings. Educational programme, holiday projects & workshop.

*Open: all year daily 10-5 (4pm Nov-Feb). (Closed Good Fri & 24-25 Dec).*
*Admission free.*
&#9855; *(ground floor only) shop* &#10013;

### Royal Academy of Arts

Burlington House, Piccadilly, W1
Central map: page 10, H6
☎ 01-734 9052

Founded in 1768 by George III, the Royal Academy of Arts is most famous for the summer exhibitions, from May to Aug. It shows works by living artists, and loan exhibitions of international importance are held throughout the year. Treasures of the academy include the Michelangelo Tondo.

*Open: daily 10-6 (incl Sun).*
*Admission charge.*
   ☕ *(licensed)* ♿ shop ✖

### Royal Air Force Museum

NW8. Entrance via M1, A41 (Aerodrome Rd, off Watford Way) or A5 (Colindale Av, off Edgware Rd) District map: page 169, 43 C5
☎ 01-205 2266 ext 38

The museum, on the former Hendon airfield, covers all aspects of the history of the RAF and its predecessors. Over 40 aircraft are on display, from the Bleriot XI to the 'Lightning'. Twelve galleries depict over 100 years of military aviation history. The Battle of Britain Museum has been built on a site adjacent to the main Museum. It contains British, German and Italian aircraft which were engaged in the great air battle of 1940. Also in the same complex is the vast new Bomber Command Museum which contains a striking display of famous bomber aircraft including the Lancaster, Wellington and Vulcan.

*Open: all year Mon-Sat 10-6, Sun 2-6. (Closed Good Fri, May Day, 24-26 Dec and 1 Jan).*
*RAF Museum Admission free.*
*Battle of Britain Museum and Bomber Command Museum admission charge.*
   ☕ *(licensed)* ♨ ♿ shop ✖

### Royal Mews Exhibition

Palace Barracks, Hampton
District map: page 168, 44 B2
☎ 01-943 3838

Housed in the 'Horse Guards' section of the Palace Barracks, which is believed to be the earliest surviving purpose-built barracks in the country, work having begun in 1689, the collection includes a wide variety of Royal transport. Exhibits include a fine French char-a-banc used by Queen Victoria for picnic and shooting parties. Also on display is her state sledge. Of particular interest to children are the model cars used by various members of the Royal Family when children. The original State Land Rover is also here.

*Open: daily Spring & Summer 10.30-5;wknds only Autumn & Winter.*
*Admission charge.*

### Royal Mews

Buckingham Palace, SW1
Central map: page 3, G4
☎ 01-930 4832 ext 634

Designed by John Nash and completed in 1825, the Royal Mews contain the state coaches, including the Gold State Coach made in 1762, with panels painted by the Florentine artist Cipriani. It has been used for every coronation since. The collection also includes the Irish State Coach, together with private

ROYAL MEWS

driving carriages and royal sleighs. In the stables are kept the Windsor Greys and Cleveland Bay carriage horses.

*Open: Wed & Thu 2-4 (Ex Royal Ascot week) and at other times when published.*
*Admission charge.*
&#x267F; *(ground floor only) shop* &#10007; *(ex guide dogs)*

## Royal Naval College

Greenwich, SE10
District map: page 169, 45 E3
&#9990; 01-858 2154

Its Thames-side setting gives this group of buildings an especial elegance. The original architect was Webb, in the late 17th century, with additions by Wren, Hawksmoor, Vanbrugh and Ripley in the 18th century. Originally a Naval Hospital, it became a Naval College in 1873. The Chapel was rebuilt in the 18th century, and the Painted Hall has a famous ceiling painted by Sir James Thornhill.

*Open: all year (Painted Hall and Chapel only) daily (ex Thu) 2.30-5 (last admission 4.45pm) (Closed Xmas day).*
*Admission free.*
*Shop* &#10007;

## St Brides Crypt Museum

Fleet Street, EC4
Central map: page 11, K6
&#9990; 01-353 1301

Internationally known as the 'parish church of the press', St Brides has been the site of seven previous churches, the existing structure having been meticulously restored to Wren's original design. The traditional three-tiered wedding cake of today is a replica of the steeple, and was first copied by a local baker in the 18th century. A wealth of history and relics can be seen on permanent display in the crypt museum.

*Open: Mon-Sat 9-5; Sun 9-8.*
*Admission free.*

## Schooner Kathleen & May

St Mary Overy Dock,
Cathedral Street, (off Clink Street)
Central map: page 12, L6
&#9990; 01-403 3965

The last British, wooden, three-masted topsail schooner, now on show to the public in a new berth at St Mary Overy Dock, on the south bank of the River Thames. Exhibitions are on board with audio visuals and films.

*Open: daily 10-5 (Nov-Mar 11-4). (Closed: Xmas & New Year.)*
*Admission charge.*
*Shop* &#10007;

## Science Museum

Exhibition Road, SW7
Central map: page 2, D4
&#9990; 01-589 3456 ext 632

The Science Museum has something for everyone. Among the extensive collection are aero-engines; agriculture; astronomy; atomic and nuclear physics; rail; road; sea and

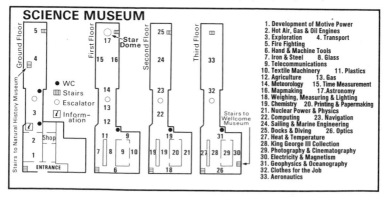

**SCIENCE MUSEUM**

1. Development of Motive Power
2. Hot Air, Gas & Oil Engines
3. Exploration    4. Transport
5. Fire Fighting
6. Hand & Machine Tools
7. Iron & Steel    8. Glass
9. Telecommunications
10. Textile Machinery    11. Plastics
12. Agriculture    13. Gas
14. Meteorology    15. Time Measurement
16. Mapmaking    17. Astronomy
18. Weighing, Measuring & Lighting
19. Chemistry    20. Printing & Papermaking
21. Nuclear Power & Physics
22. Computing    23. Navigation
24. Sailing & Marine Engineering
25. Docks & Diving    26. Optics
27. Heat & Temperature
28. King George III Collection
29. Photography & Cinematography
30. Electricity & Magnetism
31. Geophysics & Oceanography
32. Clothes for the Job
33. Aeronautics

air transport; civil, electrical, marine and mechanical engineering; telecommunications, domestic appliances, 'Gas Industry' gallery, etc. There are two galleries with items from the Wellcome Collection of the History of Medicine, galleries on Printing, Paper making and Lighting. Popular with children is 'Launch Pad', which provides an introduction to scientific ideas through the medium of exciting 'hands-on' exhibits. Exhibition on space technology now open together with a new gallery on Plastics.

*Open: all year, 10-6, Sun 2.30-6. (Closed Good Fri, May Day, 24-26 Dec & 1 Jan). Admission free.*
      ⬚ & shop ✗

## South London Art Gallery

Peckham Rd, SE5
District map: page 169, 46 E3
☎ 01-703 6120

The Gallery presents ten exhibitions a year. Exhibits include Victorian paintings and drawings, a small collection of contemporary British art and 20th-century original prints. A collection of topographical paintings and drawings of local subjects can also be seen.

*Open: only when exhibitions are in progress, Tue-Sat 10-6, Sun 3-6 (Closed Mon). Admission free. Shop ✗*

## Stock Exchange

Throgmorton St, EC2
Central map: page 12, M7
☎ 01-588 2355

This is one of the world's centres of industrial finance, where stocks and shares in individual companies are bought and sold. The trading floor may be viewed from the gallery and guides are present to describe the scene. A colour film may be seen by prior arrangement.

*Open: Mon-Fri 9.45-3.15 last guided tour 2.30. (Closed PHs). Parties must book in advance. Admission free.*
      & shop ✗

## Syon House

Isleworth, approach via Park Rd off Twickenham Rd
District map: page 168, 47 B3
☎ 01-560 0881
*(during opening hours only)*

Syon House was founded in 1415 as a monastery and remodelled in the 18th century with splendid interiors by Robert Adam, in particular the superbly coloured ante-room and the gallery library. Fine portraits and furniture are housed here. Capability Brown designed the grounds (see page 154). House overlooks River Thames. British Craft Show in Sep.

*Open: 1 Apr-29 Sep, Sun-Thu 12-5 (Closed Fri & Sat). Last tickets 4.15. Open Suns only during Oct 12-5. Admission charge.*
      ⬚ & (gardens only) shop & garden centre ✗

## Heritage Motor Museum (Syon Park)

☎ 01-560 1378

Also on display in Syon Park (see page 154) is a collection of more than 90 vehicles covering the history of much of the British motor industry. Special displays during summer.

*Open: daily 10-5.30 (4pm Nov-Mar). (Closed Xmas). Admission charge.*
      ⬚ (within 100 yds) & shop ✗

## Tate Gallery

Millbank, SW1
Central map: page 4, I3
☎ 01-821 1313 & Recorded Information 01-821 7128.

Opened in 1897, the Tate houses the national collections of British painting of all periods, modern foreign painting and modern sculpture. There is also a large collection of contemporary prints. The British works are arranged mainly in chronological order; they begin with *Man in a Black Cap*, which was painted by John Bettes in 1545. Thereafter the development of British painting up until 1920 is

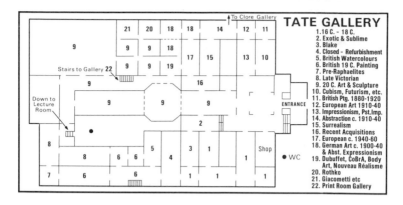

**TATE GALLERY**

1. 16 C. – 18 C.
2. Exotic & Sublime
3. Blake
4. Closed – Refurbishment
5. British Watercolours
6. British 19 C. Painting
7. Pre-Raphaelites
8. Late Victorian
9. 20 C. Art & Sculpture
10. Cubism, Futurism, etc.
11. British Ptg. 1880-1920
12. European Art 1910-40
13. Impressionism, Pst.Imp.
14. Abstraction c. 1910-40
15. Surrealism
16. Recent Acquisitions
17. European c. 1940-60
18. German Art c. 1900-40 & Abst. Expressionism
19. Dubuffet, CoBrA, Body Art, Nouveau Réalisme
20. Rothko
21. Giacometti etc
22. Print Room Gallery

followed. Hogarth, Blake, Turner, Constable and the Pre-Raphaelites are particularly well represented, and the English mastery of landscape painting is superbly illustrated. All schools of painting and sculpture from Impressionism onwards are represented in the modern and foreign collections. They include paintings by Cezanne, Matisse, Picasso, Braque, Chagall, and Paul Klee. There are also abstract paintings by such artists as Mondrian, Jackson Pollock, and Frank Stella. Sculpture by Henry Moore, Barbara Hepworth, and Alberto Giacometti, among others, is displayed, and there is a collection of kinetic and optical art. The Tate buys works almost before they are finished, and is therefore able to reflect the constantly changing emphasis of contemporary art.

*Open: all year Mon-Sat 10-5.50, Sun 2-5.50. (Closed: Good Fri, May Day, 24-26 Dec & 1 Jan.)*
*Admission free (Special exhibitions admission charge.) Free lectures, films and guided tours most days.*
*⌂ (licensed) 12-3 (closed Sun) ⌂ (coffee shop) ⌖ shop ✷ (ex guide dogs)*

### Telecom Technology Showcase

135 Queen Victoria St, EC4
Central map: page 12, L6
☎ 01-248 7444.

Two display floors here feature the past, present and future of Britain's telecommunications. There are many working exhibits charting 200 years of progress from the earliest

telegraphs, to satellites and optical fibres.

*Open: Mon-Fri 10.00-5.00. (Closed: BH.)*
*Admission free.*
*⌖ shop ✷ (ex guide dogs).*

### Thames Barrier Centre

Unity Way, SE18
District map: page 169, 48 F3
☎ 01-854 1373

Justifiably described as the 'Eighth Wonder of the World', the ⅓ mile span barrier built to save London from disastrous flooding is the World's largest movable flood barrier representing an extraordinary feat of British engineering. The nearby exhibition building has displays and an audio-visual programme explaining the flood threat and the construction of the £480 million project. Barrier gates raised for testing monthly.

*Open: daily 10.30-5 (6pm Apr-Sep). (Closed Xmas & New Year's Day).*
*Admission free.*
*⌂ (licensed) ⛱ ⌖ (ex riverside) shop ✷ (ex guide dogs)*

STOCK EXCHANGE

### Thamesworld

53-55 Greenwich Church St
Greenwich, SE10
District map: page 169, 49 E3
☎ 01-858 1198

Many kinds of audio-visual
techniques are employed here in
order to re-create the River Thames
in history, as it is today, and as it
might be in the future.

*Open: all year, daily 10-6 (Closed:
25-26 Dec.)*
*Admission charge.*
&#9855; &#9993; ✗ *Shop*

### The Monument

Monument St, EC3
Central map: page 12, M6
☎ 01-626 2717

The Monument was erected by Sir
Christopher Wren and Robert Hooke
1671-77 to commemorate the Great
Fire of 1666. Its height of 202ft is
said to equal the distance from its
base to the place in Pudding Lane
where the fire started on 2nd
September, destroying nearly 90
churches and around 13,000 houses.
From the railed-in summit, a climb of
311 steps, there are extensive views.

*Open: Apr-Sep, Mon-Fri 9-6, Sat &
Sun 2-6; Oct-Mar, Mon-Sat 9-2 & 3-4
Admission charge.* ✗

### The Sir John Soane's Museum

13 Lincoln's Inn Fields, WC2
Central map: page 11, J7
☎ 01-405 2107

The house of Sir John Soane
(1753-1837), the architect, built in
1812 and containing his collections
of antiquities, sculpture, paintings,
drawings, and books, including the
Sarcophagus of Seti (1292 BC), The
Rake's Progress and the Election
series of paintings by William
Hogarth. Architectural Drawings
Collection open by appointment. The
house itself is designed to show off
these objects in surprising and
unexpected ways.

*Open: all year (ex BH) Tue-Sat 10-5.
Admission free.*
&#9855; *(ground floor only)* ✗

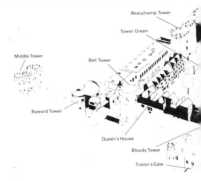

### The Thomas Coram Foundation
### for Children

40 Brunswick Square, WC1
Central map: page 10, I8
☎ 01-278 2424

The Foundation was formed in 1739
with the granting of a royal charter
to Captain Thomas Coram to open a
Foundling Hospital for destitute
children. At the instigation of
William Hogarth various works of art
were presented to the Foundation for
display in the Court Room to attract
the public and raise funds. The
present building, which was built in
1937 on the site of the old one,
houses the vast number of exhibits
which have been presented to the
Foundation over the years. Of
particular interest is the portrait of
Coram, by Hogarth, which was the
first gift.

*Open: all year, Mon-Fri 10-4
(advisable to check) (Closed BH)
Admission charge.*

### Tithe Barn Agricultural & Folk
### Museum

Hall Lane, Upminster
District map: page 169, 50 F4
☎ *Hornchurch (04024) 47535.*

This 15th-century thatched timber
building contains a large selection of
old agricultural implements, craft and
farm tools, domestic bygones and
items of local interest. In all, there
are over 2000 exhibits.

*Open: 1.30-6 on 5 & 6 Apr; 3 & 4
May; 7 & 8 Jun; 5 & 6 Jul; 2 & 3
Aug; 6 & 7 Sep; 4 & 5 Oct.
Admission free.*
&#9855; *shop* ✗

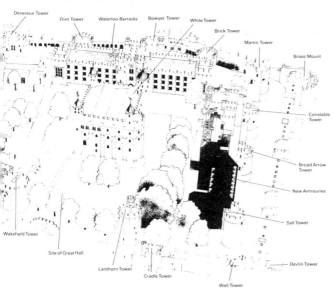

Devereux Tower · Flint Tower · Waterloo Barracks · Bowyer Tower · White Tower · Brick Tower · Martin Tower · Brass Mount · Constable Tower · Broad Arrow Tower · New Armouries · Salt Tower · Devlin Tower · Well Tower · Cradle Tower · Lanthorn Tower · Site of Great Hall · Wakefield Tower

## Tower Bridge Walkway

Tower Bridge, SE1
Central map: page 6, N5
☎ 01-407 0922

The glass-covered walkway, 142ft above the Thames, gives visitors panoramic views over London. Exhibitions illustrating the history and workings of the bridge are in both Towers. The original engine rooms may be seen on the South side of the bridge.

*Open: Apr-Oct 10-6.30; Nov-Mar 10-4.45 (last tickets sold 45 minutes before closing time). (Closed Good Fri, Xmas, New Year's day). Admission charge.*
& shop ✗

## Tower of London

EC3
Central map: page 12, N6
☎ 01-709 0765

Begun by William the Conqueror in the 11th century in the south-east angle of the wall of Roman Londinium, this is one of the world's most famous fortresses. It soon became the symbol of ultimate power, the place where even the highest and mightiest in the land could be cast down. According to tradition, 1078 marks the start of the building of the original tower (now known as the White Tower). The stronghold was enlarged in later years. Other places of particular

interest are the Bloody Tower (15th century), in which the little princes are said to have been smothered in 1483; St Peter Vincula's Chapel Royal in which Anne Boleyn, Lady Jane Grey and the Duke of Monmouth are buried; the Norman St John's Chapel, the oldest in London; and Traitors' Gate, the old water-gate. Adjoining the Beauchamp Tower, near which was the site of the scaffold, is the Yeoman Gaoler's House in which Lady Jane Grey and latterly Rudolf Hess were imprisoned. The White Tower now contains the **Royal Armouries**. These consist of the national collection of arms and armour based on the great arsenal of Henry VIII. Four of Henry VIII's personal armours may be seen. There are also displays of tournament and sporting arms, arms and armour from the Middle Ages to the 17th century and oriental armour. The crown jewels are displayed in the Jewel Tower, and also to be seen is the **Royal Fusiliers Museum**, containing uniforms, including those worn by George V as colonel-in-chief, regimental silver and china, four dioramas of famous battles, and campaign medals, among them 10 Victoria Crosses, including the prototype approved by Queen Victoria.

*Open: Mar-Oct, Mon-Sat 9.30-5, Sun 2-5; Nov-Feb, Mon-Sat 9.30-4 (Closed 1 Jan, Good Fri & 24-26 Dec. Jewel House closed Feb). Admission charge. Shop (Dept. of Environment)*

### Tradescant Trust Museum of Garden History

St Mary-at-Lambeth, Lambeth Palace Rd, SE1
Central map: page 5, J4
Enquiries to: The Tradescant Trust, 74 Coleherne Court, London SW5 0EF
☎ 01-373 4030

An historic building and newly-made period knot garden containing 17th-century plants. Nearby stand the tombs of the John Tradescants (father & son) and Captain Bligh of the 'Bounty'. Temporary exhibitions.

*Open: Mon-Fri, 11-3; Sun 10.30-5. (Closed from 2nd Sun in Dec to 1st Sun in Mar).*
*Admission free.*
  ✑ & (ground floor & gardens only) shop

### Vestry House Museum of Local History

Vestry Rd, near Hoe St, E17
District map: page 169, 51 E5
☎ 01-527 5544 ext 4391

A small museum located in a former 18th-century workhouse standing in the conservation area 'Walthamstow Village'. Historical items of local interest from the Stone Age onwards include a reconstructed Victorian parlour. The Bremer Car, probably the first British internal combustion engine car, can be seen.

*Open: Mon-Fri 10-5.30, Sat 10-5 (Closed BH).*
*Admission free.*
& (ground floor only) shop ✖

### Victoria and Albert Museum

Cromwell Rd, SW7
Central map: page 2, E4
☎ 01-589 6371 ext 372. *Recorded information service 01-581 4894*

Queen Victoria laid the foundation stone for the present building in 1899 and the building, designed by Sir Aston Webb, was opened in 1909 by Edward VII. In it were placed the art treasures from the South Kensington Museum, which had been built under the direction of Prince Albert from money derived from the Great Exhibition of 1851. It now contains one of the world's outstanding collections of fine and applied arts. In the primary British galleries there is a series of rooms decorated and equipped with the paintings, furniture and household accessories of particular periods. Amongst the exhibits on display are the enormous 16th-century *Great Bed of Ware*, an exquisite portrait miniature by Nicholas Hilliard called *Young Man leaning against a Tree*, and furniture by Chippendale. There are also primary galleries devoted to Continental arts and crafts, medieval gothic and renaissance art, Oriental art, and Islamic arts and crafts.
The subject galleries on the ground floor take in English and Continental sculpture, architecture, and costumes. The costumes, mostly English and dating from the 16th to 20th centuries, are displayed in the *Octagon Court*.
On the first floor are subject galleries covering ironwork, textiles, prints and drawings, and paintings. John

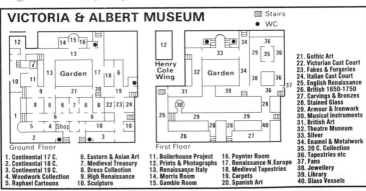

**VICTORIA & ALBERT MUSEUM**     ▥ Stairs  ● WC

Ground Floor

First Floor

1. Continental 17 C.
2. Continental 18 C.
3. Continental 19 C.
4. Woodwork Collection
5. Raphael Cartoons
6. Eastern & Asian Art
7. Medieval Treasury
8. Dress Collection
9. High Renaissance
10. Sculpture
11. Boilerhouse Project
12. Prints & Photographs
13. Renaissance Italy
14. Morris Room
15. Gamble Room
16. Poynter Room
17. Renaissance N.Europe
18. Medieval Tapestries
19. Carpets
20. Spanish Art
21. Gothic Art
22. Victorian Cast Court
23. Fakes & Forgeries
24. Italian Cast Court
25. English Renaissance
26. British 1650-1750
27. Carvings & Bronzes
28. Stained Glass
29. Armour & Ironwork
30. Musical Instruments
31. British Art
32. Theatre Museum
33. Silver
34. Enamel & Metalwork
35. 20 C. Collection
36. Tapestries etc
37. Fans
38. Jewellery
39. Library
40. Glass Vessels

Constable's brilliant evocations of the English landscape are the outstanding works of the painting galleries.

*Open: all year 10-5.50, Sun 2.30-5.50. (Closed Good Fri, May Day, 24-26 Dec & 1 Jan).*
*Admission free (donations).*
*▱ (licensed) & shop ✗*

## Wallace Collection

Hertford House, Manchester Sq, W1
Central map: page 9, F7
☎ 01-935 0687

An outstanding collection of works of art bequeathed to the nation by Lady Wallace in 1897, displayed in the house of its founders. Includes pictures by Titian, Rubens, Gainsborough and Delacroix together with an unrivalled representation of 18th-century French art including paintings, especially by Watteau, Boucher and Fragonard, sculpture, furniture, goldsmiths' work and Sèvres porcelain. Also valuable collections of majolica, European and oriental arms and armour.

*Open: all year Mon-Sat 10-5, Sun 2-5. (Closed Good Fri, May Day, 24-26 Dec & 1 Jan).*
*Admission free.*
*& shop ✗*

## Wellington Museum

Apsley House, 149 Piccadilly, W1
Central map: page 3, F5
☎ 01-499 5676

Apsley House was designed by Robert Adam, built 1771-8 and extended by Benjamin Wyatt in 1828-1830, under the direction of the Duke of Wellington who purchased it in 1817. It was presented to the nation by the 7th Duke of Wellington in 1947, and opened to the public in 1952. Exhibits include famous paintings, silver, porcelain, orders and decorations and personal relics of the first duke (1769-1852); also Canova's great marble figure of Napoleon.

*Open: all year 10-6, Sun 2.30-6. (Closed Mon, Fri, May Day, 24-26 Dec & 1 Jan).*
*Admission charge.*
*& ✗*

## Wembley Stadium

Wembley
District map: page 168, 52 B4
☎ 01-903 4864

Britain's number one stadium, built in 1923 it holds 100,000. It is the home of the English football team — venue for annual Cup Final and World events. Tour comprises 15-minute audio-visual show, visit to dressing rooms, Royal Box and retiring rooms, a walk up the Player's tunnel to pitch complete with sound effects. (Wembley Complex, see page 68)

*Tours on the hour 10-3, 4 in summer (ex 1pm).*
*(Closed Xmas, New Year's day, Thu & days before, during and after a major event).*
*Admission charge.*
*& (by prior booking) shop ✗*

## Wesley's House & Museum

47 City Rd, EC1
Central map: page 12, M8
☎ 01-253 2262

This house in which John Wesley lived and died is now a museum, containing a large collection of his personal possessions, etc. Also here is **Wesley's Chapel** built 1778, completely restored 1978. A new Museum of Methodism has been added.

*Museum open: Mon-Sat 10-4 and by arrangement. Chapel open daily.*
*Main service 11am Sun followed by lunch & tour of chapel and museum.*
*Admission charge.*
*& (ground floor only) shop ✗ (ex guide dogs)*

DUKE OF WELLINGTON

## Whitechapel Art Gallery

Whitechapel High Street, E1
Central map: page 12, N7
☎ 01-377 0107

Opened to contribute to the cultural life of the East End, this gallery has achieved widespread fame for the excellence of its temporary exhibitions. The building has an ornate *art nouveau* façade.

*Open: all year, Tue-Sun 11-5, Wed 11-8. (Closed 25, 26 Dec)*
*Admission free (ex special exhibitions).*
  ✏ *shop*

## William Morris Gallery

Water House, Lloyd Park, Forest Rd, E17
District map: page 169, 53 E5
☎ 01-527 5544 ext 4390

William Morris lived in this house, known as 'Water House', from 1848-56. There are exhibits of his fabrics, wallpapers and furniture. Also ceramics by William de Morgan, furniture by Gimson and Barnsley and work by Mackmurdo and the Century Guild. Pre-Raphaelite pictures, sculpture by Rodin.

*Open: Tue-Sat 10-1 & 2-5, and 1st Sun in each month 10-12 & 2-5 (Closed Mon & PHs)*
*Admission free.*
♿ *(ground floor and gardens) shop*
🐕

## Wimbledon Lawn Tennis Museum

Church Rd, SW19
District map: page 168, 54 C2
☎ 01-946 6131

This museum, within the grounds of The All England Lawn Tennis and Croquet Club, is the only one of its kind in the world and shows something of the games which preceded and helped in the conception of lawn tennis. Traces the development of the game over the last century. Also includes Library, the archives of which comprise collections, postcards, autographs and other ephemera. Audio visual theatre.

*Open: all year Tue-Sat 11-5, Sun 2-5. (Closed Mon & BHs).*
*Admission charge.*
*Shop* 🐕

## Wimbledon Windmill Museum

Windmill Rd, SW19
District map: page 168, 55 C2
☎ 01-788 7655

Built in 1817, this windmill houses a museum which displays the history of windmilling in pictures and models and the machinery and tools of the trade.

*Open: Etr-Oct, Sat, Sun & BHs.*
*Admission charge.*
*Shop*

## Winter Gardens

Avery Hill Park, SE9
District map: page 169, 56 F2
☎ 01-850 3217

Approximately 750 species of tropical and temperate plants in cold, temperate and tropical houses, a collection second only to the Royal Botanical Gardens at Kew. Nursery production unit open spring BH weekend. Tennis and putting available.

*Open: all year Mon-Fri 1-4, Sat, Sun & BH 11-4 (6pm in summer). (Closed 1st Mon each month & 25 Dec).*
*Admission free.*
♿

**AA**

# *Pocket Guide* *to* LONDON

# AROUND THE STREETS OF LONDON

streets, buildings, squares, churches,
monuments, bridges, etc

# The Streets and Buildings

Apart from places to visit, there is a wealth of history to be found around the streets of London.

Described on the following pages are streets, buildings, churches, monuments, statues, and plaques which mark the homes of famous people.

### Albany
(north side of Piccadilly)
Central map: page 10, H6

This secluded court dates from the early 19th century and was designed to provide exclusive apartments for gentlemen. Many famous men have lived here, including the 19th-century Prime Minister Gladstone and the poet Lord Byron (1788-1824).

### Albert Embankment
Central map: page 5, J3

The earliest section of walkway (1868) was designed by Sir Joseph Bazalgette and built as a river defence for St Thomas's Hospital. Named after the Prince Consort, it stretches between Vauxhall Bridge and Westminster Bridge.

### The Aldgate Pump
(junction of Aldgate and Fenchurch St)
Central map: page 12, N6

This disued drinking fountain stands over what was once St Michael's Well, whose water was renowned for is efficacious qualities as far back as the 15th century. For many years a 'draught (draft) on the Aldgate pump' was a facetious expression for a worthless bill.

### The Anchor Public House (Bankside)
Central map: page 12, L6

This historic pub with its Clink Bar is a reminder that it stands close to the site of the Old Clink Prison. Instruments of torture are on display in the bar — a gruesome reminder of the days when prisons were places of extreme cruelty. The pub has known pirates, smugglers and the Press Gang, who hauled men off to serve in the Navy.

### The Bank of England
Central map: page 12, M7

This most famous of national banks was founded in 1694 when City merchants decided that an independent national bank would be advantageous to all concerned. It operated from the Grocers' Hall until 1734 when the new building was opened in Threadneedle Street. The building was greatly expanded by Sir John Soane at the turn of the 18th century, and was extensively modernised between 1925 and 1939. The Bank was nationalised in 1946 and has special responsibilities for printing and issuing notes, administering the National Debt, and exchange control.

The vaults traditionally house the nation's gold reserves, and the internal security system is therefore of the highest order. After the Bank was attacked by looters during the Gordon Riots of 1780 the Bank Piquet was instituted, whereby a detachment of Guards marched to the building each afternoon and remained on watch throughout the night. This ceremony continued until 1973 when an electronic security system was installed.

### Bankside
Central map: page 12, L6

Here in Tudor times were situated the Bear Garden and the Globe Theatre, places of riotous entertainment. The whole area had an evil reputation; being outside the jurisdiction of the City, it became the centre for the darker side of life. Sir Christopher Wren is reputed to have lived at 49 Bankside during the building of St Paul's Cathedral.
Bear Garden Museum — see page 78.

### The Barbican
Central map: page 12, L7

This impressive development, built around the remaining portion of the old Roman wall, is an ambitious scheme to promote the City as a residential area rather than a place to be visited only for the purpose of daily work. It contains high-rise blocks of flats, shops, offices, pubs, the new City of London School for Girls and the 16th-century church of St Giles Cripplegate. Other features include an ornamental lake, an arts centre, and the new Guildhall School of Music and Drama.

### Barton Street
(off Gt Peter St)
Central map: page 4, I4

Barton Street contains some exceptionally well-preserved Georgian houses. Nos 1-14 (except for Nos 2 and 8) are original and carry a tablet dating them to 1722. T E Lawrence ('Lawrence of Arabia') lived at No 14. An inscription on the wall of No 2 reads: 'Peace on Thy House O Passer-by'.

### Birdcage Walk
Central map: page 4, H4

Birdcage Walk owes its name to an aviary owned by Charles II which was situated here. It contained, among other rarities, a crane with a wooden leg!

### The Bluecoat School
Caxton St
Central map: page 4, H4

William Greene, founder of what is now Watney's Brewery, established this charity school in 1688. The building itself, with its charming figure of a charity boy above the doorway, dates from 1709 and now belongs to the National Trust.

### Bond Street
Central map: page 9, G6

Famous as one of the world's most exclusive shopping streets, Bond Street is noted particularly for its jewellers and art dealers. It takes its name from Sir Thomas Bond, who, with John Hinde, a goldsmith, built it in 1686.

### Bread Street
(between Canon St and Watling St)
Central map: page 12, L6

The poet John Milton was born in this street in 1608. Its name is derived from the fact that in medieval times bakers sold their bread here.

### Bruton Place
Central map: page 9, G6

Emerging from the pavements here are several oddly-shaped bollards which were created by the simple expedient of placing redundant 19th-century cannons upright in the ground.

### Buckingham Palace
The Mall, SW1
Central map: page 3, G4

Formerly known as Buckingham House, this most famous of royal homes was built in 1703 by the Duke of Buckingham, and subsequently bought by George III in 1762. Nash altered and remodelled it for George IV in 1825, when its name was changed to Buckingham Palace. It was not much used until Queen Victoria came to the throne in 1837, when the court moved here. It has been the London home of the monarch ever since. The east wing, the side the public sees, was added in 1847 and the whole east façade was redesigned in 1913. The west wing remains largely as Nash designed it, but his great gateway, which was to have stood at the end of the Mall, proved too narrow for the State Coach, and the gate was transported bodily to its present site, Marble Arch.

The interior of the palace, with its many splendid rooms, is not open to the public. When in residence, the Royal Family live in the north wing. When the sovereign is in residence, the Royal Standard is flown. Changing of the Guard, see page 42.

### Burlington Arcade
(between Old Bond St and Royal Academy of Arts)
Central map: page 10, H6

This delightful Regency arcade is still patrolled by a beadle in traditional dress who also closes the gates at either end each night. The covered walk leads from Piccadilly to Burlington Gardens, and is lined with charming bow-windowed shops. Built in 1819, the arcade was owned by the Chesham family. Their coat of arms is still to be seen above the Piccadilly entrance.

### Carlton House Terrace
(between The Mall and Pall Mall)
Central map: page 4, I5

John Nash designed this dignified group of buildings as part of his architectural scheme for Regent Street. The terrace gets its name from Carlton House, which stood on the spot now occupied by the southern half of Waterloo Place. At No 6 is the Royal Society (formed 1660, royal charter 1662). Past members include such distinguished scientists as Sir Isaac Newton, Sir Humphry Davy, and Charles Darwin. No 12 is now the Institute of Contemporary Arts, and houses an art gallery and a theatre.

### Carnaby Street
Central map: page 10, H6

Built in the 18th century for 'poor and miserable objects of the neighbourhood', Carnaby Street was never fashionable. Then in the early 1960s a transformation took place, and the decrepit shops and houses were turned into 'boutiques', at first for men's clothes, later also for girls. By the mid 1960s it was a teenagers' paradise, but the craze lost momentum as it spread to the King's Road and High Street, Kensington.

### Caxton Hall
Caxton St
Central map: page 4, H4

The name and look of this registry office were once familiar to all followers of high society doings, as until 1977 it was the most fashionable place for out-of-church weddings.

### Cecil Court
(off Charing Cross Rd, just past Leicester Sq Station)
Central map: page 10, I6

This narrow pedestrian precinct is filled with antiquarian and secondhand bookshops.

### The Chapel of the Savoy
(junction of Strand and Savoy St)

The buildings and streets with 'Savoy' in their name stand on the site of the ancient Savoy Palace, originally built in 1241, and rebuilt as a hospital by Henry VII in 1510-16. The only part of the hospital to survive is the Queen's Chapel of the Savoy, the private chapel of the reigning monarch as Duke of Lancaster, now used by the Royal Victorian Order. Most of the present building is a 19th-century reconstruction.

### Charles Street
Central map: page 3, G5

Enormous 18th-century houses line both sides of Charles Street. Some of them have ornate ironwork on their exteriors, and all have

SIR THOMAS MORE.

sumptuous interiors. Also in the street is the curiously named 'I am the only Running Footman' pub. The humorist and author, Sydney Smith, lived at No 32.

### Cheapside
Central map: page 12, L7

This was the high street of the medieval City, a great open-air market which came to be called West Chepe (as opposed to East Cheap) from the Anglo-Saxon word for 'barter'.

### Cheyne Walk
Central map: page 2, D1/E2

This fine row of 18th-century houses has been lived in by several famous persons. A plaque at No 23 commemorates the site of Henry VIII's manor house. Henry took a fancy to the village of Chelsea while visiting his friend and Chancellor, Sir Thomas More (who lived nearby) and decided that the fresh country air was good for his children. Edward VI, Mary, and Elizabeth all lived here. Sir Hans Sloane bought the manor after his retirement in 1742 and intended to leave it to the nation as a home for his vast collection of treasures. But the government removed the collection (to form the nucleus of the British Museum) and demolished the manor. Many houses in Cheyne Walk have fragments of it built into their garden walls.

### City Livery Companies

In 1215 King John signed a charter which gave the citizens of the City of London (that is the area encompassed by the old Roman walls) the right to elect their own mayor annually, rather than accept the choice of the reigning monarch. It was at about this time that the livery companies, who over the centuries have played such a prominent part in the administration of the City, first came into existence. These companies, or guilds, evolved as friendly societies for members of a particular trade or craft, combining this function with the furtherance of their guild's business. As more guilds were founded and those already established become more influential, their leading members took to wearing distinctive costumes or liveries, many of which are still worn during special ceremonies. The original 12 Great Companies — Mercers, Grocers, Clothworkers, Fishmongers, Goldsmiths, Skinners, Merchant Taylors, Haberdashers, Salters, Ironmongers, Vintners and Drapers — have now been increased to more than 90.

During World War II only two of the guild halls — the Apothecaries' and the Vintners' — escaped bomb damage, and a number were totally destroyed. Several of the halls which exist today, most of which have been restored or rebuilt, contain historical items including ancient plate, works of art, and fine interior decorations. They are not generally open to the public, but special visits can often be arranged by the City Information Centre in St Paul's Church Yard.

Apart from their administrative responsibilities, the livery companies have considerable influence over their trades, being concerned with the binding of apprentices, and trade standards. Many of the companies have considerable charitable responsibilities — including the endowment of schools and alms houses.

Some of the more interesting halls of the companies include —

**Apothecaries,** Blackfriars Lane. A delightful 17th-century range set round a courtyard.

**Drapers,** Throgmorton Street. Some of this building dates from the 17th century but much is Victorian, and some was rebuilt after war damage.

**Goldsmiths,** Gresham Street. Handsome inside and out, this hall is Georgian.

**Mercers,** Cheapside. Thomas Becket was born in 1118 in a house which once stood here. The present hall was rebuilt after bomb damage in World War II.

**Skinners,** Dowgate Hill. This hall retains much of the fabric of the building erected after the Great Fire, although the facade is 18th-century.

**Vintners,** Upper Thames Street. The medieval courtroom here escaped the Great Fire; the rest was rebuilt in 1671.

## Clarence House
Stable Yard, St James's Palace, SW1
Central map: page 4, H5

Designed by Nash for William IV when he was Duke of Clarence, this

CLARENCE HOUSE

house was restored for Princess Elizabeth before her accession in 1952. Princess Anne was born here and it is now the home of Queen Elizabeth, the Queen Mother.

## Clink Street
Central map: page 12, L6

Gaunt 19th-century warehouses overshadow the cobbled alleyways and block the view of the Thames in this atmospheric part of South London. A plaque under the railway bridge tells the story of the 16th-century Clink Prison, from which the term 'in clink' is derived.

## The College of Arms
Queen Victoria St
Central map: page 12, L6

Sometimes called the Heralds' Office, this is the official authority in Great Britain (except Scotland) and the Commonwealth on armorial bearings and pedigrees. Its officers, who have resounding titles such as Rouge Dragon Pursuivant, also assist the Earl Marshal, an office hereditary to the Duke of Norfolk since 1672, in arranging state ceremonies such as coronations. The building itself is an imposing 17th-century structure, and stands on a site that has been occupied by the College of Arms since 1555.

## Covent Garden
Central map: page 10, I6

Until 1974, when the famous fruit and vegetable market was moved to Nine Elms, near Vauxhall, there had been a market on this site for over 300 years. The original Covent Garden owed its name to the fact that the monks

of Westminster Abbey had a 40-acre walled garden here. In 1631, Inigo Jones was commissioned to lay out the square. This grandly conceived estate, modelled on those he had seen in Italy, included a great Piazza, a church, and, on three sides, arcaded blocks of houses. The square and covered walks in front of buildings attracted market traders, and by 1670 the market had received official recognition. By the middle of the 20th century it had rapidly outgrown its site. After the market had moved, strenuous efforts were made to preserve the attractive old market buildings and these have been renovated and contain many small craft shops, business premises and restaurants.

## Crosby Hall
Danvers St
Central map: page 2, E2

This 15th-century hall once formed part of a mansion and originally stood at Bishopsgate. Fire destroyed most of the building in the 17th century, but the great hall survived, and was moved to its present site in 1911. At one time the hall was leased by Sir Thomas More, and it now stands on what was part of the gardens of the great house he built here in 1520. His house was demolished in the 1740s, but Crosby Hall still serves to remind passers-by of one of Chelsea's most famous residents.

## County Hall (former)
Central map: page 5, J5

Originally erected in 1912-32, County Hall has since been vastly expanded in size. The colonnaded front facing the River Thames is 750ft long. Formerly the administrative headquarters of the Greater London Council, it was the first component part of the projected South Bank scheme.

## Downing Street
Central map: page 4, I5

This world-famous street was built by Sir George Downing, a secretary to the Treasury, in about 1680. At first it was an unimportant residential street with a pub — the Cat and Bagpipes — on the corner. In 1732 George II offered No 10 to Sir Robert Walpole as a town house and since then it has been the official residence of the British Prime Minister. No 11 is the official residence of the Chancellor of the Exchequer. The buildings themselves have unpretentious Georgian façades, but have been extensively modified inside.

## Fleet Street
Central map: page 11, K7

Nearly every national and provincial newspaper or periodical had an office in or near Fleet Street. It is one of the most ancient thoroughfares in London, and has had links with the printing trade since about 1500. The present buildings are mostly modern.

## Gerrard Street
Central map: page 10, I6

At each end of Gerrard Street stand two beautiful Chinese gateways, erected in 1985 to mark the centre of London's Chinatown. Here and in nearby streets restaurants offer authentic Chinese cuisine. Also here is the Chinese Community

Healthcare Centre which offers both orthodox medicine and alternative Chinese medical treatments.

## Goodwin's Court
(off north end of Charlton St)
Central map: page 10, H9

This narrow alley is entirely lined with the bow-fronted windows of former shops.

## Great Russell Street
Central map: page 10, I7

Celebrated as the home of the British Museum, Great Russell Street has also had some famous residents. At No 46 lived Ralph Caldecott (1846-86), an outstanding illustrator of children's books, while No 91 was the home of George du Maurier (1834-96), who from 1860 drew for *Punch* but is probably better known for his novel *Trilby*, in which he created the character of Svengali.

Bloomsbury's association with the world of books is evident in and around Great Russell Street, where there are numerous publishers' offices and small bookshops.

## Greek Street
Central map: page 10, I6

Many famous people are associated with this street. Dr Samuel Johnson, the poet and critic, and Sir Joshua Reynolds, the English portrait painter, founded a Literary Club here; Sir Thomas Lawrence, the 18th-century portrait painter, lived and worked here for 25 years; Thomas de Quincey, who wrote *Confessions of an English Opium Eater*, indulged his addiction here; and Wedgwood had his London showroom here.

## The Greycoat Hospital
Greycoat Place (north side of Greycoat St)
Central map: page 4, H4

This charity school was founded in 1698 as a boarding school for seventy children. The original building, which dated from 1701, was partly destroyed during World War II and has now been restored in the Queen Anne style. The figures of the Greycoat boy and girl over the door are of painted wood, and may date from the early 18th century. Since 1873 it has been a day-school for girls only, who number over 600.

## The House of St Barnabas
Greek St (east side of Soho Square)
Central map: page 10, H7

One of the finest Georgian houses in London, with richly decorated ceilings, woodcarvings, and ironwork, the House of St Barnabas was founded as a charitable institution in 1846 to help the destitute in London. It is now open to the public.

## Jermyn Street
Central map: page 3, H5

Jermyn Street is famous for its many old-established shops. One of the most interesting is the ancient premises of Paxton and Whitfield, the cheese shop. Further

10 DOWNING ST.

along is the Cavendish Hotel, with its wrought-iron lamps, which although it has been rebuilt still carries memories of the eccentric hotelier Rosa Lewis, the original 'Duchess of Duke Street'.

## Jubilee Gardens
Central map: page 5, J5

These gardens were laid out as London's tribute to celebrate Queen Elizabeth II's Silver Jubilee in 1977.

## The King's Road
Central map: page 3, F3

It is hard to believe that this bustling thoroughfare was once a quiet country footpath. During the 17th century it was enlarged to become Charles II's private carriage route between St James's and Hampton Court, but did not become a public highway until the beginning of the 19th century. Mary Quant, the designer who revolutionised women's clothing, opened a boutique here in the 1950s, and the whole road promptly achieved a fashionable reputation which it has never lost.

## Lambeth Palace
Central map: page 5, J4

Much of this historic structure, which has been the London residence of the Archbishop of Canterbury for 700 years, was rebuilt during the 19th century. Extensive damage was caused by bombs during World War II. Of the old palace, the most interesting parts are the Lollards Tower and the Gatehouse, both of the 15th century, and the 13th-century Chapel Crypt. Parts of the palace, and its grounds, are open to the public.

Adjoining the south gateway of the palace is the former church of St Mary, now restored as a Museum of Garden History in memory of John Tradescant, Charles I's gardener, (see page 108). Captain William Bligh, of the *Bounty*, is buried here.

## Laurence Pountney Hill
(off south side of Canon St)
Central map: page 12, M6

Nos 1 and 2 were built in 1703 and are the finest early 18th-century houses in the City. Amid the rich carving of the doorways are two delightful cherubs playing marbles.

## Lawrence Street
(off Cheyne Row)
Central map: page 2, E2

Chelsea China was manufactured at the north end of this street from 1745 to 1784. The Chelsea factory competes with Bow for the honour of being the first to make English porcelain.

## Liberty's
Corner of Great Marlborough St and Regent St
Central map: page 10, H6

Liberty's, built in 1924, was first planned as a reproduction Tudor building throughout, but was then given a neo-classical façade to match its surroundings. The half-timbering on the north side is not purely decorative — the timbers are structural and come from genuine men-of-war. Every quarter hour, the St George on the clock which adorns the façade fights the dragon, slaying him on the hour. It is now a department store.

## Lincoln's Inn Fields
Central map: page 11, J7

LAMBETH PALACE

Lincoln's Inn Fields were laid out in the 17th century and were a famous haunt of duellists. A tablet here marks the spot were Lord William Russell was executed in 1683. Handsome buildings, including the Sir John Soane's Museum (see page 106), the Royal College of Surgeons and Lincoln's Inn (see page 89) surround the fields.

## Little Dean's Yard and Westminster School
South side of Westminster Abbey
Central map: page 4, I4

Westminster Abbey probably had its own school before 1200. When the abbey became a cathedral in 1540, the school became the King's Grammar School, with 40 scholars. It was re-founded by Queen Elizabeth I in 1560. The custom known as the Pancake Greeze is observed here every Shrove Tuesday. The cook, dressed in cap and apron, comes in with a frying-pan and has to toss a pancake over the 16ft-high iron bar which separates the old Upper and Lower Schools. As it falls, representatives from each form scramble for it, and the boy who gets the biggest piece also gets a guinea from the Dean. On the north side of Little Dean's Yard is Ashburnham House, built shortly after 1662, and the best example in London of a stately mid-17th-century house.

### The London Stone
Canon St, opposite station
Central map: page 12, M6

This is said to be the milestone from which distances were measured on the great military roads radiating outwards from Roman London.

### The Mall
Central map: page 4, H5

The Mall was originally laid out in 1660-2 as part of Charles II's scheme for St James's Park. It was transformed into a processional way in 1910.

### Marlborough House
Pall Mall, SW1
Central map: page 4, H5

Built by Wren for the Duke of Marlborough, Marlborough House was later occupied by Leopold I of Belgium. In 1850 it became the official residence of the Prince of Wales. George V was born here and after he became King it became the home of Queen Alexandra, Edward VII's widow. The house is now the Commonwealth Centre and is open by appointment.

### Meard Street
(south end of Wardour St)
Central map: page 10, H6

For those who like old houses this short 18th-century street, named after a carpenter, John Meard, is the most rewarding in all Soho. Nos 1-21 are exceptionally well preserved.

### Middlesex Guildhall
Corner of Victoria St and Parliament Sq
Central map: page 4, I4

This Renaissance-style building was opened in 1913, and stands on the site of an earlier guildhall. It once functioned as the administrative centre for the old county of Middlesex. The friezes on the façade depict Magna Carta, Henry II granting a charter to Westminster, and Lady Jane Grey accepting the crown from the Duke of Northumberland.

### Old Compton Street
Central map: page 10, H6

This street is famous for its exotic provision shops, the legacy of the 19th-century flood of immigrants — particularly French, Italians and Greeks — into the area.

### Pall Mall
Central map: page 4, H5

Pall Mall takes its name from *paille maille*, a French ball game similar to croquet, introduced into England in the reign of Charles I. Numerous famous, and usually exclusive, clubs are situated in Pall Mall. Outside the entrance to the Athenaeum Club, in Waterloo Place, are two slabs of stone, placed here as a mounting-block at the request of the Duke of Wellington.

### Paternoster Row and Panyer Alley Steps
(off south side of St Paul's station)
Central map: page 12, L7

Paternoster (Our Father) is a reminder of the participants in medieval processions who 'told' their rosaries round the precincts of Old St Paul's. Here they recited the Lord's Prayer. For several hundred years Paternoster Row was associated with the book trade, but it was entirely destroyed during the Blitz, and only the ancient name survives. The Steps commemorate the Panyer Boy, an inn whose 17th-century sign is to be seen on the side wall. It shows a baker's boy with his pannier.

### Piccadilly
Central map: page 3, G5

This famous London thoroughfare takes its name from a form of 17th-century ruff (or collar) called a 'piccadil'. At the eastern end of the street is Piccadilly Circus, always packed with shoppers and sightseers. In its centre is the statue known as Eros, erected in 1892 as a memorial to Lord Shaftesbury. This is the centre of London's West End; all around are theatres, cinemas, and restaurants. Further along Piccadilly is Fortnum and Mason's shop. Figures of Mr Fortnum and Mr Mason (who founded the shop in 1707) emerge from the clock high on the wall on the hour and bow to each other as the carillon plays a tune.

### Piccadilly Arcade
Central map: page 4, H5

This pleasant covered thoroughfare connects Jermyn Street and Piccadilly. It is adorned with hanging baskets of flowers and lined with expensive shops.

### The Post Office Tower
Central map: page 9, G7

Completed in 1964, this 619ft-high needle of concrete and glass is one of the tallest buildings in London. It has a revolving restaurant and a viewing platform which are reached by high-speed lift now closed to the public. The Tower reaches such dizzy heights in order that the telecommunication signals it receives will not be affected by the surrounding buildings.

### Queen Anne's Gate

(off Birdcage Walk)
Central map: page 4, H4

This quiet close, built in 1704, is undoubtedly one of the most charming streets in London. It has been the home of several distinguished figures in British history, including Lord Palmerston (who lived at No 20), and the statesman, lawyer and philosopher Lord Haldane (No 28). A statue of Queen Anne stands outside No 13, and No 26 still has the snuffer for extinguishing the linkman's torch after he had lighted its owners home.

### Ranelagh Gardens

Central map: page 3, F2

This garden of trees and lawns is the site of the famous 18th-century Ranelagh Pleasure Gardens. The author and wit Horace Walpole, who was here on the opening night in 1742, said that it was crowded 'with much nobility and much mob'. So for a while it continued. There was music, opera, gambling, dancing, and masquerades — and the entry fee of half-a-crown included coffee and punch. But it declined in favour towards the end of the century and finally closed its gates in 1804. The gardens were later bought by the Royal Hospital and nowadays are famous for the Chelsea Flower Show (see page 47).

### Regent Street

Central map: page 10, H6

Regent Street owes its existence to George IV, who as Prince Regent lived at Carlton House. He wanted to build a country villa on Primrose Hill and connect it to Carlton House by a new road. The villa was never built, but Regent Street was laid out in 1813-20 by the great architect John Nash (1752-1835). The total rebuilding of Regent Street that began in 1900 has made it one of the finest shopping streets in the world, at the expense of some of the greatest architecture.

### Royal Avenue

Central map: page 3, F3

The Avenue is part of a road designed by Sir Christopher Wren to link the Royal Hospital with Kensington Palace. The road was never finished but the section that remains was completed in 1694. The terraces are 19th-century.

### Royal Courts of Justice

Central map: page 11, J7

Generally called the Law Courts, the Royal Courts of Justice were designed in the Gothic style by the distinguished Victorian architect G E Street. The foundation stone was laid in 1874, but the building was not completed until 1882, after Street's death. The Central Hall contains a monument to him. The main entrance, in the Strand, has archways flanked by twin towers in which are stairs to the public galleries.

### The Royal Exchange

Central map: page 12, M7

Opened in 1568 as a meeting place for City merchants. Queen Victoria opened the present building in 1844. Important announcements such as the proclamation of new sovereigns and declarations of war are traditionally made from the broad flight of steps at its entrance.

### The Royal Hospital

Central map: page 3, F2

The Royal Hospital, Chelsea, was founded in 1682 by Charles II for veteran and invalid soldiers. Sir Christopher Wren designed most of the buildings, and his work can be seen at its finest in the Figure Court and the Chapel. Alterations and additions were subsequently made by Robert Adam and Sir John Soane. The Hospital now houses 500 army pensioners, who parade in their scarlet frock-coats on Oak Apple Day (May 29). The famous Chelsea Flower Show is held here every year (see page 47).

### Royal Opera House

Covent Garden (corner of Floral St and Bow St)
Central map: page 10, I6

The present building had two predecessors, the second one being the scene of the famous Old Price Riots — the public's protestation against the sharp increase in the costs of seats. The theatre officially opened as an opera house in 1847 and opera has flourished here ever since, achieving its greatest peaks between 1859 and 1939 when it was the leading entertainment of 'society'.

### St Anne's Soho

(corner of Wardour St and Old Compton St)
Central map: page 10, H6

The remains of a 17th-century church which was almost totally destroyed during World War II; the tower (added in 1801-3) survived. The churchyard has been laid out as a garden where memorials to the essayist William Hazlitt (*d.* 1830) and Theodore, King of Corsica (*d.* 1756), can still be seen.

### St Bartholomew's Hospital

Central map: page 12, L7

'Barts' was founded in 1123 as a religious establishment and at the dissolution of the monasteries was given to the City of London by Henry VIII. It is the oldest hospital in London on its original site. Nearby, a half-timbered Elizabethan gatehouse marks the entrance to the Norman church of St Bartholomew the Great (see page 127).

### St James's Palace

St James's Street, SW1
Central map: page 4, H5

The original palace was started by Henry VIII in 1531, and, after the destruction of Whitehall Palace, was the sovereign's official London residence. Foreign ambassadors are still appointed to the Court of St James's. The Gatehouse facing St James's Street is the main remnant of the Tudor building, and has the initials of Henry VIII and Anne Boleyn carved over the doors. The Chapel Royal was originally built by Henry VIII but was much altered in 1837. However, the ceiling by Holbein is original.

Several royal marriages have been solemnised here, including those of William III and Mary II, Queen Anne, George IV, Queen Victoria and George V. Every year on 6th January (the Festival of Epiphany) at Holy Communion in this Chapel, an offering of gold, frankincense and myrrh is made on behalf of the Queen by two of Her Majesty's Gentlemen Ushers.

In Friary Court the new sovereign is proclaimed from the balcony by the Heralds. Charles II, who was born here, made some additions to the palace, commissioning Wren to add some state apartments facing the park. James II, Mary II, Queen Anne and George IV were all born here. George IV employed Nash to restore and redecorate the palace, but Queen Victoria moved the court to Buckingham Palace when she came to the throne. St James's Palace is now occupied by servants of the Crown, and is not open to the public. However, services may be attended in the Chapel Royal between October and July.

### St James's Street

Central map: page 4, H5

Many of the best known gentlemen's clubs in London are situated in this genteel street. They include Boodle's (No 28), White's (No 37), and Brook's (No 60), all of which have been established here since the 18th century. Among the old-established shops here are James Lock, hatters for more than 200 years, still with an almost unchanged shop front, and Berry Bros and Rudd, wine merchants since the 17th century.

### St Martin's Lane

Central map: page 10, I6

St Martin's Lane is easily recognised by the globe on top of the London Coliseum, now the home of the English National Opera. Thomas Chippendale, the greatest furniture maker in England's history, opened his workshop in No 62 in 1753.

### St Paul's Gardens

(south end of New Change)
Central map: page 12, L6

In these gardens is a plaque marking the site of Old Change, a 13th-century building where bullion was stored before being taken to the Royal Mint, and which gave its name to a street, alas destroyed by bombs in 1941. New Change, a much wider street, was built after the war a little to the east of its predecessor and the reconstructed spire of the Wren church of St Augustine, Watling Street.

### Savile Row

Central map: page 10, H6

Savile Row is world-famous for its high-class tailoring establishments. No 14, the last home of the playwright Richard Brinsley Sheridan (1751-1816), is now occupied by Hardy Amies, couturier to the Queen.

ST. JAMES'S PALACE

### The Savoy Hotel
Strand
Central map: page 11, J6

In 1884, Richard D'Oyly Carte, who had already built the Savoy Theatre as a home for Gilbert and Sullivan's comic operas, decided to build a hotel to compete with the best in America. His new Savoy was famous for its 70 bathrooms — such an unheard-of number in those days that the builder asked him if his guests were to be amphibians.

### Shaftesbury Avenue
Central map: page 10, H6

Laid out in 1877-86, the Avenue is named after the great Victorian social reformer and champion of the anti-slavery cause Lord Shaftesbury. It stretches from New Oxford Street to Piccadilly Circus, and is now known chiefly for its theatres.

### Shell-Mex House
(between Strand and Savoy Place)
Central map: page 10, I6

Shell-Mex House was originally the Cecil Hotel, which, when it opened in 1886, was the largest hotel in Europe. The old-fashioned street lamp here is always alight, burning gases from the sewers below.

### Shepherd Market
(off Shepherd St)
Central map: page 3, G5

Set in the heart of Mayfair, this is one of the most delightful areas in all London. Some of the original 18th-century buildings survive, but it is the unique 'village' atmosphere which gives this tiny oasis its special charm. The present web of narrow streets was laid out by the builder and designer Edward Shepherd in 1735.

### The Sir John Cass School
(north side of Aldgate)
Central map: page 12, N6

Founded in 1710 as a charity school, this philanthrophic establishment was rebuilt in 1909. Over the doorway are two figures of school children that probably came from the original building.

### South Audley Street
Central map: page 3, G5

Sir Richard Westmacott (1775-1856), an outstanding sculptor of his day, lived at No 14. At No 57 is the famous gunsmiths, Purdey and Son. No 71 is an exceptionally fine Georgian house. Just after the crossroads with South Street is the blue and white Grosvenor Chapel, where American servicemen worshiped during World War II. It was built in 1730.

### South Bank Trees
Central map: page 5, J5

The walkway between County Hall and Hungerford Bridge is lined with London plane trees. They probably originated as a hybrid between Oriental and American planes in the 17th century, when cultivated together by the gardeners to the Stuart kings at Lambeth.

### South Bank Arts Complex
Central map: page 5, J5

This huge assembly of cultural centres was begun in 1951 when the Royal Festival Hall was built for the Festival of Britain. It is one of the most successful examples of modern architecture in London, providing comfortable seating for 3,000 people. The complex was enlarged when, in 1967, the Queen Elizabeth Hall and the Purcell Room were opened. Also here are the Hayward Gallery and the National Theatre.

### The Strand
Central map: page 11, J6

In Elizabethan times and long afterwards, the Strand was bordered by noblemen's mansions with gardens running down to the riverside or 'strand'. It is still, as it always was, the principal route between the West End and the City, running for nearly a mile from Charing Cross to the Temple Bar Memorial — where statues of Queen Victoria and Edward VII, and a griffin in the road, mark the boundary of the City. The Temple Bar itself, a triple gateway designed by Wren, was dismantled at the end of the last century and removed to Theobald's Park in Hertfordshire. In much earlier times, the severed heads of traitors and other criminals were impaled on spikes on top of the gateway to the City.

### The Temple of Mithras
(Queen Victoria St, east of Queen St)
Central map: page 12, L6

Discovered in 1954 during excavations to locate the bed of the River Walbrook, this temple dates from the 2nd century AD. The cult of Mithras, a Persian sun-god, was restricted to men and especially popular with soldiers, and the ceremonies associated with his worship were conducted in great secrecy. This temple is one of the most important Roman remains in London, and has been reconstructed near to the site where it was found.

### Tooley Street
Central map: page 6, M5

In the 19th century this area was famous for its vast trade in foodstuffs and was known as the 'breakfast table of England'. In 1861 a fire raged in the warehouses along here, which it was said produced more flames and heat than the Great Fire of London.

### Trocadero Centre
Shaftesbury Avenue/Coventry St
Central map: page 10, H6

This new three-storey complex, built behind its original facade, houses shops, restaurants and entertainment facilities including The Guinness World of Records (see page 85), The London Experience (see page 92) and Light Fantastic (see page 91).

### US Embassy
Grosvenor Square
Central map: page 9, F6

This huge building takes up the entire west side of Grosvenor Square. It was designed by Eero Saarinen, the Finnish-American architect, and completed in 1960. An eagle with a wingspan of 35 ft dominates the structure. The embassy has been seen on television many times, since it has been a focus of demonstrations of all sorts.

### Vauxhall Bridge Garden
(west side of Vauxhall Bridge)
Central map: page 4, I3

A large bollard here marks the approximate site of Millbank Penitentiary from which, between 1816 and 1867, convicts sentenced to transportation embarked on their journey. The garden also contains a sculpture by Henry Moore.

### The Victoria Embankment
Central map: page 11, J6

Stretching from Westminster Bridge to Blackfriars Bridge, the Victoria Embankment forms one of the most interesting and attractive riverside promenades in London. The principal reason for its construction was not, however, to provide a walkway, but to help solve London's pollution problem. By 1855 the river was little more than an open sewer, and the famous scientist Michael Faraday, in a letter to *The Times*, described its appearance as 'an opaque brown fluid . . . near the bridges the feculence rolled up in clouds so dense that they were visible at the surface'. The following year, 1856, became known as the Year of the Big Stink because the stench had become so overpoweringly awful. Sir Joseph Bazalgette had drawn up plans for a comprehensive sewage system by 1856, and it was decided to put these into practice. The system was designed to capture the sewage before it reached the Thames and direct it to outfalls at Barking and Crossness. The Victoria Embankment was constructed to accommodate one of the huge pipes that ran along the north bank. The York Water Gate in Victoria Embankment Gardens marks the position of the original riverbank.

### Victoria Embankment Gardens
Central map: page 6 I6

To be found here is the old York House Water Gate, the entrance to the Duke of Buckingham's garden from the Thames. In the Duke's day (the 1620s) boats bringing guests would tie up at the Water Gate, which marks the former boundary of the River Thames. There are numerous statues and memorials in the gardens. Of special interest is the little memorial to the Imperial Camel Corps (1921), statues of the poet Robert Burns and Robert Raikes, founder (1780) of Sunday Schools, a bust of the composer Sir Arthur Sullivan (*d.* 1900) and the tree commemorating Queen Elizabeth II's coronation in 1953.

### Victoria Tower Gardens
(off Millbank)
Central map: page 4, I4

In the thin triangle of Victoria Tower Gardens are the Buxton Drinking Fountain, commemorating the emancipation of slaves in the British Empire in 1834; a statue of the suffragette Mrs Emmeline Pankhurst (1858-1928); and a copy of the famous statue by Auguste Rodin (1840-1917) and called 'The Burghers of Calais'.

### Villiers Street
(off east side of Charing Cross station)
Central map: page 10, I6

In this area in the 17th century stood the mansion and gardens of George Villiers, Duke of Buckingham. He sold them for redevelopment, but insisted that every word of his name and title be preserved in the new street names: George Street, Villiers Street, Duke Street, Buckingham Street, and Of Alley (now renamed York Place). East of Villiers Street, the area between the Strand and the Thames was named the Adelphi (from the

Greek word for brothers, *adelphoi*) after the Adam brothers, who were responsible for laying out the streets in 1768-74. Much of the area has been rebuilt but the name survives in the Adelphi Theatre.

### Wardour Street
Central map: page 10, H6

During the 1920s and 1930s, Wardour Street became the home of the British film industry. But while film moguls were making (and losing) fortunes here, television was being developed in nearby Frith Street.

### William Curtis Ecological Park
Vine Lane
Central map: page 6, N5

The park, created by the Jubilee Environmental Committee, was opened in 1977, on the 100th anniversary of the publication of Curtis's *Flora of London*. It is an interesting urban nature reserve where many species of plants are cultivated. Field study facilities are available on application to the warden.

### Woburn Walk
(off east side of Upper Woburn Place)
Central map: page 10, I8

This genteel little thoroughfare has a double row of early 19th-century houses, all of which have picturesque shop fronts. The Irish poet W B Yeats (1865-1939) lived at No 5 for a while.

### Ye Olde Watling
(east end of Watling St)
Central map: page 12, L6

This interesting old pub which dates from 1668 was used as an office by Sir Christopher Wren during the building of St Paul's Cathedral.

B E R K E L E Y   S Q U A R E

# The Squares

### Belgrave Square
SW1
Central map: page 3, F4

Sheer size robs Belgrave of its square-like characteristics, because it is not possible to see from one side to the other. To all intents it is a small park, but the carefully tended lawns and gardens have an un-park-like air of exclusiveness undoubtedly lent by the elegant cream-coloured terraces that surround it. The square is one of the largest in London, and centres on attractive private gardens enclosed by ironwork entirely in keeping with the local architecture.

### Berkeley Square
W1
Central map: page 9, G6

Modern development has detracted somewhat from the original charm of this very famous square. It is doubtful whether the nightingales assigned to it in the song actually existed, though the huge plane trees in which they would have perched are there for all to see. The trees were planted in 1790, a decade before the building of the quaint Pump House that is still so much a part of the square's character. Also very much in keeping with the atmosphere of slightly time-worn elegance is the garden fountain — a nymph with a pitcher.

### Bloomsbury Square
WC1
(off north side of Bloomsbury Way)
Central map: page 10, I7

The name 'Bloomsbury' probably derives from the medieval manor of Blemund'sbury, bought by the Earl of Southampton in 1545. Bloomsbury Square was laid out on its site by one of his descendants in 1661, and was the first open space in London to be called a 'square'. The original mansions have all disappeared, but the houses on the north side date from 1800-14. The gardens were planted in about 1800 by the celebrated landscape gardener Humphrey Repton. No 6 was the home of Isaac D'Israeli, father of Benjamin Disraeli.

### Dorset Square
NW1 (West side of Gloucester Place)
Central map: page 9, F7

Long before Dorset Square was laid out its site was occupied by the original Lord's Cricket Ground. Here the MCC — the country's most famous cricket club — was begun in the 18th century. However, the grass in the square is no descendant of that upon which early matches were played, for when the square was being developed groundkeeper Thomas Lord left, taking his turf with him.

**Fitzroy Square**
W1
(north side of Fitzroy St)
Central map: page 10, H8

Designed by the famous Adam brothers in the 18th century, Fitzroy Square preserves well-built terraces typical of their designers' work, particularly on the eastern side.

**Golden Square**
W1 (east side of John St)
Central map: page 10, H6

According to popular legend, this Soho square had its name changed from 'Gelding' to 'Golden' by some of its more society-conscious residents. It is now a centre for the woollen trade.

**Gordon Square**
WC1
Central map: page 10, H8

Gordon Square is associated with the circle of 20th-century writers, critics and intellectuals known as the Bloomsbury Group. The novelist Virginia Woolf (1882-1941) lived at No 46 for a time before she married. The same house was later the home of the leading economist John Maynard Keynes (1883-1946). The critic and biographer Lytton Strachey (1880-1932) lived at No 51. At the south-west corner of the square stands the Gothic Church of Christ the King.

**Grosvenor Square**
W1
Central map: page 9, F6

Built and rebuilt on the site of a 17th-century citizen's blockade against Charles I, Grosvenor Square is now largely in the hands of a foreign power. This is immediately apparent in the vast brooding eagle

that stretches its 35ft wingspan protectively over the American Embassy, at the same time managing to encompass most of the square in that expansive gesture. The area is popularly known as 'Little America'.

The open garden around which the square is formed was designed by William Kent, a distinguished 18th-century architect and designer, and occupies some six acres. It is a pleasant patch of green amongst the buildings that loom from all sides, and echoes the transatlantic feel of the place in a memorial to one-time US President, Franklin D Roosevelt.

**Hanover Square**
W1
Central map: page 9, G6

Like Berkeley Square, Hanover Square once contained elegant Georgian houses, but many of these have now been replaced by modern offices. A statue of William Pitt the Younger stands at the south end of the square facing St George's Church.

**Leicester Square**
WC2
Central map: page 10, I6

This large square gets its name from Leicester House, a mansion built here by the Earl of Leicester in the 17th century. The open space, then known as Leicester Fields, was ideal for fighting duels. The mansion has long since disappeared, and in Victorian times the fields were laid out as a garden, with the statue of Shakespeare in the centre and busts of famous local residents at the four corners.

**Manchester Square**
W1 (between George St and Wigmore St)
Central map: page 9, F7

The leafy centre of Manchester Square contrasts prettily with the dark brick of the Georgian architecture that surrounds it. It is a quiet place, situated just far enough away from Oxford Street to be unaffected by the noise, yet close enough to be a haven for those weary of shopping in the famous thoroughfare.

**Parliament Square**
SW1
Central map: page 4, I4

The square was originally laid out by Sir Charles Barry in 1850, and redesigned in 1951 for the Festival of Britain. There are many statues of British politicians in and around the square.

**Portman Square**
W1
Central map: page 9, F7

Once second only to Grosvenor Square in the eyes of high society, Portman took 20 years to build during the 18th century. The centre of the square is occupied by a garden in which grass, shrubs, and trees combine effectively.

**Russell Square**
WC1
Central map: page 10, I8

James Burton laid out Russell Square in the early 19th century, but few of his original buildings have survived. An exception is No 21, on the north side, which is considered a good example of his work.

The pleasant central garden was originally designed by the architect Humphry Repton, but his layout was later altered.

## St James's Square
SW1
Central map: page 4, H5

At the centre of this orderly and elegant square, originally created by architect Henry Jermyn, is a garden which is particularly noted for its lovely trees. An equestrian statue of William III forms the central focal point for ranks of tall plane trees, the pastel softness of flowering almond and cherry blossom, the fragrant pyramids of lilac bloom, and golden crowns of laburnum.

## Smith Square
SW1
Central map: page 4, I4

This square is named after Sir John Smith, who owned and developed the land. Some of the houses were rebuilt after World War II, but No 5 dates from 1726. The streets leading to and from the square are lined with elegant town houses, and this is an excellent area to get a 'feel' of 18th- and early 19th-century London. In the centre of the square is Thomas Archer's fine church of St John. Concerts are often broadcast from the church, which has been specially adapted for the purpose. St John's also has its own orchestra, now of international repute.

## Soho Square
W1
Central map: page 10, H7

The name 'Soho' is said to come from the cry of huntsmen unleashing dogs to chase hares, *so* meaning 'see', and *ho* 'after him'. The Duke of Monmouth, Charles II's illegitimate son, had a mansion in Soho Square, and when he and his followers made a bid for the Crown at the Battle of Sedgemoor, 'Soho!' was their battle cry. On the east side of the square is the Roman Catholic Church of St Patrick, built in 1891-3. It has a fine Italianate interior. In the north-west corner is the French Protestant Church of London, founded in 1550 under a royal charter from Edward VI. The present building dates from 1893. Soho has been a foreign quarter since the reign of Charles II, when a great number of French Protestants fled here as the result of religious persecution. Known as 'Huguenots', they were mostly silk-weavers, and in the back gardens around Soho Square there may still be some of the mulberry trees they planted for their silkworms.

## Tavistock Square
WC1
Central map: page 10, I8

To the right of the central walk through the square's garden is a copper beech tree planted by Pandit Nehru on 13 June 1953 to mark the unveiling of the statue of Mahatma Gandhi in the centre of the garden. The statue in the south-east corner of the gardens is of Dame Louisa Aldrich-Blake (1865-1925), pioneering surgeon to the Elizabeth Garrett Anderson Hospital for women. This memorial is by Sir Edwin Lutyens, who also designed the large building of the British Medical Association on the east side of the square. This building occupies the site of a house where Dickens lived for nine years, and in which several of his novels were written. On the north side of the square is Woburn House, in which is the fascinating Jewish Museum (see page 90).

## Trafalgar Square
WC2
Central map: page 10, I6

Pigeons outnumber people in the square. They perch on heads and shoulders, and are fed, photographed, and fussed over. The square itself, dominated by Nelson's Column, was laid out in memory of Nelson and completed in 1841, but the fountains were added in 1948. On the parapet nearest the National Gallery the Standard British Linear Measures are let into the stonework.

## Trinity Square
EC3
Central map: page 12, N6

In 1465, during the reign of Edward IV, the first permanent scaffold was set up on Tower Hill. It was situated in what is now Trinity Square, and the site, with its blood-drenched memories, is marked by a rectangle of bricked paving. Public executions were held here until the 18th century; more than 125 people were put to death.

## Vincent Square
SW1
Central map: page 4, H3

Named after William Vincent, Dean of Westminster 1802-15, the square contains playing fields for the boys of Westminster School. This continues a long tradition, for in medieval times the area was part of the old Tothill Fields, where young men practised military skills such as archery and wrestling.

# Churches

The churches of central London contain some of the capital's greatest treasures, and many of the buildings themselves are architectural gems. But they are surprisingly little visited, and most are havens of tranquillity. A selection of some of the best is on the following pages.

**All Hallows-by-the-Tower**
Byward Street, EC3
Central map: page 12, M6

Preserved in the crypt here is part of the wall of a church which stood on this site in the 7th century. Also in the crypt are fragments of Roman paving, and the remains of two Saxon crosses. The shell of the church dates from the 12th to 15th centuries, but the interior, which was gutted during the Blitz, was rebuilt in the 1950s. A superb font cover designed by Grinling Gibbons escaped destruction, as did the exquisite brasses in front of the altar (Brass rubbing-see page 79). Samuel Pepys surveyed the results of the Great Fire of London from the tower.

**All Hallows**
London Wall, EC2
Central map: page 12, M7

Forming part of the boundary of the churchyard here is a stretch of the ancient wall which once surrounded the City of London. The church itself was designed by George Dance the Younger in the 18th century and has an elegant and sumptuously decorated interior. It was severely damaged during the Blitz, but was restored during the 1960s and now houses exhibitions of church art.

**All Saints**
Margaret Street, W1
Central map: page 10, H7

This striking brick-built church was erected in 1849 to the designs of William Butterfield. He was the most original architect of his time and produced plans that were initially inspired by Gothic architecture. The interior of the church is decorated with coloured bricks, and the decoration becomes much richer nearer the roof, reflecting the Victorian idea that Gothic architecture becomes more elaborate the nearer it gets to heaven.

**All Souls'**
Langham Place, W1
Central map: page 9, G7

John Nash designed this large church and had it built in this position to close the northward vista of Regent Street. It was built in 1822 and has a Classical portico surmounted by a needle spire. The interior is designed in such a way that the whole congregation can view all aspects of the services.

**Brompton Oratory**
Brompton Road, SW7
Central map: page 2, E4

This imposing Roman Catholic church was built in an Italian Renaissance style at the end of the 19th century. Its interior is rich in marble and mosaic decoration and the nave is a remarkable 51ft wide.

**Chelsea Old Church (All Saints')**
Cheyne Walk, SW3
Central map: page 2, E2

Almost totally destroyed during the Blitz, this church has been restored to its original appearance. The More Chapel, however, survived almost intact. It was built in 1528 for Sir Thomas More and his family, but it is doubtful if he was buried here. The church is extremely rich in monuments, and in the churchyard is an urn commemorating Sir Hans Sloane, the great 18th-century collector and benefactor.

**Holy Trinity**
Sloane Street, SW1
Central map: page 3, F3

This church was designed by J D Sedding, one of the principal architects of the 19th-century Arts and Crafts Movement. The interior of the church is based on 15th-century Gothic architecture and is lit by magnificent stained-glass windows designed by Edward Burne-Jones and made by William Morris.

**St Alfege**
Church Street, Greenwich, SE10
Not on map

Built in 1718 to the designs of Nicholas Hawksmoor, this church broods gloomily over its surroundings. It was

ALL SOULS'

badly damaged during the Blitz, and many of the treasures which it had contained were destroyed. The church was restored in the 1950s and houses a memorial to General Wolfe and the tomb of the 'father of English church music', Thomas Tallis (d.1585).

### St Andrew
Holborn Circus, EC1
Central map: page 11, K7

Although this church escaped the Great Fire, it was nonetheless rebuilt by Sir Christopher Wren, and is his largest parish church. It did not escape the Blitz, however, and had to be largely rebuilt. It contains a delightful memorial to Thomas Coram, who founded the Foundlings Hospital in the 18th century. The church's pulpit, font, and organ came from the chapel of the hospital. St Andrew's is a non-parochial guild church and no Sunday services are held here, but it is open for prayers on weekdays.

### St Andrew-by-the-Wardrobe
Queen Victoria Street, EC4
Central map: page 12, K6

Only the shell of this church survived the Blitz. It takes its name from the Great Wardrobe, or royal storehouse, which used to stand nearby. Now the headquarters of the Redundant Churches Fund, the church was restored in the late 1950s and contains furnishings from other London churches.

### St Andrew Undershaft
St Mary Axe, Leadenhall Street, EC3
Central map: page 12, M7

The strange name of this church is derived from the fact that a famous

maypole once stood beside it. It is essentially a 16th-century building, although the tower was restored during the 19th century. Its most notable monument is to John Stow, a 16th-century historian who wrote the first topographical description of London. Despite bomb damage in the Blitz, the church still retains some original glass in the aisle windows, and the magnificent west window dates from the 17th century.

### St Anne and St Agnes
Gresham Street, EC2
Central map: page 12, L7

Wren rebuilt this attractive little church after the Great Fire. It has a square tower and a spacious interior with a central vault supported by elegant columns. The church contains a fine collection of ecclesiastical antiquities, but is only open to the public on Sundays, when it is used for Lutheran services.

### St Anne Limehouse
Commercial Road, E14
Not on map

This was the first of Nicholas Hawksmoor's spectacular Classical-style churches, of which there are two others in the East End. It was built in 1712 and is especially notable for its imposing tower. Hawksmoor was a pupil of Sir Christopher Wren, and followed closely in the footsteps of his master.

### St Bartholomew the Great
West Smithfield, EC1
Central map: page 12, L7

St Bartholomew's is one of the few surviving examples of Norman architecture in London. It dates from the 12th

ALL SAINTS

century and is the chancel of a great Norman monastery church which once stood here. After the dissolution of the monasteries it became private property, and for 300 years was put to a variety of uses, including a factory and stables. It reverted to its original use during the 19th century and was restored by Sir Aston Webb. Its interior is dominated by huge Romanesque pillars, and contains the tomb of Rahere, the founder of the church and of St Bartholomew's Hospital. The church has a particularly interesting gateway, consisting of a half-timbered gatehouse above a battered 13th-century arch which was the original entrance to the nave.

### St Bartholomew-the-less
West Smithfield, EC1
Central map: page 12, L7

This is the chapel of St Bartholomew's Hospital, in whose grounds it stands. All that remains of the original 15th-century building is the tower and vestry, which were incorporated into an octagonal church designed by George Dance the Younger in the 18th century.

## St Benet's (Welsh Metropolitan Church)
Paul's Wharf, off Queen Victoria Street, EC4
Central map: page 12, L6

Wren put the finishing touches to this handsome little church in 1683. Its exterior has elaborately decorated window surrounds and the interior has an abundance of carved woodwork, including the galleries and altar. The church has been used by Welsh Episcopalians since 1879 and is only open for Sunday services.

## St Botolph Aldgate
Aldgate High Street, EC3
Central map: page 12, N7

A church has occupied this site for more than 1,000 years, but the present building dates from the 18th century, when it was rebuilt by the architect George Dance the Elder. J F Bentley, the architect responsible for Westminster Cathedral, added the figured ceiling in 1889, and further extensive alterations were made after a fire in 1965.

## St Botolph
Aldersgate St, EC1
Central map: page 12, L7

Founded in the 11th century and rebuilt in the 18th century, this church stands near the site of one of the old City gates.

St CLEMENT DANES.

The simple but very attractive exterior has a brick-built square tower with a cupola capped by a wooden bell turret. The beautifully decorated interior is lit by an odd mixture of stained glass windows, the best of which is undoubtedly an 18th-century representation of the Agony in the Garden.

## St Botolph's
Bishopsgate, EC2
Central map: page 12, M7

St Botolph's was rebuilt in the 18th century by James Gold with the help of George Dance the Elder. It is an impressive brick building surmounted by a clock tower and steeple. The interior was altered in the 19th century and has a coved ceiling supported by huge Corinthian columns.

## St Bride
Fleet Street, EC4
See page 103

## St Clement Danes
Strand, WC2
Central map: page 11, J6

A church has stood on this site since the 9th century. Sir Christopher Wren rebuilt it in the 1680s, and it was rebuilt once more after it had been virtually destroyed during World War II. It is the memorial church of the Royal Air Force, and the crests of some 900 squadrons and Commonwealth air forces are let into the flooring. Many of the church's fixtures and furnishings have been donated by overseas air forces. The 115-ft tower houses the bells that are immortalised in the famous lines of the nursery rhyme: 'Oranges and Lemons say the bells of St Clement's'.

ST ETHELBURGA THE VIRGIN

## St Clement Eastcheap
Clements Lane, EC4
Central map: page 12, M6

Of particular interest in this little church is the beautiful 17th-century woodwork, seen at its best in the canopied pulpit. The church itself was built by Wren in 1683.

## St Dunstan-in-the-West
Fleet Street, EC4
Central map: page 11, K7

Although founded in the 13th century, the present church on this site dates only from the early part of the 19th century. It is an octagonal building with a prominent lantern tower. Many monuments from the church that once stood here have been preserved, and include one to the mythical King Lud and his sons. Also of interest is the clock, which was made in 1671, and was one of the first clocks in London to have minute divisions. The famous angler Izaak Walton is depicted in the north-west window, and it was in Fleet Street that *The Compleat Angler* was published.

## St Edmund The King and Martyr
Lombard Street, EC3
Central map: page 12, M6

This church is dedicated to a king of East Anglia who was killed by the Danes in AD870. It was rebuilt by Sir Christopher Wren in 1670, and has a distinctive spire.

## St Ethelburga-the-Virgin
Bishopsgate, EC2
Central map: page 12, M7

Entered by a 14th-century doorway, this tiny medieval building is one of the best preserved of the City's pre-Fire churches. It was once famous for the picturesque shops which obscured the front, but were demolished in 1932.

## St Etheldreda, or Ely Chapel
Ely Place, EC1
(off Charterhouse St)
Central map: page 11, K7

Originally built in the 13th century, this little chapel was allowed to deteriorate over the centuries, and was finally almost totally destroyed during the Blitz. Only the façade and some Roman foundations survived, and these have been incorporated into the present structure. The chapel is two-storeyed and has a massive vaulted undercroft dating from 1252. It is the oldest pre-Reformation Roman Catholic church in London.

## St George
Bloomsbury Way, WC1
Central map: page 10, I7

Noted for its striking façade, this 18th-century church was built by Nicholas Hawksmoor. It has a Corinthian portico supported by six columns, and a tower and spire crowned by a statue of George I wearing a Roman toga.

## St George
Borough High Street, Southwark, SE1
Central map: page 6, L5

Rebuilt by the architect John Price in 1734-36, this church has a spired tower with octagonal upper stages. The galleried interior is watched over by Victorian carvings of cherubs affixed to the ceiling.

## St Giles Cripplegate
Fore Street, EC2
Central map: page 12, L7

Only the nave and tower of the original church built here in the 14th century survive. It was largely rebuilt in the 16th century, with further additions made to the tower a century later, and was badly damaged during World War II. It has now been restored. Among the many famous people buried here are Sir Martin Frobisher and the poet John Milton.

## St George Hanover Square
St George's Street, W1
Central map: page 9, G6

Many fashionable weddings have taken place in this church since it was built in the early part of the 18th century. It is an impressive Classical-style building with a galleried interior lit by 16th-century Flemish windows. Among those married here have been Benjamin Disraeli and Theodore Roosevelt.

## St Giles-in-the-Field
St Giles High Street, WC2
Central map: page 10, I7

This church's fine 161ft Baroque steeple makes it a prominent landmark. A church was founded on this site by Matilda, the wife of Henry I, in the 12th century, but the present building dates from the 18th century. It was beautifully restored in 1952-53, and has superb interior fittings, many of which were made for the church in the 18th century.

ST HELEN, BISHOPGATE

## St Helen Bishopsgate
Great St Helen's, EC3
(off Bishopsgate)
Central map: page 12, M7

One of the largest churches in the City, this magnificent structure was built in the 13th century and was originally two churches joined by an arcade of pillars. There are two naves, one of which served a monastery, and the other for the parish. The church is famous for its beautiful brasses, which are usually protected by carpets. Permission must be obtained before rubbings can be made. There is much else of interest in the building, including several excellent monuments, two fine sword-rests (one dating from 1665 and very rare), and a Jacobean pulpit which is beautifully carved.

## St James-the-Less
Thorndyke Street, off Vauxhall Bridge Road, SW1
Central map: page 4, H3

G E Street, one of the most accomplished of Victorian architects, designed this splendid church in 1858. Its plain exterior encases a majestic vaulted interior which is lit by windows made by the famous firm of Clayton and Bell.

**St James Garlickhythe**
Upper Thames Street, EC4
Central map: page 12, L6

Founded as long ago as the 12th century, the present church on this site was built by Wren after the Great Fire, and is one of his more elaborate designs. Its most distinguishing exterior feature is the handsome spire. The interior, which was restored after bomb damage, has excellent woodwork, as well as ironwork hat racks and sword rests. The church reputedly owes its name to the fact that garlic was once sold nearby.

**St James's**
Piccadilly, W1
Central map: page 10, H6

This church was originally built for the Earl of St Alban by Wren in 1676. It was extensively damaged during the Blitz, and was restored to its former glory in 1954. It has a magnificent galleried interior beneath a barrel-vaulted ceiling. The font, reredos, altarpiece and organ case are all the work of the master-woodcarver, Grinling Gibbons. The organ itself was a gift from Mary II in 1690, and came from Whitehall Palace. (Brass rubbing — see page 79)

**St John**
Smith Square, SW1
Central map: page 4, I4

When the architect of this church, Thomas Archer, asked Queen Anne what style she would like it built in, she is reputed to have kicked over a stool, pointed at it and said 'build me one like that'. In fact the four large towers at each corner of the building serve a strictly functional purpose, in that they

were specially designed to prevent the whole structure sinking into the marsh upon which it was built. The church was gutted during World War II, and now serves as a music and cultural centre.

**St John's Church**
Church Row, Hampstead
Not on map

St John's is the parish church of Hampstead, rebuilt 1745-7, and subsequently added to and altered in the 19th century. The handsome wrought-iron gates to the churchyard date from the 18th century, and were brought from the mansion of the Duke of Chandos in Edgware when it was demolished. Many famous local residents are buried in the churchyard. In the south-east corner lies the painter John Constable (1776-1837), in the newer part north of the road the actor-manager Sir Herbert Beerbohm Tree (1853-1917), the historian of London, Sir Walter Besant (1836-1901), and George du Maurier.

**St Katherine Cree**
Leadenhall Street, EC3
Central map: page 12, N7

This church was built in 1631, and is one of the few London churches that escaped damage both in the Great Fire, and World War II. It is built in the Classical style, and is now the headquarters of the Industrial Christian Fellowship.

**St Lawrence Jewry**
Gresham Street, EC2
Central map: page 12, L7

Rebuilt by Wren on the site of a medieval church, this church stands in the forecourt of the Guildhall. The name Jewry has survived from

the period between 1066 and 1290 when the neighbourhood had a large Jewish population. The church was rebuilt after bomb damage, and the present spire incorporates a replica of the incendiary bomb which gutted the interior. It is the guild church of the Corporation of London, and pews are set aside for the lord mayor, sheriffs, and other City dignitaries.

**St Leonard**
Shoreditch High Street, E1
Central map: page 12, N8

Restored by George Dance the Younger between 1736 and 1740, this church has an imposing portico and a 192ft steeple. There have been subsequent renovations following bomb damage in World War II, but the organ console dates from 1756. There are old stocks and a whipping post in the churchyard.

**St Magnus the Martyr**
Lower Thames Street, EC3
Central map: page 12, M6

The church which originally stood on this site, dating from Saxon times, overlooked the northern approach to the old London Bridge. It was destroyed in the Great Fire, and was rebuilt by Sir Christopher Wren. A portion of timber from an 8th-century Roman wharf, and a stone from the first arch of old London Bridge, dating from 1176, are preserved in the churchyard near the main entrance. Today the church is hemmed in by tall buildings, but its fine tower is still prominent. Inside, much of the 17th-century woodwork and wrought ironwork has been preserved.

## St Margaret's Lothbury
Lothbury, EC2
Central map: page 12, M7

Rebuilt by Wren between 1686 and 1690, this church contains a good deal of ancient woodwork from other City churches, including the screen and pulpit from All Hallows the Great, Upper Thames Street, which was demolished in 1894. The Scientific Instrument Makers' Company hold their services here, and the church is also a venue for music recitals.

## St Margaret's Westminster
Parliament Square, SW1
Central map: page 4, I4

Dating from the late 15th century, St Margaret's has been the official church of the House of Commons since 1614. Although it is rather overshadowed by its mighty neighbour, Westminster Abbey, it is equally worthy of attention, and is especially notable for its wealth of monuments. The glass in the east window, 16th-century work from the Netherlands, is considered to be the finest in London. Chaucer and William Caxton were famous early parishioners, and both Samuel Pepys and Sir Winston Churchill were married here.

## St Margaret Pattens
Rood Lane, Eastcheap, EC3
Central map: page 12, M6

This church was redesigned by Wren, and contains much interesting woodwork, including the only 17th-century canopied churchwardens' pews in the City, and a beadles' pew complete with a low punishment bench where members of the congregation who misbehaved were made to sit for the remainder of the service. The name Pattens is thought to derive from the wooden soles, mounted on iron rings called pattens, designed to raise the wearer above the debris of London's streets, which were made and sold in a nearby lane.

## St Martin-within-Ludgate
Ludgate Hill, EC4
Central map: page 12, K7

It is thought that a church stood on this site some 13 centuries ago, but reliable records date only from the 12th century. It was rebuilt in 1437, destroyed in the Great Fire, and subsequently rebuilt by Wren in 1684. He incorporated the remains of the old tower into the fabric of the new church. The interior is magnificently decorated, and contains carved woodwork by Grinling Gibbons, and a double 17th-century church warden's chair, believed to be the only one of its kind in existence.

## St Martin-in-the-Fields
Trafalgar Square, WC2
Central map: page 10, I6

The medieval church on this site, then surrounded as its name suggests by open fields, was extensively rebuilt by James Gibbs in the early 18th century. It has an imposing temple-like portico, and a spacious galleried interior. Buckingham Palace is within the parish boundaries, and there are royal boxes at the east end of the church. The vaulted crypt contains a 16th-century chest and an 18th-century whipping post, but is better known for the fact that it is opened each evening as a shelter for the homeless. This carries on the tradition of H R L Sheppard, a World War I army chaplain, who, on his return from the Front, always kept the church open for servicemen or others who were stranded.

## St Mary's
St Marychurch Street, SE16
Not on map

Rebuilt during the 18th century, this church has close connections with the sea and sailors. The altar table and sanctuary chairs were made from timber from the 18th-century warship *Fighting Temeraire*, and the nave columns are made from ships' masts enclosed in plaster.

## St Mary Aldermary
Queen Victoria Street, EC4
Central map: page 12, L6

One of the few churches that Wren rebuilt in the Gothic style after the Great Fire, this church was greatly altered during the 19th century. However, the beautiful fan-vaulted ceilings survive, as do Wren's pulpit and font.

## St Mary Abchurch
Abchurch Lane, EC4
(off Cannon St)
Central map: page 12, L6

Wren rebuilt this church about 15 years after the Great Fire had destroyed the original, and subsequent renovations have done nothing to alter the late 17th-century appearance. It stands in a secluded courtyard, and is noted for its painted ceiling by William Stow, and rare Grinling Gibbons reredos. Most of the original fittings have survived, notably the pulpit , font, and finely carved pews.

### St Mary-at-Hill
off Eastcheap, EC3
Central map: page 12, M6

Since it was damaged during the Great Fire, this church has been restored and rebuilt several times, beginning with Wren's work of about 1672. Its modest exterior encloses one of the finest church interiors in the City. There is much fine plasterwork, and the fittings are superb. The only complete set of box pews in the City can be seen here, and there are some magnificent Georgian sword rests.

### St Mary-le-Bow
Cheapside, EC2
Central map: page 12, L6

Restored by Wren after the Great Fire, this church was extensively fire-damaged during the Blitz. Wren's steeple survived, however, and its lofty spire, crowned by a 9ft weathervane in the form of a dragon, still towers over Cheapside. The famous Bow Bells originally rang as a curfew and it was their distinctive peal which is said to have recalled Dick Whittington from Highgate Hill. Those born within their sound are said to be true Cockneys. The bells were recast after severe damage in 1941, and rang out anew in 1961.

### St Mary-le-Strand
Strand, WC2
Central map: page 11, J6

The present building on this site, designed by James Gibbs in the early 18th century, is one of the best examples of Italian-influenced church architecture in London.

### St Mary Woolnoth
Lombard Street, EC3
Central map: page 12, M6

Partly damaged in the Great Fire, and subsequently restored by Wren, this church was completely rebuilt by Nicholas Hawksmoor between 1716 and 1727 in a highly original, almost fortified style. The interior has a tremendous feeling of sumptuous spaciousness which is heightened by the groups of Corinthian columns supporting the ceiling.

### St Michael-upon-Cornhill
Cornhill, EC3
Central map: page 12, M6

This church was built by Wren after the Great Fire, and its fine Gothic tower was added by Hawksmoor in 1721. Sir George Gilbert Scott restored and embellished it. The font and the altar-table date from the late 17th century, but the most unusual, and decorative, object is the carved wooden pelican by George Paterson, which dates from 1775.

### St Michael Paternoster Royal
College Hill, EC4
(off Queen St)
Central map: page 12, L6

Dick Whittington met the cost of rebuilding this church in 1409 and he was buried here in 1423, but his tomb was destroyed during the Great Fire. Wren rebuilt the church, but it was badly damaged by a flying bomb in 1944, and the restored building was not consecrated until 1968.

### St Nicholas Cole Abbey
Queen Victoria Street, EC4
Central map: page 12, L6

One of the first churches which Wren worked on after the Great Fire, St Nicholas was gutted by incendiary bombs in 1941. The architect Arthur Bailey undertook the rebuilding in 1962, adhering to Wren's design, and preserving the unusual spire, which has an inverted trumpet shape and is crowned by a weathervane in the shape of a ship.

### St Olave
Hart Street, EC3
(opposite Pepys St)
Central map: page 12, N6

Samuel Pepys and Admiral Sir William Penn saved this 15th-century church from the Great Fire by having the surrounding buildings torn down. No one, however, could prevent bomb damage in 1941. Access to the church from Seething Lane is via an unusual gateway decorated with skulls, which Dickens describes as belonging to the church of St Ghastly Grim in his *Uncommercial Traveller*. Pepys and his wife Elizabeth are buried here.

ST-MARY-LE-STRAND

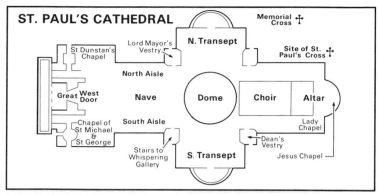

ST. PAUL'S CATHEDRAL

Memorial ✝ Cross

St Dunstan's Chapel

Lord Mayor's Vestry

N. Transept

Site of St. ✝ Paul's Cross

North Aisle

Great West Door

Nave

Dome

Choir

Altar

Chapel of St Michael & St George

South Aisle

Lady Chapel

Stairs to Whispering Gallery

S. Transept

Dean's Vestry

Jesus Chapel

### St Paul's Cathedral
EC4
Central map: page 12, L7
☎ 01-248 2705

This is Wren's masterpiece. It was built of Portland stone in 1675-1710 to replace the former Gothic cathedral of the 13th century, which was altered early in the 17th century by Inigo Jones and finally destroyed in 1666 by the Great Fire of London. The cathedral rises to a height of 365ft and in the south-west tower is 'Great Paul', a bell weighing some 17 tons. The west façade of the cathedral is 180ft wide and the famous dome, 112ft in diameter, is buttressed by twelve massive supports. Within the dome is the famous 'Whispering Gallery', where whispered words can be heard quite clearly 112ft away across the void. Carved woodwork by Grinling Gibbons and ironwork by Jean Tijou are features of the cathedral interior. The crypt contains the tombs of Wren, Nelson, Wellington, Reynolds and Turner. The Whispering Gallery and Golden Gallery may be visited for a small charge. Open: daily Apr-Sep, 8-6; Oct-Mar, 8-5, subject to special services. Admission free (Donations).

### St Paul's Church
Covent Garden WC2
Central map: page 10, I6

The first new Anglican church to be built in London after the Reformation, St Paul's was designed by Inigo Jones for the 4th Earl of Bedford, between 1631 and 1633. It has long associations with the theatre since both the Theatre Royal, Drury Lane and the Royal Opera House are in the parish. Amongst the famous buried here are Claude Duval the highwayman, Grinling Gibbons, Thomas Arne, composer of *Rule Britannia*, and the actress Vivien Leigh. J M W Turner was baptised here.

### St Paul
Deptford High Street, SE8
Not on map

Built between 1712 and 1730 to a distinctive Baroque design by Thomas Archer, this church has a fine circular portico supported by Tuscan columns and surmounted by a slim tower. The square interior is galleried and has many Dutch oak fittings.

### St Peter-upon-Cornhill
Cornhill, EC3
Central map: page 12, M6

This church, which stands on the highest ground in the City, is believed to occupy a site on which a church has stood since the 2nd century. This makes it by far the oldest church site in London. The present church was built by Wren after the Great Fire, and contains many fine fittings, including a 17th-century font and two Wren-type churchwardens' pews. However, the most outstanding feature is the chancel screen, designed by Wren and his 16-year-old daughter. Lunchtime recitals are held in the church, and the Players of St Peter-upon-Cornhill perform colourful plays selected from medieval mystery plays.

### St Sepulchre
Holborn Viaduct, EC1
Central map: page 11, K7

Wren assisted in the rebuilding of this church after the Great Fire. It is the largest of the City parish churches, and contains some 17th-century pews and a fine Renatus Harris organ, dating from 1677. The churchyard was so popular with bodysnatchers during the

18th century that a Watch House was erected so that the corpses could be guarded. This was restored following war damage. St Sepulchre's is known as the Musicians' Church, and the Musicians' Chapel contains the ashes of Sir Henry Wood, founder of the Promenade Concerts.

### St Stephen Walbrook
Walbrook, EC4
(next to Mansion House)
Central map: page 12, M6

This church is one of Wren's masterpieces, and has what is believed to be the first dome built into any English church. It was badly damaged during World War II, and restored during the 1950s.

### St Vedast
Foster Lane, EC2
(off Cheapside)
Central map: page 12, L7

The most noteworthy feature of this Wren church is its elegant steeple. Inside there are a number of ancient fittings from defunct City churches.

### Southwark Cathedral
Borough High Street, SE1
Central map: page 6, M5

A church has stood on this site since the 7th century, but it was not

until 1905 that the basically 16th-century parish church of St Saviour was elevated to cathedral status. Despite rebuilding, particularly during the 19th century, its medieval Gothic style has remained largely intact, and parts of the church date back to at least the 13th century. There are many monuments in the building, including an unusual one to a 17th-century quack doctor called Lyonell Lockyer. Ancient tombs include that of Edmund Shakespeare, William's younger brother.

### Westminster Abbey
Parliament Square, SW1
Central map: page 4, I4
☎ 01-222 5152

A church has stood on this site since at least as early as Saxon times. The church later built here was enlarged by Edward the Confessor and made the crowning place of English sovereigns. Henry III rebuilt the cathedral (1216-72) in tribute to Edward. Henry VII added the chapel at the eastern end (1503-19). The 225ft-high towers were added in the mid 18th century by Nicholas Hawksmoor. Many generations of English sovereigns are buried here in beautifully carved

THOMAS CARLYLE

tombs. Elsewhere are memorials to the nation's great statesmen, politicians, scientists, poets and others. (Brass rubbing — see page 79.)

Open: daily 8-6 (8pm Wed) Choir and chapels Mon-Fri 9-4.45 (5.45 Sat)

### Westminster Cathedral
Ashley Place, SW1
Central map: page 4, H4
☎ 01-834 7452

The largest and most important Roman Catholic church in England; a Byzantine structure completed in 1903 just seven years after the foundation stone was laid. Built entirely of red brick with contrasting bands of Portland Stone, its interior is ornamented with marble and beautiful mosaics.

Open: daily, 7am-8pm Admission free (Donations).

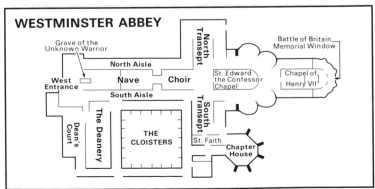

## WESTMINSTER ABBEY

Grave of the Unknown Warrior

North Transept

Battle of Britain Memorial Window

North Aisle

West Entrance

Nave    Choir

St. Edward the Confessor Chapel

Chapel of Henry VII

South Aisle

South Transept

Dean's Court

The Deanery

THE CLOISTERS

St. Faith

Chapter House

# Statues, Monuments and Plaques

London has more statues than any other city in the world, and there are hundreds of 'blue plaques' commemorating famous people's homes. Described on the following pages is a selection of London's more interesting monuments, statues and plaques.

### Achilles
Hyde Park, W1
Central map: page 3, F5

Sculpture by Sir Richard Westmacott, 1822.
This statue of the Greek god was made from a cannon captured during the Peninsular Wars, and erected in 1822.

### Prince Albert
The Albert Memorial, Kensington Gore, SW7 (opposite Royal Albert Hall)
Central map: page 2, D4

Sculpture designed by Sir Gilbert Scott, 1872.
This enormous and imposing memorial is a monument not only to Prince Albert, but also to the benevolent aspects of Victorian Imperialism. The memorial was commissioned by Queen Victoria in memory of her husband. The sculpture of the Prince, which was made by John Foley, sits under an ornate and intricately decorated canopy. The Prince is depicted reading a catalogue of the Great Exhibition of 1851, for which he was largely responsible.

### Alfred the Great
Trinity Church Square, off Trinity Street, SE1
Central map: page 6, L4

Thought to date from 1395, this is the oldest statue in London.

### Queen Anne
Front of St Paul's Cathedral, EC4
Central map: page 12, L7

Sculpture by Richard Belt, 1886.
This marble statue is a copy of the one by Francis Bird, 1712, and erected to commemorate the completion of St Paul's.

### Queen Boadicea
Westminster Bridge, SW1
Central map: page 4, I5

Sculpture by Thomas Thornycroft, 1902.
Queen Boadicea (or Boudicca) is depicted in her war chariot, accompanied by her daughters.

### Robert Burns
Victoria Embankment Gardens, WC2
Central map: page 10, I6

Sculpture by Steeller, 1884.

### The Burghers of Calais
Victoria Tower Gardens, SW1 (off Millbank)
Central map: page 4, I4

Sculpture by Rodin.
Rodin's superb group of figures represents the citizens of Calais who surrendered to Edward III in 1340 to save their town from destruction.

### Lord Byron
Hyde Park Corner, SW1 (opposite Achilles)
Central map: page 3, F5

Sculpture by Richard Belt, 1880.

### George Canning
Parliament Square, SW1
Central map: page 4, I4

Sculpture by Richard Westmacott, 1832.
This bronze statue of the statesman in a toga is chiefly notable for the fact that while it was still in the sculptor's studio it fell over and killed a man.

### Thomas Carlyle
Cheyne Walk, SW3
Central map: page 2, E2

Sculpture by Sir Edgar Boehm, 1900.
This statue shows the 'Sage of Chelsea' sitting in Cheyne Walk Gardens.

### Edith Cavell
Junction of St Martin's Lane and Charing Cross Rd, WC2
Central map: page 10, I6

Sculpture by Sir George Frampton, 1920.
Memorial to the First World War nurse who was shot in Belgium (1915) for helping prisoners to escape.

### The Cenotaph
Whitehall, SW1
Central map: page 4, I5

Monument by Sir Edwin Lutyens, 1919.
Set in the middle of Whitehall, the Cenotaph is a simple pillar of Portland stone unveiled in 1920 on the anniversary of Armistice Day. It was originally built to the memory of the men who lost their lives in World War I. Now memorial services for the dead of both world wars are held here every year on the second Sunday in November.

**Sir Charles Chaplin**
Leicester Square, W1
Central map: page 10, I6

Sculpture by John
Doubleday, 1981.

**Charles I**
Trafalgar Square, SW1
Central map: page 10, I6

Sculpture by Hubert le
Sueur, 1633.
Cast in bronze, this
statue was to have been
melted down during the
Commonwealth period
but was hidden and re-
erected in 1660. It was
moved to Mentmore in
Buckinghamshire during
World War II and was
replaced in 1947 with a
new sword. The original
sword is said to have
been dislodged by a
photographer in 1867
and stolen while a
procession was in
progress.

**Sir Winston Churchill**
Parliament Square, SW1
Central map: page 4, I4

Sculpture by Ivor
Roberts-Jones, 1973.
This bronze statue of the
great statesman and war
leader depicts Churchill
in a typically pugnacious
attitude.

**Cleopatra's Needle**
Victoria Embankment
Central map: page 11, J6

Mehemet Ali, a viceroy
of Egypt, presented this
famous landmark to
Great Britain in 1819. It
was not erected in its
present position until
1879, after an eventful
sea journey which cost
the lives of six seamen.
Originally the Needle
stood in Heliopolis,
where it was one of a
pair erected 3,500 years
ago. Its twin now stands
in Central Park, New
York, and neither of
them has any
connections with
Cleopatra.

**Oliver Cromwell**
Old Palace Yard, SW1
(outside Westminster
Hall)
Central map: page 4, I4

Sculpture by Sir William
Thornycroft, 1899.

**Edward VII**
Waterloo Place, SW1
(Junction of Pall Mall and
Regent St)
Central map: page 4, H5

Sculpture by Sir Bertram
Mackennal, 1921.

**Eros**
Piccadilly Circus, W1
Central map: page 10, H6

Sculpture by Sir Alfred
Gilbert, 1833.
One of London's most
famous landmarks, this
figure of an archer was
erected as a memorial to
a Victorian reformer and
philanthropist, the Earl of
Shaftesbury. The archer
actually represents the
Angel of Christian
Charity, not Eros.

**The Fat Boy**
Giltspur Street, EC1
Central map: page 12, K7

This peculiar little gilded
figure marks the
spot, originally known as
Pie Corner, where the
Great Fire was halted in
1666.

**Mahatma Gandhi**
Tavistock Square, WC2
Central map: page 10, I8

Sculpture by Fredda
Brilliant, 1968.

**George III**
Corner of
Haymarket/Trafalgar
Square
Central map: page 4, I5

Statue by Wyatt, 1836.
Fine equestrian statue.

**George IV**
Trafalgar Square, SW1
Central map: page 10, I6

Sculpture by Chantrey,
1834.

**George V**
Old Palace Yard, SW1
(Outside Westminster
Hall)
Central map: page 4, I4

Sculpture by Sir William
Reid Dick, 1947.

**The Griffin**
Strand, EC4
Central map: page 11, J6

The Griffin, the unofficial
badge of the City of
London, stands at the
point where the Strand
ends and Fleet Street
begins. Originally this
was the site of the Old
Temple Bar gateway, and
the spot traditionally
marks the western limit
of the City.

**Sir Henry Irving**
St Martin's Place, WC2
(Trafalgar Square)
Central map: page 10, I6

Sculpture by Thomas
Brock, 1910.
Irving is regarded as
being one of the greatest
actors who ever lived.

**James II**
Trafalgar Square, WC2
(outside National Gallery)
Central map: page 10, I6

Sculpture by Grinling
Gibbons, 1686.
Usually regarded as the
finest statue in London,
this figure of the King is
shown in Roman
costume.

**Dr Edward Jenner**
Italian Gardens,
Kensington Gardens, W2
Central map: page 8, D6

Sculpture by William
Calder Marshall, 1858.
Pioneer of vaccination,
notably discoverer of
smallpox vaccine.

**Dr Samuel Johnson**
St Clement Danes,
Strand, WC2
Central map: page 11, J6

Sculpture by Percy
Fitzgerald, 1910.

### President John F Kennedy
1 Park Crescent, W1
Central map: page 9, G8

Sculpture by Jacques Lipchitz, 1965.
Bronze bust which was paid for by readers of the *Sunday Telegraph.*
Unveiled by his brothers Edward and Robert Kennedy.

### Abraham Lincoln
Parliament Square, SW1
Central map: page 4, I4

Sculpture copy of Saint-Gaudens, 1920.
Replica of statue in Chicago, it shows Lincoln in a frock coat standing in front of his Grecian chair.

### Monument
Monument Street, EC3
Central map: page 12, M6

See page 106

### Sir Thomas More
Cheyne Walk, SW3
(corner of Old Church St)
Central map: page 2, E2

Sculpture by Cubitt Bevis, 1969.

### Lord Nelson
Trafalgar Square, WC2
Central map: page 10, I6

Sculpture by E H Bailey, 1843.
This 17ft 4in statue stands on the top of the famous column. Together they reach a combined height of almost 185ft. Four identical lions, cast from a single original by Sir Edwin Landseer, guard the base of the column. This memorial to the nation's greatest sailor was set up between 1842 and 1867.

### Florence Nightingale
Waterloo Place, SW1
(Junction of Pall Mall and Regent St)
Central map: page 4, H5

Sculpture by A Walker, 1915.

The statue of the 'Lady with the Lamp', immortalized for her work to wounded servicemen, stands adjacent to the Guards Crimean War memorial.

### Peter Pan
Kensington Gardens, W2
Central map: page 2, D5

Sculpture by Sir George Frampton, 1911.
This statue of Sir James Barrie's immortal character has delighted several generations of children.

### Sir Walter Raleigh
Banqueting House, Whitehall, SW1
Central map: page 4, I5

Sculpture by William Macmillan, 1959.
Raleigh was beheaded near this spot in 1618. The bronze statue, in Elizabethan dress, is extremely small, reflecting Raleigh's diminutive stature.

### Richard I
Old Palace Yard, SW1
(outside Westminster Hall)
Central map: page 4, I4

Sculpture by Baron Carlo Marochetti, 1860.
This spirited equestrian statue of Richard the Lionheart was made for the Great Exhibition.

### Franklin D Roosevelt
Grosvenor Square, W1
Central map: page 9, F6

Sculpture by Sir William Reid Dick, 1948.

### Royal Regiment of Artillery Memorial
Hyde Park Corner, SW1
Central map: page 3, G5

Sculpture by C Sargeant Jagger, stone base by Lionel Pearson, 1925.
Magnificent memorial of stone field gun with over-life size bronze gunners. In remembrance

of the 49,076 men of all ranks who lost their lives in the 1914-18 war.

### Captain Robert Falcon Scott
Waterloo Place, SW1
(Junction of Pall Mall and Regent St)
Central map: page 4, H5

Sculpture by his widow Lady Scott, 1915.

### William Shakespeare
Leicester Square, WC2
Central map: page 10, I6

Sculpture by Giovanni Fontana, a copy of one by Scheemakers in Westminster Abbey, 1874.

### Field Marshall Jan Christian Smuts
Parliament Square, SW1
Central map: page 4, I4

Sculpture by Jacob Epstein, 1958.

### South Bank Lion
Central map: page 5, J5

The lion standing on a plinth on the east side of Westminster Bridge previously surmounted the Lion Brewery, which was demolished to build the Royal Festival Hall. It was made from Coade's famous artificial stone which had superb weathering qualities. Unfortunately the formula — which was a closely guarded secret — was lost after the factory was demolished.

**Queen Victoria**
Queen Victoria
Memorial, The Mall,
SW1
Central map: page 4, H5

Sculptures by Sir Thomas
Brock, 1911.
This elegant group of
statuary stands in front of
Buckingham Palace. It
was designed by Sir
Aston Webb.

Kensington Gardens,
WC2
(near the Round Pound)
Central map: page 1, C5

Princess Louise, one of
Queen Victoria's
daughters, made this
statue in 1893.

**George Washington**
Trafalgar Square, WC2
(outside National Gallery)
Central map: page 10, I6

Sculpture, replica of
original in Richmond,
Virginia, USA by Jean-
Antoine Houdon.
Presented by Virginia in
1921.

**The 1st Duke of
Wellington**
Hyde Park Corner, W1
Central map: page 3, G5

Sculpture by J E Boehm,
1888.
The Duke is shown here
riding Copenhagen, the
horse he rode throughout
the Battle of Waterloo.

**King William III**
St James's Square, SW1
Central map: page 4, H5

Sculpture by John Bacon
the Younger, 1808.
Portrayed as a Roman
General. Under the
horse's hoof is the
molehill which caused
his fatal accident while
riding at Hampton Court.

**Duke of York**
Carlton House Terrace,
SW1 (off The Mall)
Central map: page 4, I5

Sculpture by Sir Richard
Westmacott, 1833.
This 112ft granite pillar,
crowned by a statue of

DUKE OF WELLINGTON

the Grand Old Duke of
York, commemorates the
second son of George III
and was designed by
Benjamin Wyatt. The
cost of its erection is
supposed to have been
largely defrayed by
stopping a day's pay
from every man in the
army.

## BLUE PLAQUES — Famous People

Blue plaques to commemorate the residences of famous people have been
erected in London since 1866. Today the number exceeds 500. The first
plaque commemorated Byron's home at 24 Holles Street. It was made from
deep-blue terracotta with white lettering. Since then various designs have
been used:

| | |
|---|---|
| 1867-1900 | The tablets were made by Minton in chocolate-brown terracotta with white lettering |
| 1907-1921 | Introduction of additional rectangular design in bronze, stone and lead |
| 1921 | Doulton glaze adopted as standard material for plaque. During the 1920s after various use of colours the 'blue' plaque was adopted as the standard colour |
| 1937 | Plain design still used today was adopted |
| 1939 | White edging was added to the plaques |
| 1955 | Plaques manufactured by Carter's at Poole, Dorset |
| 1982/83 | Plaques manufactured by Alan Dawson of Staffordshire |

Listed below are a few of the famous residences:

| NAME | ADDRESS | PLAQUE ERECTED |
|---|---|---|
| BADEN-POWELL, Robert (1857-1941) founder of the Scouting movement | 9 Hyde Park Gate Central map: page 2, D4 | 1972 |

| NAME | ADDRESS | PLAQUE ERECTED |
|------|---------|----------------|
| BAIRD, John Logie (1888-1946)<br>In 1926 he demonstrated<br>television in this house | 22 Frith Street<br>Central map: page 10, H6 | 1951 |
| BALDWIN, Stanley (1867-1947)<br>Prime Minister | 93 Eaton Square<br>Central map: page 3, G4 | 1969 |
| BLIGH, William (1754-1817)<br>Captain of the 'Bounty' | 100 Lambeth Road<br>Central map: page 5, K4 | 1952 |
| CANAL, Antonio, (Canaletto) (1697-1768)<br>Venetian Painter | 41 Beak Street<br>Central map: page 10, H6 | 1925 |
| CARLYLE, Thomas (1795-1881)<br>Essayist and historian<br>(see page 81) | 24 Cheyne Row<br>Central map: page 2, E2 | 1907 |
| CHURCHILL, Lord Randolph (1849-1895)<br>Statesman | 2 Connaught Place<br>(off Bayswater Road)<br>Central map: page 7, E6 | 1962 |
| CLIVE OF INDIA, Lord (1725-1774)<br>Soldier and<br>administrator | 45 Berkeley Square<br>Central map: page 9, G6 | 1953 |
| DANCE, George, the younger (1741-1825)<br>Architect | 91 Gower Street<br>Central map: page 10, H8 | 1970 |
| DICKENS, Charles (1812-1870)<br>Novelist<br>(see page 83) | 48 Doughty Street<br>Central map: page 11, J8 | 1903 |
| DISRAELI, Benjamin, Earl of Beaconsfield<br>Statesman, born here 1804 | 22 Theobalds Road<br>Central map: page 11, J8 | 1948 |
| DISRAELI, Benjamin Earl of Beaconsfield<br>(1804-1881)<br>Statesman, died here | 19 Curzon Street<br>Central map: page 3, G5 | 1908 |
| ELGAR, Sir Edward (1857-1934)<br>Composer | 51 Avonmore Road<br>Central map: page 1, A3 | 1962 |
| ELIOT, George (Mary Ann Cross)<br>(1819-1880)<br>Novelist | 4 Cheyne Walk<br>Central map: page 2, E2 | 1949 |
| FRANKLIN, Benjamin (1706-1790)<br>American Statesman | 36 Craven Street<br>(off N side of<br>Northumberland Ave)<br>Central map: page 4, I5 | 1914 |
| GLADSTONE, William (1809-1898)<br>Statesman | 11 Carlton House Terrace<br>(off N side of The Mall)<br>Central map: page 4, I5 | 1925 |
| HANDEL, George (1685-1795)<br>Musician | 25 Brook Street<br>Central map: page 9, G6 | 1952 |
| HILL, Sir Rowland (1795-1879)<br>Postal reformer | 1 Orme Square<br>(off Orme Lane)<br>Central map: page 7, C6 | 1907 |
| HUXLEY, Thomas (1825-1895)<br>Biologist | 38 Marlborough Place<br>Central map: page 7, C9 | 1910 |
| IRVING, Sir Henry (1838-1905)<br>Actor | 15a Grafton Street<br>(N end of Albemarle St)<br>Central map: page 9, G6 | 1950 |
| JOHNSON, Dr Samuel (1709-1784)<br>Writer | 17 Gough Square<br>Central map: page 11, K7 | — |
| KIPLING, Rudyard (1865-1936)<br>Poet and writer | 43 Villiers Street<br>(off John Adams St)<br>Central map: page 10, I6 | 1957 |
| LAWRENCE, T E (1888-1935)<br>'Lawrence of Arabia' | 14 Barton Street<br>(off Gt Peter St)<br>Central map: page 4, I4 | 1966 |

| NAME | ADDRESS | PLAQUE ERECTED |
|---|---|---|
| MARCONI, Guglielmo (1874-1937)<br>Inventor of wireless communication | 71 Hereford Road<br>Central map: page 7, B6 | 1954 |
| MARX, Karl (1818-1883)<br>Philosopher | 28 Dean Street<br>Central map: page 10, H6 | 1967 |
| MOZART, Wolfgang Amadeus (1756-1791)<br>Composer | 180 Ebury Street<br>Central map: page 3, G3 | 1939 |
| NEWTON, Sir Isaac (1642-1727)<br>Scientist and philosopher | 87 Jermyn Street<br>Central map: page 4, H5 | 1908 |
| NIGHTINGALE, Florence (1820-1910)<br>Nurse and hospital reformer | 10 South Street<br>Central map: page 3, F5 | 1955 |
| NOVELLO, Ivor (1893-1951)<br>Actor, song writer and dramatist | 11 Aldwych<br>Central map: page 11, J6 | 1973 |
| PEPYS, Samuel (1633-1703)<br>Diarist, Secretary        also at<br>of the Admiralty | 12 Buckingham Street<br>14 Buckingham Street<br>(off John Adam St)<br>Central map: page 10, I6 | 1947 |
| PITT, William, Earl of Chatham<br>(1708-1778)<br>Prime Minister | 10 St James's Square<br>Central map: page 4, H5 | 1910 |
| also<br>STANLEY, Edward, Earl of Derby<br>(1799-1869)<br>Prime Minister<br>GLADSTONE, William (1809-1898)<br>Prime Minister | | |
| PITT, William (the Younger) (1759-1806)<br>Prime Minister | 120 Baker Street<br>Central map: page 9, F7 | 1949 |
| ROSSETTI, Dante (1828-1882)<br>Artist and Poet | 110 Hallam Street<br>Central map: page 9, G7 | 1906 |
| SCOTT, Captain Robert (1868-1912)<br>Antarctic explorer | 56 Oakley Street<br>Central map: page 2, E2 | 1935 |
| SHERATON, Thomas (1751-1806)<br>Cabinet maker | 163 Wardour Street<br>Central map: page 10, H6 | 1954 |
| TWAIN, Mark, (Samuel Langhorne Clemens)<br>(1835-1910)<br>Writer | 23 Tedworth Square<br>Central map: page 3, F2 | 1960 |
| VAUGHAN WILLIAMS, Ralph (1872-1958)<br>Composer | 10 Hanover Terrace<br>(off Outer Circle)<br>Central map: page 8, E8 | 1972 |
| WHISTLER, James (1834-1903)<br>Artist | 96 Cheyne Walk<br>Central map: page 2, E2 | 1925 |
| WILBERFORCE, William (1759-1833)<br>Abolition of slavery | 44 Cadogan Place<br>Central map: page 3, F4 | 1961 |
| WILDE, Oscar (1854-1900)<br>Dramatist | 34 Tite Street<br>Central map: page 3, F2 | 1954 |
| WREN, Sir Christopher (1632-1723)<br>Architect | 49 Bankside<br>Central map: page 12, L6 | — |

ST. PAUL'S CATHEDRAL

# Thames Bridges

The first bridge across the Thames was built in Roman times, and it was that bridge which helped London to grow into one of the most important cities in the world. It remained the lowest bridging point of the river for many centuries; most of the other bridges were built only in the 19th century. The bridges to be seen today are extremely varied in design, and some are of considerable beauty. Given below are brief details of the bridges from Hampton to the Tower.

## Hampton Court Bridge
District map: page 168, B2

Built in 1933 to the designs of Sir Edwin Lutyens, this elegant bridge connects Hampton Court with East Molesey. The River Mole flows through East Molesey to enter the Thames just below the bridge. To the north of the bridge is Hampton Green, where there is a splendid group of mainly 18th-century buildings. Amongst these is Old Court House, which was the home of Sir Christopher Wren for a while, and the Royal Mews, which now houses the headquarters of the Horse Rangers Trust. On the other side of the Green is Hampton Court House, an imposing structure dating from the middle of the 18th century.

## Kingston Bridge
District map: page 168, B2

Kingston owes its origins to the fact that here was one of the two safe fords across the Thames above Westminster. It made Kingston an extremely important place. A bridge had been built here by the 12th century, and for centuries the only bridge below it was London Bridge. The present bridge was built between 1825 and 1828. An excellent tow path leads upstream from it to Hampton Court.

## Richmond Bridge
District map: page 168, B3

Excellent views up and down the Thames may be obtained from this majestic bridge. It was built in 1777 to the designs of James Paine in a pleasing Classical style.

## Chiswick Bridge
(on A316)
District map: page 168, C3

This concrete bridge was built in 1933 to the designs of the architect Sir Herbert Baker. Just downstream from it, opposite the Ship Inn, is the finishing point of the Oxford and Cambridge Boat Race. Between the bridge and the inn is an attractive group of houses of varying dates, and beyond them, on the south bank, is the huge Mortlake Brewery.

## Hammersmith Bridge
District map: page 168, C3

Sir Joseph Bazalgette, the architect who did so much to change the appearance of the Thames in central London, designed this fanciful suspension bridge in 1887. Just downstream from the bridge, on the north bank, is the converted warehouse used by Riverside Studios, a flourishing arts centre. On the opposite bank is Harrods Furniture Depository, an imposing building decorated in *art-nouveau* style. Below this is Barn Elms Park, which once comprised the

grounds of a mansion that was demolished in 1954. The history of the mansion goes back to Tudor times, when it was the home of Sir Francis Walsingham, Secretary of State to Elizabeth I. The park is now used for recreational activities.

## Putney Bridge
District map: page 168, C3

Graceful Putney Bridge is a 19th-century replacement of an earlier wooden toll bridge. It marks the starting point of the Oxford and Cambridge boat race, and all along the riverside there are well-kept boat and clubhouses.

## Albert Bridge
Central map: page 2, E2

This combined cantilever and suspension structure resembles a gigantic iron cobweb and is one of the most distinctive of all London's bridges. It was designed by R M Ordish and opened in 1873.

## Chelsea Bridge
Central map: page 3, G2

This handsome suspension bridge was opened in 1937 and replaced a similar structure of 1858. The river here is the widest reach west of London Bridge and was once the scene of extravagant aquatic displays. During the reign of Charles II it was so popular that it became known as 'Hyde Park on the Thames' or

'Pall Mall afloat'.
Between Chelsea Bridge
and Grosvenor Bridge
the entry to the now
disused Grosvenor Canal
can be seen. A large
pumping station
dominates the scene
here.

### Vauxhall Bridge
Central map: page 4, I3

Dating from 1900, this
bridge is decorated with
several enormous figures,
one of them holding a
model of St Paul's
Cathedral.

### Westminster Bridge
Central map: page 4, I4

The present bridge was
designed by Thomas
Page and completed in
1862. It replaced a stone
bridge of 1750 on which
Wordsworth composed
his famous sonnet in
1802. At the western end
stands a statue of Queen
Boudicca.

### Waterloo Bridge
Central map: page 11, J6

John Rennie's beautiful
Waterloo Bridge, which
had been built in the
early part of the 19th
century, began to show
signs of structural
weakness in 1923. In
1934 demolition work
began, and the old
bridge was replaced by
the present structure in
1939. It was designed by
the architect Sir G G
Scott and is considered
to be the most graceful
bridge in London.

### Blackfriars Bridge
Central map: page 11, K6

This bridge, designed by
James Cubitt in 1899,
replaced an 18th-century
structure. Its name is
derived from the
Dominican Priory which
once stood nearby.
Beneath the bridge the
Fleet River — which runs
below the streets of
London for almost its
entire length — can be
seen flowing from a
culvert into the Thames.

### Southwark Bridge
Central map: page 12, L6

Sir Ernest George
designed this
undistinguished bridge in
1919. Many
archaeological finds have
been made on the north
bank of the river here.
They include Roman
artifacts and the
foundations of Baynard's
Castle, a Norman fortress
originally built by one of
William the Conqueror's
followers. It was
demolished and rebuilt
several times, and the
site was not finally
cleared until the 1880s.

### London Bridge
Central map: page 12, M6

London Bridge was first
built in stone between
1176 and 1209. It
became almost a town
on its own, having
houses, shops, a chapel,
fortified gates, and even
water mills built upon it.
All the buildings were
pulled down in 1760,
and the bridge itself was
replaced in 1832 as it
was rapidly being eroded
away. The present
structure dates from
1968, at which time its
predecessor was
dismantled stone by
stone and reassembled in
the USA.

### Tower Bridge
Central map: page 6, N5

This fairy-tale structure,
with its Gothic towers,
steel lattice-work
footbridge and road
drawbridge was designed
by Sir John Barry and
Isambard Kingdom
Brunel in 1886-94. It was
opened by the then
Prince of Wales. The
twin bascules, or
drawbridges, weighing
1,100 tons each, were
operated by four steam
hydraulic engines until
1975, when these were
replaced by electric
motors as they had
become uneconomical.
The pedestrian walkway
was reopened to the
public in 1982
(see page 107).

TOWER BRIDGE

# ROYAL AND PUBLIC PARKS

A touch of countryside in London

# The Royal Parks

## Bushy Park

*District map,
page 168, B2*
☎ *01-977 1328*

*Open: all year 7 —
½ hour before dusk
(vehicles 6.30-midnight)*
☞ ♿

Hampton Court Road separates its namesake park from less formal acres of Bushy Park, an engagingly pastoral area that recreates the seeming randomness of the real countryside. With one notable exception, that is — Sir Christopher Wren's magnificent Chestnut Avenue. This superb double row of enormous trees is best seen in spring, when the candle-like blooms form a frothy pink and white line that bisects the park from north to south.

Close to the Hampton Court end of the avenue is the Diana Fountain, which once stood in the grounds of the great house, but now marks the junction of the chestnut way with an avenue of limes. The latter is a smooth, formal highway through an otherwise wild part of the park.

North of the limes is the Longford River. Although it looks entirely natural, it was in fact built on the order of Charles I to supply Hampton Court with water, and still feeds many of the park's water features. At one point it flows through the mature woodland and picturesque glades of Waterhouse Plantation, where it hurls itself over an artificial ledge in the heart of one of the most beautiful rural retreats in the country.

Most visitors to the park congregate near the cricket ground and children's playground— both well worth visiting, but not to the exclusion of all else. Bushy House, a handsome 18th-century building, contains the National Physical Laboratory.

## Green Park

*Central map,
page 3, G5*
☎ *01-930 1793*

*Open: 5am — midnight*

This is indeed a green park. Its close turf, graduating towards a more carefree rankness round the roots of lovely old trees, might have been borrowed from the sheep-cropped slopes of the Sussex Downs. There are no flowerbeds, though in springtime the grass is sprinkled with the flowers of daffodils and crocuses. There is no visible water in the park, but the Tyburn Stream

GREEN PARK.

flows just beneath the surface and is the reason for the park's verdancy.

Just across the thin tarmac boundary of The Mall is St James's Park, but even without the road the two areas would be distinct from one another. It is easy to forget their shared history in picturesque St James's, where the magical combination of water and flowers masks the memory of violent crimes that have been enacted on its lawns. In the slightly severe greenness of Green Park, however, stories of past events spring easily to mind.

The ghosts of duellists battle in the damp shadows of the trees at twilight, the slightest breeze entices an almost human sigh from the gnarled plane tree near Piccadilly, and occasionally the setting sun turns patches of grass an unsettling red.

The times of violence have gone from the park now, along with Charles II's constitutional stroll that gave its name to Constitution Hill, and the walls of the ice house that he built to keep his wines cool in summer.

## Greenwich Park, Greenwich

*District map,*
*page 169, 36 E3*
☎ *01-858 2608*

*Open: Summer 7 —*
*dusk. Winter 7 — 6*
🖨 ✦

It is difficult to consider Greenwich Park without involving the magnificent Wren buildings that rise from the foot of the valley. It is a matter of taste; those interested in architecture will find the park an apt foil to those masterly designs, while others might thank providence that they complement rather than spoil the Thames-side greenness lapping at their walls.

The park was enclosed in medieval times, used as a hunting chase by the Tudor monarchs, and formalised by the Stuarts. Several tumuli, traces of a Roman villa, and records of a castle demolished by Charles II show that the area now occupied by the park was inhabited fairly constantly from prehistoric times.

The most extensive changes were made by the great French landscaper Le Nôtre, who was commissioned by Charles II. His love of symmetry, and of the straight line opposed by the curve, is very much in keeping with another of the park's aspects — as a place of science. Here stood the old Royal Observatory, now pensioned off as a museum, and here also is the Meridian — a stone-set strip of brass that marks zero degrees Longitude, the point on which such measurements all around the world are based.

Away from all this, in the park's eastern corner, is the Wilderness, 13 acres of bracken and wild flowers inhabited by a herd of fallow deer. Close by is a delightful flower garden. Everywhere there are trees, and the sense of not being far from running water. On the park's northern perimeter is the largest children's playground in any of the Royal Parks, facilities for cricket and football near the Ranger's House, and, in the centre of the park, the historic 20ft stump of Queen Elizabeth's Oak. (see also Old Royal Observatory, page 99)

## Hampton Court

*District map,
page 168, 19 B2*
☏ *01-977 8441*

*Open: Gardens and
grounds daily, summer
7 — 9 (or dusk) winter
9 — dusk.*
🛒 *shop* ♿

Before Macadam made the biggest single revolution in road building since the Romans, the River Thames was the main access to London. That, and the sylvan beauty of its wild valley, must have been the deciding factors in Cardinal Wolsey's choice of site for Hampton Court, the most magnificent house of the Tudor age.

Nestling inside an elbow of Britain's premier river is an outstanding collection of formal gardens and little architectural conceits — stunning herbaceous borders and long, shaded walks lined by ancient trees. The combination of flowers, statues, and fountains in the Privy Garden is considered to show formal gardening at its very best, and the heady breath of the elaborate Herb Garden intoxicates the senses.

There is water here too. The magnificent Long Water was created by Charles II in French-canal style, and the very old Pond Garden demonstrates that strange, botanical no-man's land between dry and submerged habitats.

The Rose Garden grows in what was once the hoof-hammered lists of Henry VIII's Tiltyard, and the modern Knot Garden recreates the almost tortured complexity that was sought after by gardeners during the 16th century.

Above all Hampton Court is a place of opposites, contrasts that are summed up in just two of its features — the charming Wilderness dell which is surrounded by a carpet of daffodils in springtime and the geometric perfections of the famous Maze.
(see also Hampton Court Palace, page 86)

## Hyde Park

*Central map, page 2,
E5, F5*
☏ *01-262 5484*

*Open: 5am — midnight*

Hyde Park merges imperceptibly with Kensington Gardens, which makes it seem a lot larger than it is, but there is a marked character difference between the two parks.

Before Henry VIII enclosed the area as a hunting chase, the park was a wild tract of countryside that once formed part of a vast primeval forest. It was watered by the little River Westbourne, a tributary of the Thames. After it was dammed to form the enchanting Serpentine lake the Westbourne vanished underground.

LION GATE,
HAMPTON COURT.

The Serpentine is undoubtedly the main feature of the park. It is the habitat of wild creatures that find scant sanctuary elsewhere in the city centre. It is also a source of pleasure to humankind, a large silvery flatness that rests easily on the eye and murmurs to the dip of oars or the swish of sailing dinghies. Its shrub-covered islands are the homes of breeding waterfowl, sanctuaries guarded from the tread of man. At the eastern end of the Serpentine is the Dell, often considered the park's most picturesque feature. At its centre is a large block of granite called the Standing Stone; it is in fact all that remains of a 19th-century drinking fountain.

Here the horse is still welcome, whether it be of the King's Troop of the Royal Horse Artillery come to fire a salute, or a civilian out for a casual canter along the *Route du Roi* — now known as Rotten Row. There was once an enclosure in the park called The Tour where courtiers drove a circular route in an ostentatious parade of fashion. Ever since the Stuart Kings threw open the gates, Hyde has been a people's park. Its history is one of gaiety, of racing and sports, folk dancing, and minor self indulgence. This spirit of relaxed tolerance, of democratic freedom, is nowhere more typified than at Speaker's Corner. Here, at the Marble Arch corner of the park, anyone can stand up and say just what they please, so long as they can tolerate the remarks of their audience.

## Kensington Gardens

*Central map, page 2, D5*
☎ *01-262 5484*

*Open: dawn — dusk*

The boundary between Kensington Gardens and Hyde Park which were one and the same place before William III enclosed his palace garden, runs north to south across the Serpentine Bridge. Both parks have the Serpentine waters in common, though in Kensington Gardens it is called The Long Water.

It is not until the walker has penetrated some distance into the gardens that the individual characteristics of the areas become apparent.

The gardens become more orderly. The manicured greenery of Hyde Park gives way to colourful regimentation. Avenues of trees shade the pathways, and sculpture adds excitement to the views. Kensington Palace is the focal point providing a dignity characterised by the unmistakable workmanship of Sir Christopher Wren, which can be glimpsed through a cloak of trees. The beautiful sunken gardens round the rectangular pond in front of the palace is the culmination.

There is fantasy here too. In the children's playground the pixies and other small creatures of Ivor Innes' imagination rampage over the Elphin Oak in the frozen motion of carved wood near playground swings donated by the writer J M Barrie. A statue of Barrie's eternal youth Peter Pan stands beside The Long Water, and serves as a reminder of his enchanting story, much of which is set in the gardens. The tranquillity of Kensington Gardens is as deliberate as its formality; note the 'sail only' rule for model boats on the Round Pond. Monthly exhibitions of contemporary art are held in the Serpentine Gallery under the auspicies of the Arts Council.

### Primrose Hill

*Central map, page 9, F9*
☎ *01-486 7905*

*Open: at all times*

Once part of the same hunting forest as its neighbour Regent's Park, Primrose Hill retains in its name the rural character that it undoubtedly had in the past. It lost a great deal of charm during World War II, when it was cleared and used for allotments, but it is gradually recovering its attractiveness. The view from the summit is panoramic and encompasses virtually the whole of central London.

The hill's height made it prominent in the otherwise flat farmland that surrounded it, and it became an obvious place for the quenching of revenge by dark deed or duel.

In 1842 it gained gaslights, a gymnasium, and respectability as a Royal Park. It also gained a fence to keep the public out, but nowadays its 62 acres are open to anybody wishing to enjoy them.

### Regent's Park

*Central map, page 9, F9*
☎ *01-486 7905*

*Open: 5am — dusk*

After the execution of Charles I, the great royal hunting ground of Marylebone Park fell into the hands of Oliver Cromwell, who sold its timber and deer to pay his war debts. Further erosion occurred when Charles II sold leases on the ground to various noblemen, and it was not until the early 19th century that any attempt was made to regain what had been lost. Then, however, it became part of the Prince Regent's grand design for a vast neo-classical redevelopment under the talented hand of John Nash — hence 'Regent's' Park. Nash's original plans were never completed. That would have meant building on the park itself, and the Prince Regent decided that the open space was preferable to more development. The focus of the overall design was the Inner Circle. This now encloses the lovely Queen Mary's Garden, which has an attractive little lake, cascades of delicate and many-hued rockery plants, and one of the most beautiful rose gardens in the capital.

The subterranean Tyburn River fills the lake and pours into the boating pond from the only visible stretch on its route to the Thames.

PRIMROSE HILL.

The park's other waterway, the Regent's Canal, makes a much more definite impact on the landscape. A pleasure-boat service carries passengers to Regent's Park Zoo from the terminal in Little Venice. The elegant charm of the park is enhanced by several Victorian garden ornaments, notably two large flower vases on the Broad Walk. Near the lake is a group of fossil tree trunks which are the only surviving reminders that the Royal Botanical Gardens were once situated here. The park has many public amenities, including games fields, facilities for archery and tennis, and sailing on the lake.

(see also London Zoo, page 94)

### Richmond Park

*District map, page 168, B2*
☏ 01-948 3209

*Open: dawn — ½ hour before dusk*
⌨ ♿

This vast tract of virtually wild countryside on the very doorstep of London's urban sprawl remains from an ancient forest that once covered much of southern England.

Charles I enclosed the park area as part of a royal estate, and successive monarchs have shaped the land to suit their hunting needs. The deer that they so avidly sought no longer display the furtive timidity of the hunted. Instead they wander unharmed among copses and spinneys high above the Thames Valley, and are not averse to bullying the picnicking tourist into parting with a sandwich or two. The ultimate irony must be the deers' freedom of the slopes of King Henry VIII's Mound, which the monarch had built so that he could watch their slaughter.

In the 18th century severe restrictions on public access to Richmond Park were imposed by the Crown, but — thanks to a brewer called John Lewis — today's public can wander there at will. Lewis fought to preserve a public right of way through the park, and won.

A formal garden can be seen at Pembroke Lodge, and the various plantations show a wealth of exotic shrubs and wild flowers. Model sail boats are allowed on Adam's Pond, where the deer drink, and 18-acre Pen Ponds have been specially made for angling (a fishing permit is required).

RICHMOND PARK

## St James's Park

*Central map, page 4,*
*H5*
☎ *01-930 1793*

*Open: 5am — midnight*

Here, on the fringe of one of London's busiest shopping and entertainment centres, is a green oasis of peace.

St James's is a reminder of the countryside, a great contrast to the city greyness that surrounds it. In autumn it is one of the few places in the West End where the commuter can see the first frosts; in summer it is full of relaxing office workers, many of whom have made a habit of feeding the park's flourishing population of birds.

Medieval St James's was a vastly different place, a brooding, marshy waste where the morning breeze stirred mist round a hospital for female lepers. Things changed in the 16th century when Henry VIII swept away the hospital, built St James's Palace and converted the surrounding area into a deer park. The Stuart kings drained the marsh and formed the lake, and Charles II transformed the land into a Versailles-type formal garden. At this time the lake was a featureless strip known as the Canal, but it was waterscaped in 1828 when the great architect John Nash was employed to remodel the park. Today pleasant walks and paths thread through a mixture of flower borders, shrubs and trees. The nucleus of the park is formed by the lake, which is almost oriental in flavour with its fringe of weeping willows and resident ornamental ducks floating serenely upon it. Duck Island in the centre provides a lush haven for water birds, the most famous being the pelicans which parade its banks with a proprietary air.

# The Public Parks

## Battersea Park, SW11

*Central map, page 3,*
*F1*
☎ *01-871 7530*

*Open: 7.30 — dusk*

Amongst the attractions in this riverside park are a deer park, sub-tropical garden, and wildflower garden. Facilities specifically for children include playing fields, a small zoo, and a miniature railway.

## Crystal Palace Park, SE19

*District map,*
*page 169, E2*
☎ *01-778-7148*

*Open: Park, summer*
*7.30 — dusk*
*winter 8 — dusk.*
*Sport facilities, boating,*
*pony rides, Admission*
*Charge. Children's zoo,*
*adventure playground*
*and park, Admission*
*free.*

This 200-acre park is named after the huge glass-and-iron structure that was built in 1851 for the Great Exhibition. It was moved here from Hyde Park in 1854, and destroyed by fire in 1936. Situated in the park, whose hill-side site commands extensive views, is an Olympic-standard swimming pool and a superb sports stadium. The only survivors of the Great Exhibition are the life-sized models of prehistoric creatures which are to be found on an island in the lake. These brightly-coloured denizens are perennial favourites with children and photographers.

PREHISTORIC ANIMALS, CRYSTAL PALACE PARK.

### Holland Park, W8

*Central map, page 1,A4*

*Open: 7 — dusk*

Less than 30 years ago Holland Park was the garden of a private house, and even now it retains that air of intimacy that is so peculiar to the inviolate. Its flock of peacocks and gaggle of geese mount solemn guard for long-gone inhabitants of the house, and visitors stroll on smooth lawns where open-air Kensington teas may have been held not too many summers ago.

In the 18th and 19th centuries the house here was a popular meeting place for the literary and political personalities of the day. Only part of it now faces across the elegant quadrangle that it once dominated, but it is easy to imagine the intellectuals of the time threading through lighted rooms at the end of a summer evening. Macauley called Holland Park the 'Favourite resort of wits and beauties, painters and poets, scholars, philosophers, and statesmen'. Such people, jaded by the effort of creation or wearied by their excursions into the labyrinthine politics of high social life, must have found the park easy on the eye and relaxing to the mind.

That feeling remains, though the sparkling company and locked gates have gone. In springtime the Dutch and Iris Gardens are a constant delight to the visitor — especially the person who has unexpectedly stumbled upon this strange little haven while lost in the masonry heart of Kensington. Other flowerbeds show a wide range of plants, including the original Caroline Testout roses, and a charming show of native British plants. Also here is a *yucca* garden, where the Mexican *yucca* plant guards its delicate clusters of white flowers with bunches of spear-like leaves.

In contrast with the formal path-and-lawn layout, given a military air by the uniformed nannies who take their small charges for walks here, is the free-play area. This is woodland that has been left to its own devices for the benefit of older children.

*District map,*
*page 168, B3*
☎ *01-940 1171*
*ext 4118*

*Open: Gardens 10 to*
*between 4 & 8pm*
*(depending on season);*
*museum & glasshouses*
*from 10am, some*
*buildings close*
*lunchtime. (Closed*
*Xmas day & New*
*Year's day.)*
*Admission charge.*
☕ ♿ *shop ✗ (ex*
*guide dogs)*

## Kew Gardens, Kew (Royal Botanic Gardens)

London Zoo may be the showcase of the animal
kingdom, but when it comes to plants there is
nowhere to beat the Royal Botanic Gardens at
Kew. Here, firmly established on 300 acres of
Thames-side London, are exotics from all over the
world — the mice and the mammoths of botany.

The garden's facilities for research are unrivalled,
but it is not as a purely scientific establishment
that Kew is known. The great beauty and
strangeness of its charges are part of London
legend, and its earthen 'laboratory' beds have
been laid out to be pleasing to the eye.

The first nine acres of gardens were laid out by
George III's mother, Princess Augusta, some 200
years ago, and they really began to flourish during
the reign of her son. Their present-day success is
largely due to the eminent 19th-century botanist
Sir Joseph Banks, a close friend of the king, who
worked with Head Gardener William Aiton to lay
the basis for the superb collection that now exists.
Royal patronage continued, even after the gardens
came into public ownership in 1841. Today's
visitors can be thankful for this as they enjoy the
conserved wildness of the Queen's Cottage and
grounds — a gift from Queen Victoria.

The largest living collection in the gardens is the

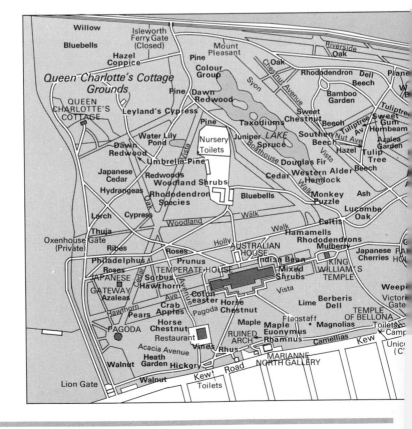

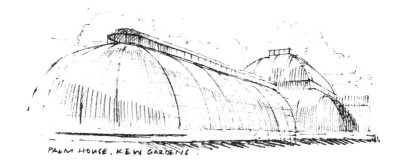

PALM HOUSE, KEW GARDENS.

Arboretum, where many species of trees and shrubs grow harmoniously. The Tropical and Palm Houses are interesting too, while magnificent flower borders of the Herbaceous Section are a constant delight. Great cushions of alpines grow amongst sandstone outcrops and beside the stream of the Rock Garden, and the woodland garden around The Mound exudes a green coolness that is at once relaxing and a tonic.

(see also Kew Palace and Queen Charlotte's Cottage, page 91)

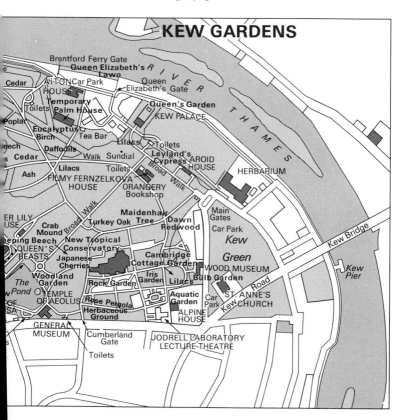

**KEW GARDENS**

## Osterley Park, Osterley

*District map,*
*page 168, 38, B3*
☎ *01-560 3918*

*Open: daily 10-8*
⌨ ♿

Osterley is indeed a 'green lung' for London, or at least for the city's heavily built-up western suburbs. Nearby the M4 motorway carries its never-ending metallic stream into the warrens of the capital, growling to itself in a constant monotone of labouring car and lorry engines. Yet nothing detracts from the park.

Its delightfully informal landscape preserves the character and tranquillity of the English countryside. The 120 acres of level ground that it covers has been cleverly and sympathetically landscaped so that the flatness is not apparent. Trees have been planted singly and in copses to break the lie of the land still further, and the whole is complemented by enchanting lakes.

Osterley House — the reason for all this carefully contrived rurality — stands amid smooth lawns and fragrant stands of old cedars (see page 100).

The house and park complement each other well. Adam's elegant lines rise grandly from the formal gardens laid out around the house, throwing the 'wild' parkland into a rugged relief that it might not have achieved on its own.

## Syon Park, Isleworth

*District map,*
*page 168, 47, B3*
☎ *01-560 0881*

*Open: 18 Mar-28 Oct*
*daily 10-6; 29 Oct-17*
*Mar 10-dusk. (Closed*
*Xmas). Conservatory*
*closed during Winter*
*months.*
*Admission charge.*
⌨ *(licensed)* ♿
*(gardens only) shop*
*garden centre* 🐕

Close to Kew Gardens in spirit, but divided from it by the waters of the Thames, is Syon Park — the country's first national gardening centre.

Its horticultural reputation goes back to the 16th century, when the use of trees as purely decorative contributions to its layout was looked upon with amazement. The park that exists today, however, is the work of that master of landscape design — 'Capability' Brown. As such it is a valuable cultural record, as well as a beautiful retreat from the bustle of modern town life.

There is water in plenty. The capital's major artery flows sedately past the 16th-century exterior of Syon House, and the picturesque lake supports large colonies of water-loving plants.

The focal point of Syon, if not the house, must certainly be the Great Conservatory. This vast crescent of metal and glass, with small pavilions at either end and a lofty central dome, was the first construction of its type in the world. It was also the inspiration for the ill-fated Crystal Palace, but apart from all this it houses one of the finest private collections of tropical plants in the country. It is the only place in Britain where the coconut palm has reached full maturity.

A particularly beautiful — if somewhat overwhelming — feature of the park is the six-acre Rose Garden.

All this, just nine miles from the centre of London, is open to the public — though admittance to the house and park is by separate entrances. (See also Syon House and Heritage Motor Museum, page 104).

# CENTRAL LONDON

## Key to map pages

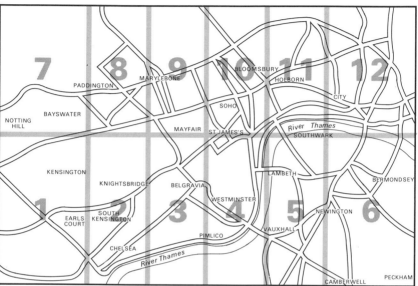

## Legend

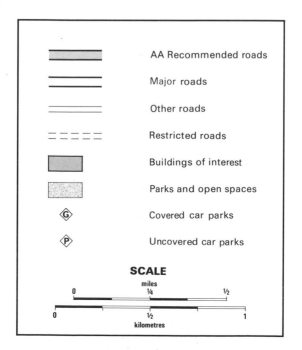

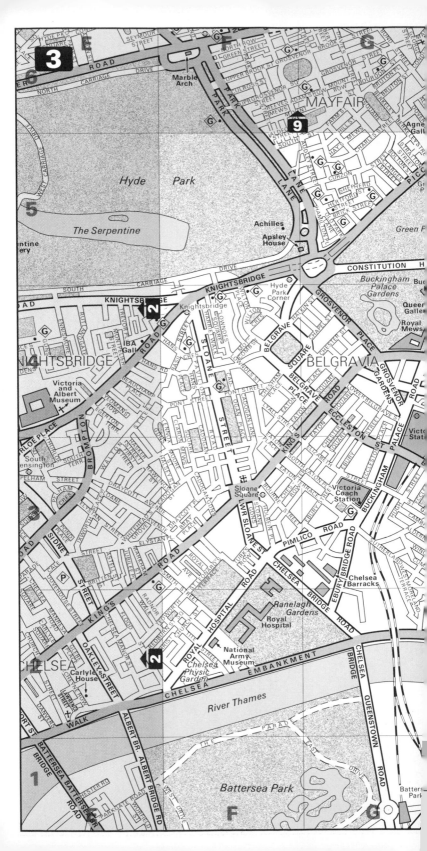

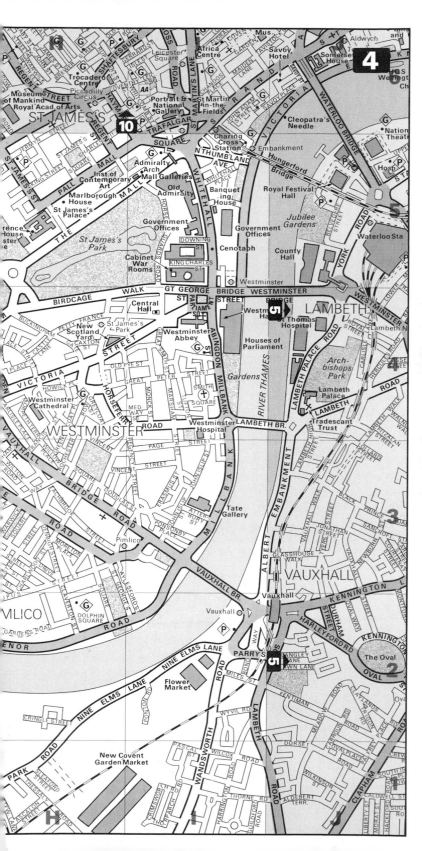

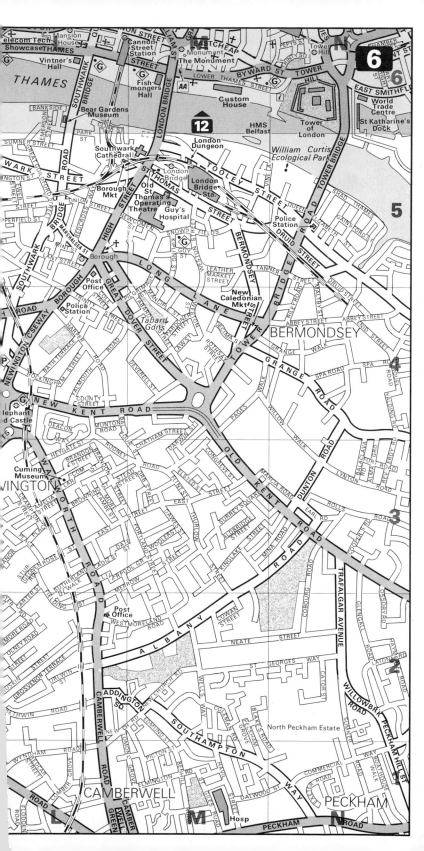

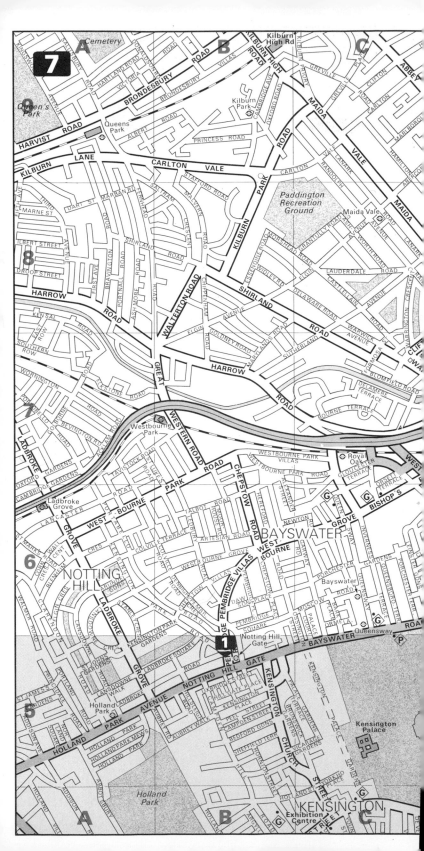

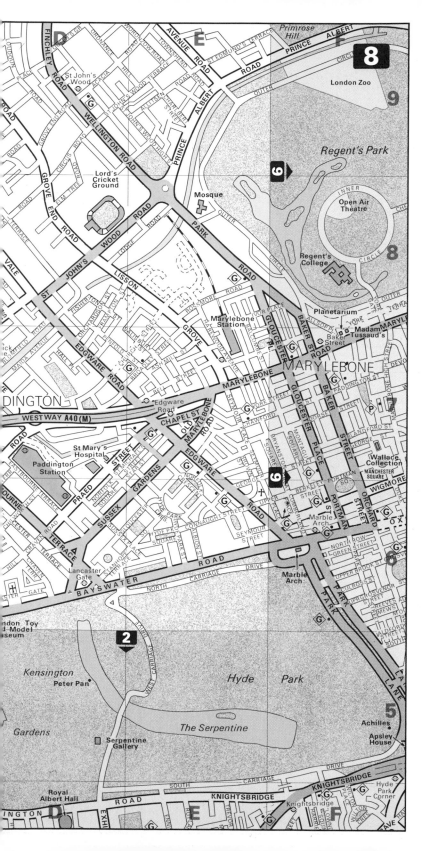

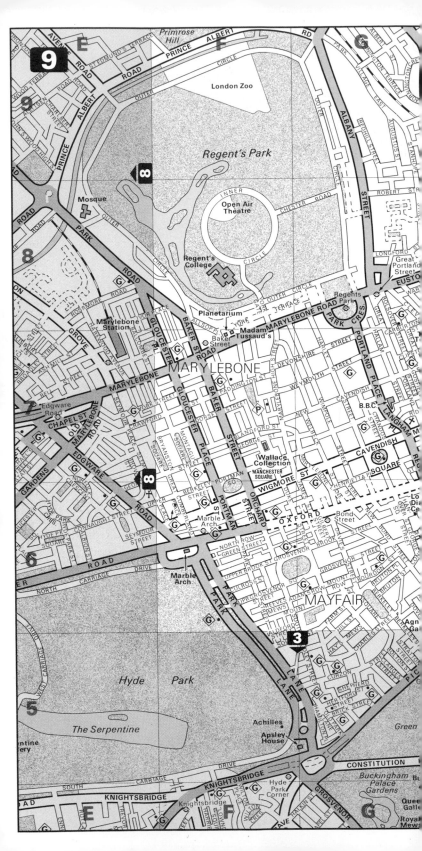

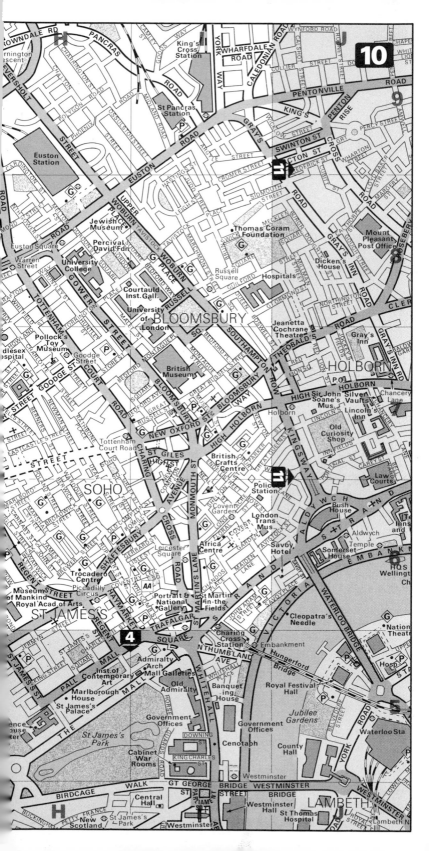

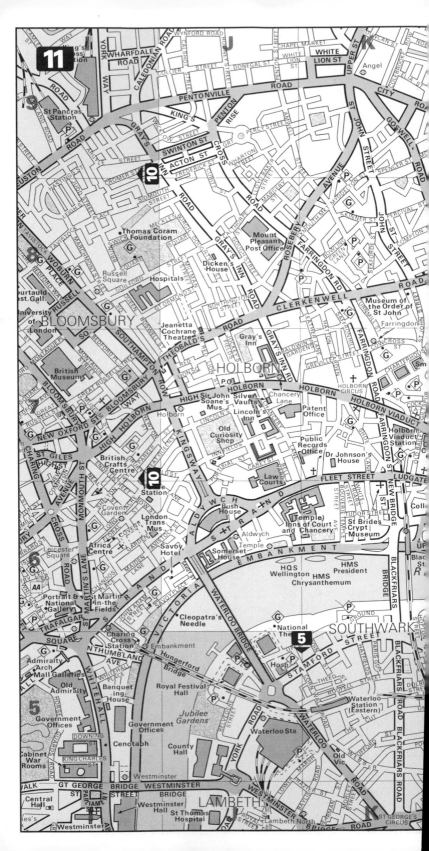

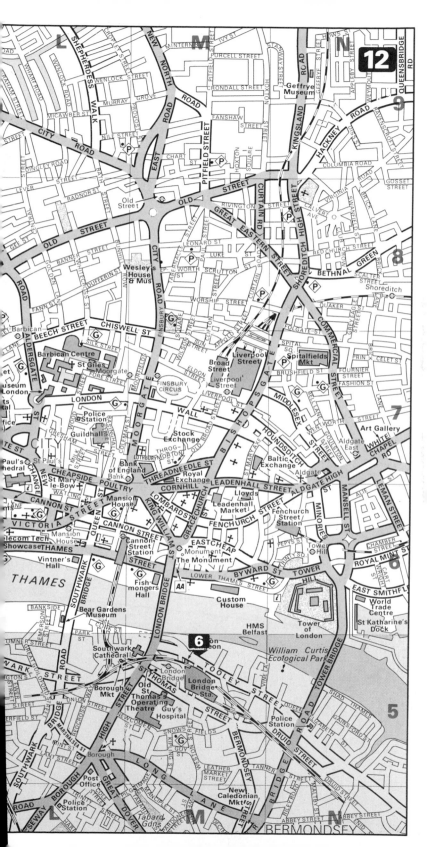

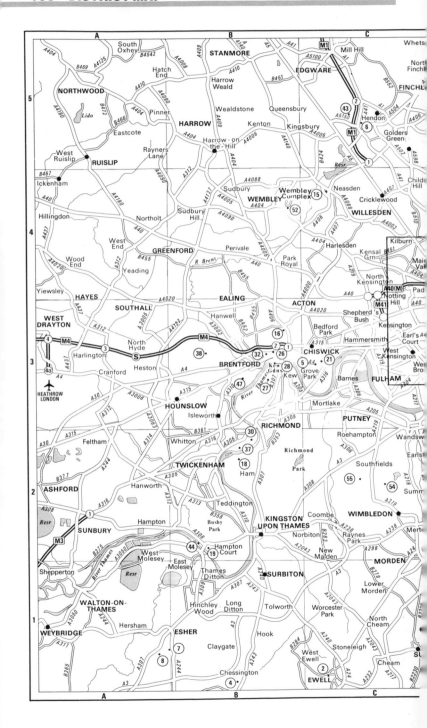

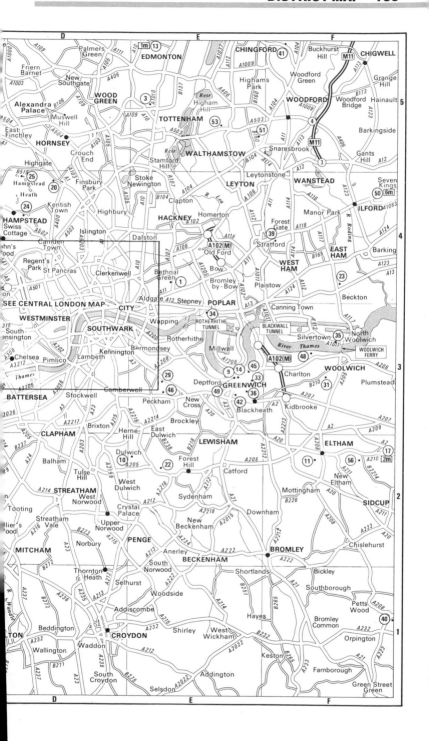

## STREET INDEX
## CENTRAL LONDON